OLD
TESTAMENT
AND
RELATED
STUDIES

The Collected Works of Hugh Nibley

The Collected Works of Hugh Nibley will
include volumes on the following subjects:

The Old Testament and related studies
Ancient history
The Pearl of Great Price
Early Christianity
The Book of Mormon
The Doctrine and Covenants and Mormonism
Education, politics, and society

The Collected Works of Hugh Nibley: Volume 1

OLD TESTAMENT AND RELATED STUDIES

Hugh Nibley

Edited by
John W. Welch
Gary P. Gillum
Don E. Norton

Deseret Book Company
Salt Lake City, Utah
and
Foundation for Ancient Research and Mormon Studies
Provo, Utah

First printing March 1986

Library of Congress Cataloging-in-Publication Data

Nibley, Hugh, 1910–
  Old Testament and related studies.

  Includes index.
  1. Bible. O.T.—Criticism, interpretation, etc.
  2. Mormon Church—Doctrines. 3. Church of Jesus
  Christ of Latter-day Saints—Doctrines. I. Title.
  BS1171.2.N53   1986   221.6   85-27544
  ISBN 0-87579-032-1

Printed in the United States of America   18961-4783
20   19   18   17   16   15   14   13   12   11

Contents

Foreword

This volume is the first in a series, the Collected Works of Hugh Nibley. The series will gather together all of Hugh Nibley's published books and articles, as well as many other previously unpublished papers and transcribed talks.

Hugh Nibley has had a prolific presence in the Latter-day Saint academy and community over the last forty years. During that time, he has stirred many minds and touched many hearts. His work, which this series memorializes, sets many stages upon which the drama of Mormon thought over the coming generations will undoubtedly be played out.

But as Hugh Nibley himself would be quick to point out, the collection of his written works into one place by no means implies that his work or this work is complete. Some of the materials appearing in this series are obviously still in somewhat rough form. Minor editorial changes have been made by the editors and by Dr. Nibley, but the informal or exploratory character of many of these pieces has been preserved. The Nibley style is, in the final analysis, indelible. Beyond that, all the footnotes have been rechecked for accuracy and have been modified where necessary to make them complete and consistent.

For Hugh Nibley's seventy-fifth birthday in March 1985, the following tribute was prepared. With slight modification, it usefully serves to introduce Hugh Nibley—the man behind these texts—to the readers of this series. That tribute, entitled "A Doorkeeper in the House of the Lord," reads as follows:

The last person in the world who is interested in celebrating Hugh Nibley's seventy-fifth birthday [or in seeing the publication of the Collected Works of Hugh Nibley, for that matter] is Hugh Nibley. He has never asked for such a thing; he avoids recognition like the plague. In complete candor, he faithfully describes himself as follows:

"I have always been furiously active in the Church, but I have also been a nonconformist and have never held any office of rank in anything. I have undertaken many assignments given me by the leaders, and much of the work has been anonymous: no rank, no recognition, no anything. While I have been commended for some things, they were never the things which I considered most important. That was entirely a little understanding between me and my Heavenly Father which I have thoroughly enjoyed, though no one else knows anything about it. . . . I would rather be a doorkeeper in the House of the Lord than mingle with the top brass in the tents of the wicked."

Many similar words come to mind as others try to describe Hugh Nibley. His life is a rare combination of faith and scholarship, of teaching and research, of orthodoxy and eccentricity, of rigor and homily, of spontaneity and tedium, of anonymity and legend, of an intimidating genius with a genuine humility. "Who is this Nibley?" many visiting scholars have asked.

He is sincerely comfortable thinking of himself as a doorkeeper in the House of the Lord. He loves the temple and the gatherings of the Saints and would rather be there than anywhere else. His scholarly and religious endeavors over the past four decades have posted him at important portals through which Mormon generations will pass for years to come. His prolific writings have distilled the comings and goings of millennia of human traffic. With a watchman's panoramic vision, he sees the span of social and intellectual developments from Enoch and Abraham, to Peter and Paul, to Joseph and Brigham. He paces the halls of human knowledge, sometimes charting the territory with great detail, at other times simply unlocking doors that lead down passageways that others will be exploring for years to come.

Hugh Nibley was born March 27, 1910, in Portland, Oregon. He was perceptive and preceptive from the beginning. His experiences in the natural environment of pristine Oregon awakened in him an enduring sensitivity to mankind's stewardship over the earth. Memorizing much of Shakespeare led him inexorably to the study of Old English, then Latin, then Greek, then Arabic, and on and on. For Hugh Nibley, one profound thing has always led to another.

After serving a mission in Germany and carrying out a special assignment in Greece, he completed his A.B. in history at UCLA, graduating *summa cum laude* in 1934. Although he was born in wealth, the family fortune evaporated in the Great Depression, leaving Hugh to struggle for books and graduate school tuition. He was a university fellow at the University of California at Berkeley (1936-37), where he earned his doctorate in 1938, studying with such luminaries as the great Semitist William Popper. His dissertation, entitled *The Roman Games as the Survival of an Archaic Year-Cult*, was composed in three weeks.

Following an appointment as lecturer in social philosophy at the Claremont Colleges in Pomona, California, and after several intense years of service as an army intelligence noncommissioned officer in World War II, he dedicated his promising academic career to service of The Church of Jesus Christ of Latter-day Saints. At the behest of John A. Widtsoe, Hugh Nibley joined the history faculty at Brigham Young University in 1946, leaving—as Robert Thomas has put it—the "glory that was Greece and the grandeur that was Rome for the modesty that was Provo."

He and his wife, Phyllis, became the goodly parents of eight fine children. Their home has been a haven. Its doors have always been open to numerous students and family friends. Their family life has been filled with music, lively discussions about drama and literature, archaeological excursions, the arts and sciences.

He was promoted to the rank of professor of history and religion in 1953. His academic career has been punctuated with a visiting professorship at Berkeley (1959-60), where he lectured on ancient rhetoric and studied Coptic;

with a trip to Jordan in 1964, where he examined the Dead Sea Scrolls; and with advanced studies in Egyptian at the Oriental Institute in Chicago in 1966.

His publications over the past forty years cover a wide range of topics, including ancient history, politics, classics, education, science, Egyptology, early Israel, the Apocrypha and Pseudepigrapha, Christian origins, the Book of Mormon, the Pearl of Great Price, temples and temple worship, Church history, and society and the gospel. Though he considers it spiritually irrelevant, most of his nearly two hundred titles are classics. A good synopsis of his academic interests can be gleaned by scanning a few of those titles: For example, *No Ma'am That's Not History* (1946); "The Arrow, the Hunter and the State" (1949); *Lehi in the Desert and the World of the Jaredites* (1952); *The World and the Prophets* (1954); *An Approach to the Book of Mormon* (1957); "Christian Envy of the Temple" (1959-60); "How to Write an Anti-Mormon Book" (1962); "The Expanding Gospel" (1965); *Since Cumorah* (1970); "Brigham Young on the Environment" (1972); "What is Zion?" (1972); "Beyond Politics" (1974); *The Message of the Joseph Smith Papyri: An Egyptian Endowment* (1975); "The Early Christian Prayer Circle" (1978); "Patriarchy and Matriarchy" (1980); *Abraham in Egypt* (1981); and "Work We Must, but the Lunch Is Free" (1983). All the while, he has carried on voluminous correspondence, magnified his distinctive calling in life as Church teacher and speaker, and been a major contributor to Church magazines over the years—often on short notice and under considerable pressure from publication deadlines.

His works are characterized by several unmistakable traits. He harbors an urgent sense of placing immediate priority on eternal values. He knows that the door is about to close, that time is running out, that money is not worth it, that the extreme situations involving total extermination of nations in the Book of Mormon are relevant for our day—and for him all these realizations trivialize many pedantic projects and issues. He is relentless in his examination of documents and in providing abundant documentation. His curiosity is inexhaustible. He still feeds his memory a steady diet of vocabulary cards. Discoveries constantly amaze him. His writings often draw parallels or offer new characterizations that others have failed to perceive. His interests are usually ahead of their time. He incisively exposes the shortcomings of scientific absolutism and the fundamental flaws of both gospel detractors and zealots. His works are typically bold and daring, challenging but reassuring, resourceful and creative, innovative if not revolutionary, sensitive and insightful.

Still, he does not take himself at all seriously. Repenting and giving thanks are the things he thinks he does best. He sees his learning as forever tentative, incomplete, and accumulating. Once discovered, his innovative insights are so painfully obvious that it is hard for him to see why he had not noticed them before. He willingly describes himself as a buffoon and, from time to time, as a frustrated fiction writer, waiting for the real scholarship to begin.

As a university community and as a people, we owe an immeasurable debt to Hugh Nibley for his unique contributions to our lives. His work has changed us all. Few students can talk coherently about their first class from Hugh Nibley. For many it has been viewed as a necessary rite of passage, while for others it was an electrifying baptism in the waters of ideas and ideals. Hugh Nibley's manner of speech—tempered hyperbole—instills an extraordinary sense of vitality. His unfailing encouragement to students to satisfy their *own* curiosity—not *his*—is the kind of faith that has moved many inert cerebral mountains.

In a word, Hugh Nibley is no ordinary doorman. But then, as far as that goes, he doesn't stand by ordinary doorways either.

Of that, readers of the Collected Works of Hugh Nibley may see for themselves.

JOHN W. WELCH

Sources and Acknowledgments

"Historicity of the Bible" is the edited transcript of an address given to the Seminary and Institute faculty at Brigham Young University on June 19, 1956.

"Archaeology and Our Religion," accompanied by two cover letters dated September 16, 1965, was originally intended to be included in the "I Believe" series in the *Instructor*. On January 18, 1982, it appeared in the *Seventh East Press*, pp. 4-7, 12.

"Myths and the Scriptures" was published in the October 1971 *New Era*, pp. 34-38.

"Before Adam" is the edited text of an address given to the BYU community on April 1, 1980.

"Patriarchy and Matriarchy" was first delivered on February 1, 1980, to the annual women's conference at Brigham Young University. It was subsequently published in the proceedings of that conference, *Blueprints for Living: Perspectives for Latter-day Saint Women* (Provo: Brigham Young University Press, 1980), pp. 44-61.

"Unrolling the Scrolls—Some Forgotten Witnesses," a talk given in Glendale, California, in 1967, has been transcribed and edited from a tape recording.

"Treasures in the Heavens: Some Early Christian Insights into the Organizing of Worlds" was published in *Dialogue: A Journal of Mormon Thought* 8 (Autumn/Winter 1973): 76-98, and reprinted in *Nibley on the Timely and the Timeless* (Provo: BYU Religious Studies Center, 1978), pp. 49-84.

"Great are the Words of Isaiah" is an address given at BYU's sixth annual Sidney B. Sperry Symposium on January 28, 1978. It subsequently appeared in the proceedings of that symposium, pp. 193-207, published by Brigham Young University Press in 1978.

"More Voices from the Dust" appeared in the *Instructor* (March 1956), pp. 71-72, 74.

"The Dead Sea Scrolls: Some Questions and Answers" was originally an address given to the Seminary and Institute faculty at BYU on July 5, 1962. It then appeared in the *Instructor* 98 (July 1963): 233-35.

"Qumran and The Companions of the Cave" first appeared in *Revue de Qumran* 5 (April 1965): 177-98. It was reprinted in *Nibley on the Timely and the Timeless* (Provo: BYU Religious Studies Center, 1978), pp. 187-212.

Introduction

This volume gathers together eleven Hugh Nibley articles and talks that deal essentially with the Old Testament or topics related to it. The first four papers address several problems raised by opponents of the Bible. These are mainly claims of one kind or another against the historicity of the creation account and early narratives in Genesis. Answers are given to the skeptical views of existentialist theologians, textual critics, overconfident scientists and archaeologists, demythologizing historians, and evolutionists. Guiding principles are articulated through the eyes of faith, through the unifying threads of culture and ritual, and through the miraculous and insightful perspectives of revealed scripture found in the Book of Mormon and the Book of Abraham.

The next three papers are related to the study of the biblical creation account. First is a discussion of the roles of men and women in the world, followed by two papers on the composite picture of the creation of the world as seen from numerous apocryphal and pseudepigraphic texts, as well as passages from the Dead Sea Scrolls, the Nag Hammadi library, and early Christian materials. The assumption here, only thinly veiled, is that ritual threads connect this worldview with the meaning of the Latter-day Saint temple ceremony.

After the paper on Isaiah, which discusses the human qualities Isaiah finds most pleasing to God, the final three papers report discoveries relative to the Dead Sea Scrolls. Two articles are early announcements of the potential significance of the Dead Sea Scrolls for Book of Mormon studies—a theme explored further by Hugh Nibley in a series of articles in the *Improvement Era* that soon thereafter

appeared in his book *Since Cumorah*, first published in 1967.
The final article raises issues about possible connections between the Dead Sea Scrolls and certain later Arabic texts,
showing an intriguing persistence and pervasiveness of
the traditions known at Qumran.

As editors, we caution that this volume is neither
exhaustive nor independent. Subsequent volumes in this
collection will also contain materials relevant to Old Testament studies, for many other Hugh Nibley writings deal in
one way or another with the Old Testament. There is, one
will quickly find, a high degree of interrelatedness in much
of what Hugh Nibley has written. This makes it somewhat
artificial, if not impossible, to carve up the works of Hugh
Nibley into distinct topical compartments. His works on
Enoch and Abraham, for example, do not appear in this
volume; they will be published in separate subsequent volumes. Those two figures belong as much to the Pearl of
Great Price as to the Old Testament. Our main goal as
editors has been to organize these materials along the lines
of those gospel themes and scriptural connections that
themselves have been the fixed beacons along Hugh Nibley's research paths. We hope that our design adds coher-
ence and comprehension to this collection.

1

Historicity of the Bible

The problem of the historicity of the Bible is exactly the same today as it has been since the days of the first apologists. One reads the Bible and decides for himself what is history in it and what is allegory, and what is myth, and what is legend, and what is interpolation.

There are two main schools of thought on the subject. There are the fundamentalists, who believe that everything put forth in the Bible as history actually happened as they find it stated; and there are the liberals, who about the year 1925 (according to the study of Eduard König)[1] reached the general consensus that the historical value of the Bible is nil. The LDS people have always stood between these two extremes.

Thirty years ago there was such a solid consensus of learned opinion about the real nature of the Bible and the ancient Hebrew and Christian religions in both camps, both fundamentalist and liberal, that a student needed only to consult any handbook to put him in harmony with the "scholars" on all major issues. That is no longer the case: today all is doubt and confusion.

The principal cause of this confusion has been what one scholar calls "the breakthrough of the eschatological interpretation," which he compares to a strategic military breakthrough that throws a whole army into panic and disorder.

Before we describe the breakthrough, it is important to know what eschatology is. The eschatological viewpoint is that which sees and judges everything in terms of a great eternal plan. Whether we like it or not, we belong to the

"Historicity of the Bible" is the edited transcript of an address given to the Seminary and Institute faculty at Brigham Young University on June 19, 1956.

eternities; we cannot escape the universe. All our thoughts and deeds must be viewed against an infinite background and against no other. *Eschatos* means "ultimate" and refers to that which lies beyond all local and limited goals and interests. Limited objectives are commendable in their way, but only as contributing to something eternal. Extreme as this doctrine may seem, the only alternative, as the philosophers of old repeatedly observed, is a trip to nowhere, a few seconds of pleasure in an hour of pain, and after that only "the depth of emptiness." But the eschatological view of life is more than a philosophy; it is a specific religious tradition, teaching that there actually was a great plan agreed upon at the foundation of the world, and that all that has transpired on earth since the beginning or shall take place hereafter is to be understood as showing forth the operation or attempted frustration of that plan. (An interesting corollary to that is that all things are party to this plan, so that when man sins he puts himself at cross-purposes with all nature, which becomes his enemy and crosses and checks him with all kinds of diseases and allergies. These are simply forms of frustration that the rabbis believe resulted from the fact that we are trying to go one way while the universe insists on going another way. We do not belong anymore.) Everything is in terms of this plan.

    This "eschatological breakthrough" was the realization, climaxing a generation of cumulative study and discovery, that the eschatological view of man's life on earth, though highly distasteful to the doctors and teachers of conventional Christianity and Judaism, was nonetheless the very heart of the original Christian faith and was firmly held by important groups of Jews in ancient times. Accordingly, "since the breakthrough of the eschatological interpretations of the concept of the Kingdom of God in the preaching of Jesus, the question of the content and meaning of Jesus' message has never been satisfactorily settled." Conventional and long-established views of the nature of the Christian religion, whether liberal or fundamentalist, are so completely out of line with the new discoveries that there is now afoot an extremely widespread movement to put the whole Christian faith on a new "existentialist" footing that will ignore history altogether. An eminent Christian scholar, S. G. F. Brandon, commenting on this movement, observes, "It is eloquent witness to the increasing embarrassment felt by Christian thinkers about the assumed historicity of their faith. Such a suggestion of embarrassment in this connection may possibly cause surprise and provoke an instant denial that such a situation exists in any significant academic circle. However, the historical character of Christianity, which was once proclaimed apologetically as the greatest argument for the validity of that faith, has gradually been found to be a source of great perplexity if not of weakness."[2] Until now, according to this authority, Christian scholars have willingly accepted "the claim that, if Christianity derives its authority from certain events which took place at a specific place and time, then that claim must be investigated by the most austere standards of historical judgment. For many decades under the aegis of the liberal tradition of scholarship, this task was undertaken with fervent conviction, and great was the knowledge amassed by such methods of research about Primitive Christianity. But in time this process of investigation into Christian origins has gradually revealed itself to be a journey ever deeper into a morass of conjecture about the imponderables which lie behind or beyond the extant literary documents."[3]

Note there that what is found wanting is not the Bible, but man's interpretations of it, the root of the trouble being that they simply do not have enough evidence to go one way or the other.

If this is true today, it was even truer thirty, forty, or fifty years ago—but the scholars did not know. On both sides they felt convinced that they had the final answer. (The Swede, Olaf Linton, wrote a very good dissertation on that.)[4] They could both speak with perfect confidence because of what I call the gas law of learning, namely, that any amount of information no matter how small will fill any intellectual void no matter how large. A simple and natural misunderstanding lies at the root of almost any biblical study you can find from around 1900: that was the belief that since the New Testament is, after all, the *whole* of our evidence on such things as the life of Christ and the Apostolic Church, it must necessarily tell the *whole* story. This theory that we know all there is to know is a very flattering one, but during the last twenty years it has been subject to a series of fatal blows.

In the business of scholarship, evidence is far more flexible than opinion. The prevailing view of the past is controlled not by evidence but by opinion. The scholars, like the fundamentalists, have believed what they wanted to believe. The liberals have in the past been more willing than their rivals to change their opinions in the face of overwhelming evidence. But now things have come to an impasse with them; they are in open revolt against history. The findings of the last two decades have been of supreme significance, but they have *not* confirmed the preconceptions of the liberals, who now propose simply to ignore them. The existentialism of Bultmann, Barth, and the Roman Catholic Marcel as a champion of Thomistic theology, is, says Brandon, "a truly vehement repudiation" of history.[5] They say we must reject all historical study of Christianity as "negating its present relevance by demonstrating its relevance to the environment in which it took its origin."[6] What is relevant to life and conditions of one age cannot possibly be relevant to another (the Book of Mormon clearly and fully disproves this thesis, which is based on Spengler's *Unwiederkehrlichkeit*); if a thing happens once it can never happen again. Here we have as the very essence of the apocalyptic pattern of history the doctrine that things happen in cycles and recur. Both Harnack and Schweitzer laid great emphasis on the claim that virtually nothing is or can be known about a historical Jesus. This freed them to work out a kind of a Jesus that pleased them. "We are thankful," wrote Schweitzer, "that we have handed down to us only gospels, not biographies of Jesus."[7] When new discoveries come out, they receive, to say the least, a very cold reception. If the real Jesus walked in on them, they would invite him to leave. They have the Jesus they want, and they do not want more. The scholars made their own Jesus: Kierkegaard and Dilthey decided that if we must take history we can at least make it into a thing expressive of our own experience; this led to the existentialism of today, in which the individual rejects as myth anything he does not feel inclined to accept. It is the negation of the open mind. Bultmann writes: "It is impossible to make use of electric light and radio, and, in case of illness, to claim the help of modern medical and clinical methods and at the same time believe in the New Testament's spirits and miracles."[8] On the other hand, I have heard General Authorities cite the electric light and radio as proof of the possibility of miracles. Bultmann's statement is simply untrue, but it is very significant as demonstrating how scholars control evidence instead of being controlled by it. The case of the radio can be taken as equally convincing evidence for or against miracles, depending on how one *wants* to take it. Bultmann sees in it only evidence against miracles—it apparently never occurs to him that it might provide an argument for the other side. He believes what he wants to, and frankly admits it when he tells us, if history does not suit our theory of religion, to throw out the history.

In all this, it is not the weakness of the scriptures but the willfulness of men that is exposed. It has taken a hundred years of guessing and counterguessing to convince the learned that they were not solving the problem of "the content and the meaning of Jesus' message"; the discovery, instead of teaching them humility, has turned them bitterly against the scriptures, whose historical claims

Bultmann and his school now attack with "truly vehement repudiation." The eminent Jewish scholar Torczyner tells us how the old established ideas about the uniform nature of the Bible have had to be given up: "This uniform picture of Biblical criticism has finally been forced to shatter, after the first faint suspicions of certain individuals had gradually grown up to the stature of the *communis opinio*. Scientific investigation has disclosed the richness and variety of the Biblical literature . . . revealing as it does both life and individuality, contradiction and differentness."[9] Torczyner's own reaction to this recognition of a fact familiar to all Latter-day Saints since the founding of the Church has been to turn him violently against the Bible as history, declaring it to be a "total misconception—or even falsification—of the real state of things."

"It is a heavy loss," writes another Hebrew scholar, "that the old historical works no longer survive intact and independent, but only as worked-over materials inserted into the structure of a late compilation and buried under the rubble of many re-editings. The only hope lies in textual analysis, but in the end even that can give us no more than a lot of fragments, whose connection with each other is largely damaged or totally destroyed." Over one hundred years ago, the Prophet Joseph Smith shocked the world by announcing that the very first verse of the Bible has been altered and corrupted by "some old Jew without any authority." If he offended the fundamentalists as much as the liberals, the new discoveries have been equally damaging to both.

Out of this hopeless inadequacy of man's knowledge has grown what now goes by the name of "the Modern Predicament," which is "that man seems to be faced with an unbridgeable gulf between . . . knowledge and faith. . . . Religion was born in a world different from ours—a tiny, comfortable world. . . . That ancient world has been nibbled away by science and the question arises whether against a new and scientific background religion in any form will find it possible to survive."[10] It was just that "tiny, comfortable world" of conventional Christianity that was so mortally offended by the coming forth of latter-day prophecy; the mighty revelations of the Book of Mormon, Doctrine and Covenants, and Pearl of Great Price were an unpardonable affront to the established barriers of time, place, and custom. The Christian world is now for the first time learning how wrong it was, and the experience is not a pleasant one. In all the journals, Catholic and Protestant, a cry of distress goes up: "What is left to us," they ask, "if the things we have always been taught are not so?"

It is hard to believe that men would search for "a religion without faith," yet that is the title of a book designed to guide modern religious thinking. The author begins with a quotation from David Strauss: "The religious area of the human soul is like the region of the Redskins in America, which is becoming inexorably smaller from year to year." This leads to the question "What remains for the man who does not believe? What can we salvage of religion and its benign influence for the confirmed agnostic who is *convinced* that we can know nothing of another world?" Incidentally, since we cannot prove a negative, being convinced of one is a pure act of faith. In other words, how can we enjoy the fruits of faith without any faith at all? "Modern humanity," says a contemporary theologian with a nod of approval, "is for the most part of the same opinion as Pliny, . . . that belief in a rebirth or life after death is simply a sop for children." Since Pliny was an ancient dilettante and not a modern scientist, we cannot lay this state of mind to the charge of science; in their ways of disbelief the clergy have led the field. This can be seen in Marneck's final definition of a "religion without faith," for in the end he recommends "to the *non*-believing person access to religious feelings through the substitution *(Auslösung)* of religious feelings by like feelings of a non-religious nature." These "non-religious" feelings which are accessible to the complete "non-believer" are found in social good-works, aesthetic experience, brotherly love, the psychological search for the deeper self, and the Ethical Gospel. But these are the very things that for many years have made up the substance of religion as taught in liberal theological seminaries everywhere: truly a "religion without faith." "Never before," says a leading Egyptologist, viewing our times against a sweeping background of world history, "was the human race . . . farther from the divine than it is today. It has in this respect sunk to the lowest abyss."

It is not only in the field of religions but in all ancient studies that preconceived ideas are being uprooted on all sides. The religious take it harder than others because they are committed to a "party line"—usually so deeply committed that a major readjustment produces disillusionment and even disaffection. Yet the discoveries that have proven so upsetting should have been received not with hostility but joy, for if they have a way of shattering the *forms* in which the labors of scholarship have molded the past, they bring a new *substance* and reality to things that the learned of another age had never thought possible. The same discoveries that to their dismay are rebuking the favorite theories of the doctors are at the same time vindicating that *Bible* world that they had consigned to the realm of myth. Years ago the celebrated Niebuhr observed that ancient history is always treated "as if it had never really happened"—it is a thesis, a demonstration, an intellectual exercise, but not a real account of real people. "Ingrained in our subconscious," says a recent study of ancient Egypt, "is a disbelief in the actual existence of those times and persons, which haunts us through the schools and in the theaters and libraries and impregnates the whole concept of 'Antiquity.'" In a word, artificiality is to this day the very substance of ancient history.

From this mood of precious academic make-believe, the learned are now rudely aroused to face another world entirely. We live in a time of the reexamination and reevaluation of all ancient documents now extant. They are being

completely gone over from beginning to end. They are not
as we thought they were at all. This may seem a late date to
ask, for example, "What is the Book of Mormon?" It should
seem far stranger to ask, "What is the Iliad?" "What is the
Apocrypha?" "What is the Book of the Dead?" or "What is
the Bible?" Yet those questions are being more seriously
considered today than at any other time. Up until the present, scholars have thought they had a pretty good idea of
what the historical, literary, philosophical, or religious
writings of the past were all about. Not so today! The whole
question of ancient records is now undergoing a thorough
reinvestigation.

How this state of things has come about may best be illustrated by considering the case of the famous Eduard
Meyer. In 1884 the first volume of his great *History of the Ancient World (Geschichte des Altertums)* appeared, presenting
to the world "for the first time a history of the Ancient East
in a scientifically satisfying form, a work which at the time
produced a veritable sensation." Before many years, however, the author was hard at work revising the whole thing,
for the history of the ancient world must be constantly re-
written. By considering a few of the things that happened
between Meyer's two editions of his own work, one may
gain some idea of the tempo of discovery in our times. As
Walter Otto summarizes the developments:

> The History of the Ancient East had taken on a to-
> tally different aspect. . . . Times and areas which for-
> merly had been almost or completely unknown were
> brought to light; we have become acquainted with com-
> pletely new languages and learned to use them as
> sources; peoples known formerly only by name now
> stand before us as concrete realities; the Indo-germanic
> element, which serious scholarship had long concluded
> was of no significance for the Ancient East, . . . now
> shows more clearly every day as an important historical
> element even in the more ancient periods; empires, such
> as the Mitanni and especially the Hittite, of whose history

and structure not long ago only a few scattered details were known, have recently emerged as worthy rivals of the great traditional empires of the east, who actually recognized the Hittites as their equal.[11]

In the two decades since those words were written, things have gone faster than ever. To mention only a few of the developments, there is afoot today a general reevaluation of the oldest Egyptian texts and a far-reaching reinterpretation of the very essentials of Egyptian religion; the origin and background of Sumero-Babylonian civilization is being reconsidered completely in the light of excavations made along the periphery of that area and of epic texts whose real significance has just begun to dawn on the experts; the unearthing of the oldest known villages gives us a new and unexpected picture of a civilization that "seems to have come into being with relative (even revolutionary) suddenness," instead of with that evolutionary gradualness with which all such things were once supposed to have happened; the involvement of the Hebrew Patriarchs, especially Abraham, with our own Indo-European relatives has called for a wholly new picture of Old Testament times and peoples; the application of new methods of dating has cut down the conventional time scale, especially for the earlier periods (for example, as at Jericho) abruptly and drastically; the discovery of a new date for Hammurabi has called for a thoroughgoing revamping of ancient chronology; "the Hurrians have emerged from total obscurity and have come to occupy a stellar role. . . . A new planet has appeared on the historical horizon and an area that was formerly dark has been flooded with a new and strange light." Within the last five years with the discovery of a single inscription a whole world of Greek myth and legend has been transmuted into the category of flesh-and-blood reality; within the same short period the decipherment of the Minoan Script B has with a single sweep rubbed out two hundred years of laborious speculation and acid controversy on major aspects of the Homeric problem, and shown us the Greeks writing good Greek a thousand years before anyone had credited them with literacy; at the same time the mystery of Etruscan has been solved, and the true nature of the mysterious Runic writing of our Norse ancestors explained; today nearly all scholars accept the original identity of the Hamitic, Semitic, and Indo-European languages—a thing that the less informed and more opinionated gentlemen of a few years ago laughed to scorn as a fundamentalist pipe-dream.

In all this fever and ferment of discovery and reevaluation, no documents have been more conspicuously involved than those relating to Israel's past and that of the earliest Christian church. Since World War II the greatest discoveries ever made in these fields have come to light. In the great days of "scientific" scholarship, when the only safe and respectable position for any man of stature to take was to give a flat "no" to any suggestion that the Bible might contain real history, not the least sensational of Eduard Meyer's many ingenious pronouncements was the startling declaration that the Old Testament was not only history but very good history—by far the most accurate, reliable, and complete history ever produced by an ancient people, with the possible exception of the Greeks, who came much, much later. Time and research have strikingly vindicated this claim.

Eduard König treats the subject in a study that deserves to be summarized here.[12] He tells how all the scholars brushed aside the account in Genesis 23 of Abraham's dealings with the Hittites as a fabrication or a mistake—until the Amarna discoveries proved that the Bible was right and they were wrong. The account of Judah's seal-ring in Genesis 38:18 was treated as a clumsy anachronism until about 1913, when the use of seals in early Palestine was proven by excavation. The favorite creed that the early history of Israel rested entirely on oral tradition was blasted by discoveries proving widespread literacy in the earliest days of Israel. The universal belief that Israel had no interest in real history is disproven by the care with which memorial stones, trees, and so on were designated, and by the fullness and detail of early accounts. It was taken for granted that the early histories of Israel did not reflect the ancient times they purported to describe, but depicted actually the much later periods in which they were written; yet archaeological, ethnological, and philological findings in and around Israel show that these texts do *not* depict the Aramaic times but give an authentic picture of a much earlier world. Naturally it was assumed that the early historians of Israel knew nothing about the correct use of sources and evidence; yet they are careful to cite their sources (often now lost), have keen eyes for historical changes, and often include comments and sidelights from various related sources. The prevailing conviction that Israelite history was a "harmonizing and rationalizing" piece of free composition is disproven by the very scholars who make the charge when they claim they are able to detect a great variety of styles and levels of composition—in other words, that the texts have not been harmonized. The very common claim that the history of Israel was all painted over and prettied up so as to quite conceal the original, runs contrary to the many unsavory and uncomplimentary things said about Israel and her founders throughout these writings; the weaknesses of Israel's heroes are not concealed, as such things are in other ancient histories, and the actions of the nation are certainly not "bathed in a golden light," as the scholars claimed.

It is hard now to realize that as recently as 1908 Eduard Meyer could announce to the Berlin academy: "Twenty-five years ago there existed not *a single historical document*" to confirm the early history of Israel as given in the Bible. It was quite suddenly in the late 1800s that such documents began to appear, and then it was like the coming of our spring floods, with the great collections of stuff—no mere trickle—pouring out year after year in a breathtaking sequence that appears not yet to have reached its crest.

The present decade has seen epoch-making departures in the direction of new and daring comparative studies. Enough documentary material is now available to justify bold attempts at generalization that would have been out of the question less than a generation ago. As late as 1930 a leading Egyptologist, T. E. Peet, while marveling at the amazing parallels between them, could stoutly affirm that the literatures of the Egyptians, Babylonians, Hebrews, and Greeks were each the result of separate and independent evolutions, and even as he was writing the Ras Shamra, records were being unearthed to establish beyond a doubt the interdependence of these "independent" cultures. The ancient world is now all one. It was a favorite thesis of Eduard Meyer that Greece and Israel produced parallel historical literature in complete ignorance of each other. What would he say today to serious studies of such themes as "Homeric Epics in the Ancient East" or "Linguistic Relationships between the Ancient Orient and the British Isles"? These are no mere crackpot aberrations.

The greatest linguist of our day (Hrozny) could write not long ago: "Accepted today beyond all possible doubt is the close affinity of the Hamitic with the Semitic races and languages . . . and of the Indoeuropean with them!"[13] and go on to explain this phenomenon in terms exactly corresponding to those of the Tower of Babel story. Yet such a thesis is far less radical than those that now emphasize the extreme suddenness of the emergence of languages, whole linguistic families appearing full-fledged and completely made within a decade! The vast range of these comparative studies, most of which, of course, are still highly conjectural, we cannot examine here. We bring them up only to show what is going on and to make it clear that the picture of man's life and thought and action in the past is by no means the one we were taught to accept in our childhood.

It is especially important to note that the easy, lazy, flattering evolutionary bias that once solved all questions of
the past from an armchair, by a simple rule of thumb,
simply won't work any longer. This can be illustrated by
the effect of the Ugaritic texts of Ras Shamra, texts that
showed Professor Peet to be wrong in attributing the
growth of Hebrew literature to an evolutionary process,
leading the great orientalist A. H. Sayce to confess that his
own conception of the primitive beginnings of the record
was a mistaken one: "There is no longer any difficulty," he
wrote, "in believing that there were abundant literary
documents for compiling the earlier books of the Old Testament. . . . Consequently there is no longer any need of our
believing as I formerly did that cuneiform tablets lie behind
the text of the earlier Biblical books. . . . In the Mosaic
period the Oriental world was as well stocked with books
and what we would call public libraries as it was in the
Greek epoch."[14] Using the same texts, Dr. Gordon has concluded that the fundamental criteria of the higher critics in
their reconstruction of a hypothetical evolution of the Old
Testament text are not binding: "It is against the background of Ugaritic that we must evaluate the multiplicity of
God's name. . . . Elohim and Yahwe need not imply dual
authorship in a chapter of the Bible any more than Baal and
Hadd do in a Ugaritic myth."[15] No less questionable than
the names of God as a key to the structure of the Bible are
variations in style, heretofore believed to indicate with perfect certainty changes of authorship within the various
books: "The rediscovery of the lost literature of the Bible
world shows us that most biblical books could be accepted
in Israel as single compositions. . . . The magnificent
structure of the Old Testament higher criticism is not to be
brushed aside; but its individual results can no longer be
accepted unless they square with the Hebrew text as we
can now understand it in the light of parallel literatures
from the pagan forerunners and contemporaries of the Hebrews, in Bible lands."[16]

Haldar, studying priestly and prophetic institutions, reaches a similar conclusion regarding accepted principles of the higher criticism: "It follows that the evolutionary view of the Old Testament prophets cannot be accepted; instead . . . heavy stress must be laid on continuity."[17] "The greatly increased knowledge of the world surrounding Israel in the ancient Orient" shows, according to Mowinckel, "that the 'sources' of the Old Testament at any rate might be much more ancient than those held by the prevailing evolutionary view of literary criticism."[18]

The major shift in orientation in Bible study from the old literary to what Mowinckel calls the "traditio-historical method" has been the result of a growing necessity of seeing the Bible in a much broader setting than it has heretofore been placed in. As Gordon said, the results of Bible criticism "can no longer be accepted unless they square with the rediscovered 'lost literatures of the Bible World.'" The Bible World is no longer the world made by the Bible, but the much wider world in which the Bible finds itself along with other books, sacred and profane. Today, we are told, "the Old Testament horizon must be expanded and its history interpreted against this larger background. Here, indeed, we must learn to hold converse with the whole universe." "The Bible strikes root into every ancient Near Eastern culture," writes Albright, "and it cannot be historically understood until we see its relationship to its sources in true perspective."[19] The same may be said of any other ancient text: all fields of study seem to be converging at present on the single theme of the oneness of the ancient world. The interrelationships between ancient writings are being drawn closer all the time; they are already so close, in fact, that Haering can now proclaim that all ancient literature, sacred and profane, Jew and Gentile, may be regarded and must be read as a single great book!

A century and a quarter ago, a young man shocked and angered the world by bringing out a large book that he set up beside the Bible not as a commentary or a key to the scriptures, but as original scripture—the revealed word of God to men of old—and as genuine history. The book itself declares that it is an authentic product of the Near East; it gives a full and circumstantial account of its own origin; it declares that it is but one of many, many such books that have been produced in the course of history and may be hidden in sundry places at this day; it places itself in about the middle of a long list of sacred writings, beginning with the patriarchs and continuing down to the end of human history; it cites now-lost prophetic writings of prime importance, giving the names of their authors; it traces its own cultural roots in all directions, emphasizing the immense breadth and complexity of such connections in the world; it belongs to the same class of literature as the Bible, but along with a sharper and clearer statement of biblical teachings contains a formidable mass of historical material unknown to biblical writers but well within the range of modern comparative study, since it insists on deriving its whole cultural tradition, even in details, directly from a specific time and place in the Old World.

The Book of Mormon is God's challenge to the world. It was given to the world not as a sign to convert it but as a testimony to convict it. In every dispensation the world must be left without excuse. It is given without reservation or qualification as a true history and the word of God: "A record of a fallen people, and the fulness of the Gospel of Jesus Christ to the Gentiles and to the Jews also." The bold claims of this book were meant to invite comment and question. If the Book of Mormon is to be the guiding star for a world that has lost its bearing, "proving to the world that the Holy Scriptures are true" (D&C 20:11), it must stand firm and unmoved without any external support. The Bible has been systematically dismantled by men who in the end did not want to believe it. For a hundred years they have been whittling away at it with dogged determination, and now they are all out to "demythologize" and "deeschatologize" it for good. But the Book of Mormon cannot be so dismantled, even by those most determined to reject it. It is a single monolithic block, given to the world at one time and place. Unlike the Bible, it cannot lead "into a morass of imponderables" due to the obscurity of its sources, for it is not the product of centuries or generations of editing and transmission. Unlike the Bible, it cannot be partly true, for the Book of Mormon itself closes the door on such a proposition.

Throughout the Middle Ages wild reports circulated through Europe and Asia from time to time that a letter had fallen from heaven. These reports caused an immense sensation among Christians everywhere, and though they always turned out to be false, the world never ceased hoping that someday a letter or some other tangible thing from heaven would fall into the eager hands of a yearning Christendom. We may smile and ask, "Is anything as crass and tangible as a letter from heaven to be taken seriously by right-thinking people? Must one hear voices and see visions or otherwise have experiences unfamiliar to everyday experience? Are such things necessary?" Whether one likes it or not, Christianity is a very literal-minded religion. The recent attempt to "demythologize" it, that is, to treat as expendable everything in it that smacks of the miraculous, supernatural, or literal has met with a surprisingly vigorous storm of protest from ministers everywhere who, when confronted with a flat "either-or" have been forced to admit that Christianity with the miraculous, the apocalyptic, and the tangible elements removed would not be Christian at all.

In the Book of Mormon, the world finally has, so to speak, its "letter from heaven." Those other epistles were easily tested and found wanting; though sometimes written and presented with considerable skill, they could not fool for long even the unscientific and uncritical ages in which they came forth. There is no reason why the Book of Mormon should not be subjected to every possible test, textual, literary, and historical, for it pleads no special immunity of any kind. It says in 2 Nephi: "Ye have closed your eyes, and ye have rejected the prophets. . . . the Lord God shall bring forth unto you the words of a book, and they shall be the words of them which have slumbered. . . . The learned shall not read them, for they have rejected them, and I am able to do mine own work. . . . For behold, I am God; and I am a God of miracles; and I will show unto the world that I am the same yesterday, today, and forever; and I work not among the children of men save it be according to their faith. . . . For the wisdom of their wise and learned shall perish, . . . the terrible one is brought to naught, and the scorner is consumed. . . . they also that erred in spirit shall come to understanding, and they that murmured shall learn doctrine." (2 Nephi 27:5-6, 20, 23, 26, 31, 35.)

In the Book of Mormon the very questions about the Bible that now oppress the liberal and fundamentalist alike, to the imminent overthrow of their fondest beliefs, are fully and clearly treated; no other book gives such a perfect and exhaustive explanation of the eschatological problem; here we learn how the Christian and Jewish traditions fit into the world picture, and how God's voice has been from the very beginning to all men everywhere; here alone one may find a full setting forth of the exact nature of scripture, and of the vast range and variety of revelation; here you will find anticipated and answered every logical objection that the intelligence or vanity of men even in this sophisticated age has been able to devise against the preaching of the word; and here one may find a description of our own age so vivid and so accurate that none can fail to recognize it—all these things and much more by way of "proving to the world that the holy scriptures are true." (D&C 20:11.)

So you see that when Joseph Smith brought forth the Book of Mormon, he shocked and angered the world. You remember that within a week the announcements started coming out in the papers: "the Book of Mormon—Blasphemy," and so on. He shocked and angered the world by setting up beside the Bible another book as original scripture.

I think we may see it come to pass that the Book of Mormon will prove to the world that the scriptures are true. There are things in the Bible that are historical and things that are not. The guide to follow is the Book of Mormon.

NOTES

1. König, Eduard, "Ist die jetzt herrschende Einschätzung der hebräischen Geschichtsquellen berechtigt?" *Historische Zeitschrift* 132 (1925): 289-302.

2. Brandon, Samuel George Frederick, "The Historical Element in Primitive Christianity," *Numen* 2 (1955): 156.

3. Brandon, p. 157.

4. Linton, Olaf, *Das Problem der Urkirche in der neueren Forschung* (Uppsala: Almquist und Wiksell, 1932), n.p.

5. Brandon, p. 157.

6. Bultmann, Rudolf, "History and Eschatology in the New Testament," *New Testament Studies* 1 (1954): n.p.

7. Schweitzer, Albert, *Geschichte der Leben-Jesu-Forschung* (Tübingen: J. C. B. Mohr, 1913), p. 2.

8. Bultmann.

9. Torczyner, Harry, "Das Literarische Problem der Bibel," *Zeitschrift der deutschen Morgenländischen Geschichte* 85 (1913): 287-88.

10. Paton, Herbert James, *The Modern Predicament* (New York: Macmillan, 1955), p. 374.

11. Otto, Walter F., "Zur Universalgeschichte des Altertums," *Historische Zeitschrift* 146 (1932): 205.

12. König, pp. 289-302.

13. Hrozny, Bedrick, *Ancient History of Western Asia, India and Crete* (Prague: Artia, 1940), p. 52.

14. Sayce, Archibald Henry, *Monument Facts and Higher Critical Fancies* (London: Religious Tract Society, 1910), n.p.

15. Gordon, Cyrus, *Ugaritic Literature* (Rome: Pontifical Institute of the Bible, 1949), n.p.

16. Gordon.

17. Haldar, Alfred Ossian, *Association of Cult Prophets among the Ancient Semites* (Uppsala: Almquist und Wiksell), p. 199.

18. Mowinckel, Sigmund, *Religion und Kultus* (Göttingen: Vandenhoeck & Ruprecht, 1953), n.p.

19. Albright, William Foxwell, *Archaeology and the Religion of Israel* (Baltimore: Johns Hopkins Press, 1946), n.p.

2

Archaeology and Our Religion

Nothing illustrates better than archaeology the inadequacy of human knowledge at any given time. It is not that archaeology is less reliable than other disciplines, but simply that its unreliability is more demonstrable. Meteorology (to show what we mean) is quite as "scientific" as geology and far more so than archaeology—it actually makes more use of scientific instruments, computers, and higher mathematics than those disciplines need to. Yet we laugh at the weatherman every other day; we are not overawed by his impressive paraphernalia, because we can check up on him any time we feel like it: he makes his learned pronouncements—and then it rains or it doesn't rain. If we could check up on the geologist or archaeologist as easily when he tells us with perfect confidence what has happened and what will happen in the remotest ages, what would the result be? Actually, in the one field in which the wisdom of geology can be controlled, the finding of oil, it is calculated that the experts are proven right only about 10 percent of the time.[1] Now if a man is wrong 90 percent of the time when he is glorying in the complete mastery of his specialty, how far should we trust the same man when he takes to pontificating on the mysteries? No scientific conclusion is to be trusted without testing—to the extent to which exact sciences are exact they are also experimental sciences; it is in the laboratory that the oracle must be consulted. But the archaeologist is denied access to the oracle. For him there is no neat and definitive demonstration; he is doomed to plod along, everlastingly protesting and fum-

"Archaeology and Our Religion," accompanied by two cover letters dated September 16, 1965, was originally intended to be included in the "I Believe" series in the *Instructor*.

bling, through a laborious, often rancorous running debate that never ends.

To make a significant discovery in physics or mathematics or philology, one must first know a good deal about the subject; but the greatest archaeological discoveries of recent years were made by ignorant peasants and illiterate shepherd boys. From that it follows, as the handbooks on archaeology never tire of pointing out, that the proper business of the archaeologist is not so much the finding of stuff as being able to recognize what one has found. Yet even there the specialist enjoys no monopoly. Dr. Joseph Saad, who directed the excavations at Khirbet Qumran, tells of many instances in which the local Arabs were able to explain findings that completely baffled the experts from the West, to the rage and chagrin of the latter. Hence Sir Mortimer Wheeler warns the archaeologist: "Do not ignore the opinion of the uninstructed. 'Everyone knows as much as the savant. . . . ' Emerson said so and he was right."[2]

With everybody getting into the act, it is not surprising that the history of archaeology is largely the story of bitter jealousies and frightful feuds. Archaeology mercilessly accentuates certain qualities characteristic of all research but often glosses over the exact sciences. The elements of uncertainty, surprise, and disappointment, and the pervasive role of speculation and imagination, with all the unconscious conditioning and prejudice that implies, are not merely regrettable defects in archaeology—they are the very stuff of which the picturesque discipline is composed. "What in fact is Archaeology?" asks Sir Mortimer, and answers, "I do not myself really know. . . . I do not even know whether Archaeology is to be described as an art or a science." Even on the purely technical side, he points out, "There is no right way of digging, but there are many wrong ways."[3]

Duel in the Dark

The idea of archaeology as the key to a man's origin and destiny was introduced as a weapon of anti-clerical polemic in the revolutionary movements of the eighteenth and nineteenth centuries. Reimar's "hate-filled pamphlet" on history and the New Testament launched the "scientific" attack on the Bible,[4] and when Boucher de Perthes, a child of the French Revolution, found stone "hand-axes" among the flints of Abbeville he published them in five stately volumes entitled, with pontifical finality, "On the Creation."[5] These objects, whose use and origin are still disputed, were to be nothing less than the key to the creation. Such fantastic leaps of the mind reveal the fierce determination of the first modern archaeologists to "get something" on the Bible. It was inevitable that biblical archaeology should become little more than "an offshoot of Darwinism."[6] The great Lamarck, before he even came up with his explanation of the creation, was animated "by a severe . . . philosophical hostility, amounting to hatred, for the tradition of the Deluge and the Biblical creation story, indeed for everything which recalled the Christian theory of nature."[7] And Darwin writes of himself in his twenties: "I had gradually come, by this time, to see that the Old Testament from its manifestly false history of the world and from its attributing to God the feelings of a revengeful tyrant, was no more to be trusted than the sacred books of the Hindoos [sic], or the beliefs of any barbarian. . . . By further reflecting . . . that the more we know of the fixed laws of nature the more incredible do miracles become—that the men at that time were ignorant and credulous to a degree almost incomprehensible to us. . . . This disbelief crept over me at a very slow rate, but was at last complete. The rate was so slow that I felt no distress, and have never since doubted for a single second that my conclusion was correct."[8]

This is a very revealing statement, a rich compound of cliches, a testament of Victorian smugness: "manifestly false . . . revengeful tyrant . . . any barbarian . . . fixed laws of nature . . . never doubted for a single second." Those are the words of a man who knows all the answers and is proud rather than ashamed of his unflinching loyalty to his adolescent prejudices. Just how much would a young English theology student in the 1820s know about the *real* history of the world, books of the Hindus, or "the beliefs of any barbarian"? Next to nothing, is putting it mildly, but it was enough to put the stamp of "complete disbelief" on Darwin's thinking forever after. Students commonly assume that it was the gradual amassing of evidence that in time constrained such men to part company with the Bible. Exactly the opposite is the case: long before they had the evidence, they brought to their researches such an unshakable determination to discredit the book of Genesis that the discovery of the evidence was a foregone conclusion. It was Darwin's bosom friend and spokesman who blurted out the real issue with characteristic bluntness: "Darwin himself avoided attacking the Bible, but for Huxley, his doughty champion against all comers," writes J. C. Greene, "the battle against the doctrine of inspiration, whether plenary or otherwise, was the crucial engagement in the fight for evolution and for freedom of scientific enquiry."[9] The battle was against revelation, and evolution was the weapon forged for the conflict. We must not be misled by that inevitable tag about "freedom of scientific enquiry." When a Tennessee high-school teacher was fired for teaching evolution in 1925, the whole civilized world was shocked and revolted at such barbaric restriction on freedom of thought; yet at the same time there was not an important college or even high school in the country that would hire a man who dared to preach *against* evolution. Freedom of thought indeed.

The great debate between "science" and "religion" has been a duel in the dark. How do things stand between the picture that "archaeology" gives us of the past and the picture that the scriptures give us? Take the biblical image first: the best efforts of the best artists back through the years to represent a clear picture of things described in the Bible look to us simply comical. Even the conscientious Flemish artists, using the best Oriental knowledge of their time, paint Solomon or Holofernes as boozy Landgraves at a fancy dress ball, while the masters of the Italian Renaissance show their prophets and apostles affecting the prescribed dress and stock gestures of traveling Sophists of the antique world. We are no better today, with our handsome "Bible Lands" books, based on diligent research, showing Jesus or Elijah in the garb of modern Bedouins or Ramallah peasants moving through the eroded terrain of modern Palestine or discoursing beneath arches and gates of Norman and Turkish design. The moral of this is that no matter where we get our information, our picture of the Bible is bound to be out of focus, for it will always be based on inadequate data, and it will always be of our own construction. And at no time did the Christian world have a more distorted picture of the Bible than in the nineteenth century. To the Victorians, creaking with culture and refinement, it was easy and pleasant to assign all other creatures their proper place and station in the world—for that is what evolution does. Their outspoken objection to Mormonism was that it was utterly barbaric, an intolerable affront to an enlightened and scientific age. Huxley declared with true scientific humility that the difference between a cultivated man of his own day and a native of the forest was as great as that between the native and a blade of grass. What possible understanding could these people have of the real Bible world? Taken at face value the Bible was a disgustingly primitive piece of goods—"poor stuff," John Stuart Mill pronounced it; the work of people "ignorant and credulous to a degree almost incomprehensible to us," as Darwin said, for this, of course, was the Bible that Darwin rejected: in it he was attacking an image that was the product of his own culture and nothing else.

The Mind's Eye

Archaeology today "in our universities and schools," according to Wheeler, "forms innocuous pools of somewhat colorless knowledge—mostly a refined Darwinism—in which our kindergartens are encouraged to paddle."[10]

Again, everybody gets into the act. My own children, long before they could read, write, or count, could tell you exactly how things were upon the earth millions and millions of years ago. But did the little scholars really know? "What is our knowledge of the past and how do we obtain it?" asks the eminent archaeologist Stuart Piggott, and answers: "The past no longer exists for us, even the past of yesterday. . . . This means that we can never have direct knowledge of the past. We have only information or evidence from which we can construct a picture."[11] The fossil or potsherd or photograph that I hold in my hand may be called a fact—it is direct evidence, an immediate experience; but my interpretation of it is *not* a fact, it is entirely a picture of my own construction. I cannot experience ten thousand or forty million years—I can only imagine, and the fact that my picture is based on facts does not make *it* a fact, even when I think the evidence is so clear and unequivocal as to allow no other interpretation. Archaeology brings home this lesson every day, as Sir Flinders Petrie pointed out, for in no other field does interpretation count for so much.[12] "The excavator," writes Sir Leonard Woolley, "is constantly subject to impressions too subjective and too intangible to be communicated, and out of these, by no exact logical process, there arise theories which he can state, can perhaps support, but cannot prove. . . . They have their value as summing up experiences which no student of his objects and notes can ever share."[13] Yet what makes scientific knowledge scientific is that it *can* be shared. "There are fires," writes a leading student of American archaeology, "which man may, or may not, have lit—animals he may, or may not, have killed—and crudely flaked stone objects, which those most qualified to judge think he did not make. By weight of numbers these finds have been built into an impression of probability, but the idol has feet of clay."[14] This is the normal state of things when we are dealing with the past: "If one certainty does emerge from this accumulation of uncertainties," writes an

eminent geologist, "it is the deep impression of the vastness of geologic time."[15] An "accumulation of *un*certain-
ties" leaves the student ("by weight of numbers") with an
"impression" which he thereupon labels a *"certainty."*

Yet with examples gross as earth to exhort him, the archaeologist is constantly slipping into the normal occupa-
tional hazard of letting the theory rather than the facts call
the tune. For years archaeologists always assumed that
pieces could be chipped from the surface of stones merely
by exposure to the burning sun—they never bothered to
put their theory to the test, though no one ever was present
when the sun did its chipping.[16] From Breasted's *Ancient
Times*, millions of high-school students have learned how
primitive man woke one morning in his camp in the Sinai
Peninsula to find that bright copper beads had issued from
the greenish rocks with which he banked his fire that night.
It was not until 1939 that a scientist at Cambridge actually
went to the trouble to see if copper could be smelted from
an open fire, and discovered that it was absolutely impossible.[17] Nobody had bothered to check up on these simple
things—like the Aristotelians who opposed the experi-
menting of Galileo, the men of science felt no need to question the obvious. If man had been on the earth for, say,
100,000 years, scattered everywhere in tiny groups subsisting
on a near-animal level, could we possibly find the cultural
and linguistic patterns we do in the world today? After fifty
thousand years of local isolation, is it conceivable that languages at opposite ends of the earth should be recognizably
related? Only in our day are such elementary questions beginning to be asked—often with surprising and disturbing
results. But however vast the accumulation of facts may become,
our picture of the past and the future will always be, not
partly but wholly, the child of our own trained and con-
ditioned imaginations. "The world will always be different
from any statement that science can give of it," a philosopher of science writes, and he explains: "that is, we are
looking for an opportunity to restate any statement which

we can give of the world. . . . We are always restating our statement of the world."[18] Scholarship is also an age-old, open-ended discussion in which the important thing is not to be right at a given moment but to be able to enter seriously into the discussion. That I cannot do if I must depend on the opinion of others, standing helplessly by until someone else pronounces a verdict, and then cheering loudly to show that I too am a scholar.

Because interpretation plays an all-important role in it, archaeology has been carried on against a background of ceaseless and acrimonious controversy, with theory and authority usually leading fact around by the nose. If the great Sir Arthur Evans decided eighty years ago that the Minoans and Mycenaeans were not Greeks, then evidence discovered today must be discounted if it shows they were Greeks; if it was concluded long ago that the Jews did not write in Hebrew at the time of Christ, then Hebrew documents from that time if they are discovered today must be forgeries. "Does our time scale, then, partake of natural law?" a geologist wonders. "No. . . . I wonder how many of us realize that the time scale was frozen in essentially its present form by 1840 . . . ? The followers of the founding fathers went forth across the earth and in Procrustean fashion made it fit the sections they found even in places where the actual evidence literally proclaimed denial. So flexible and accommodating are the 'facts' of geology."[19] "Science," said Whitehead, "is our modern-day dogmatism." There is something cozy and old-fashioned, almost nostalgic, in the archaeology of forty years ago with its invincible meliorism and romantic faith in man's slow, steady, inevitable onward and upward march. But archaeology is the science of surprises, and the most desperate efforts of accommodation have not been able to discredit the sensational changes of our day.

"One of the most exciting results of the radio-carbon dating," writes Piggott, " . . . has been to emphasize how rapidly and severely the environment was modified."[20] Extreme and rapid changes of environment have long been anathema to science. "Darwin's secret, learned from Lyell,"[21] according to H. F. Osborn, was (in Lyell's own words) that "all theories are rejecting that which involves the assumption of sudden and violent catastrophies."[22] In a world of nuclear explosions this seems downright funny, but it "was a perfect expression," as Egon Friedell has written, "of the English temperament and comfortable middle-class view of the world that refused to believe in sudden and violent metamorphoses, world uprising, and world calamities."[23] One of the most militant evolutionists of our day says that "it remains true, as every paleontologist knows, that most new species, genera, and families, and nearly all categories above the level of families, appear in the record suddenly, and are not led up to by known, gradual, completely continuous transitional sequences."[24] One wonders why if *most* species appear on the scene *suddenly* without millions of years of evolutionary preparation leading up to them, the human race cannot have done the same. "Because it didn't," we are told. For a hundred years, thousands of scientists have devoted their lives to proving that it didn't; yet all they have to offer us as proof to date is a large and cluttered science fair of bizarre and competing models, interesting but mutually damaging.

The New Uniformity

Through the years the writer, who is no archaeologist, has had to keep pretty well abreast of the journals and consult occasionally with archaeologists in order to carry on his own varied projects. Anyone who has any contact at all with what is going on is aware that the significant trend since World War II has been the steady drawing together of far-flung peoples and cultures of antiquity into a single surprisingly close-knit fabric. Early in the present century an "Egyptologist" could make fun of the "amusing ignorance" of the Pearl of Great Price, in which "Chaldeans and Egyptians are hopelessly mixed together, although as dissimilar and remote in language, religion, and locality as are today's American Indians and Chinese."[25] Today a ten-year-old would be reprimanded for such a statement, since now we know that Chaldeans and Egyptians were "hopelessly mixed together" from the very beginning of history. Even as late as the 1930s so eminent a scholar as T. E. Peet had to exercise extreme caution—suggesting that there might be any resemblance between the literatures of Babylonia, Palestine, Egypt, and Greece.[26] Today we know better, as every month establishes more widely and more firmly the common ties that knit all the civilizations of the ancient world together.

A hundred years ago, investigators of prehistory already sensed "the essential unity of the earlier Stone Age cultures throughout the Old World." From the very beginning of the race "at a given period in the Pleistocene," writes Piggott, "one can take, almost without selection, tools from South India, Africa and South England which show identical techniques of manufacture and form. . . . What happened at one end of the area seems to be happening more or less simultaneously at the other."[27] I have never seen any attempt to account for this astounding worldwide coordination in the industries of primitive beings who supposedly could communicate to their nearest neighbors only by squeals and grunts. In the mid-nineteenth century the folklorists were beginning to notice that the same myths and legends turned up everywhere in the Old and New Worlds, and philologists were discovering the same thing about languages; today Hockett and Asher are bemused by the "striking lack of diversity in certain features of language" and make the astounding announcement that "phonological systems [of all the languages of the world] show much less variety than could easily be invented by any linguist working with pencil and paper."[28] The same authorities note that "man shows an amazingly small amount of racial diversity," and pardonably wonder "why human racial diversity is so slight, and . . . why the languages and cultures of all communities, no matter how diverse, are elaborations of a single inherited 'common denominator.' "[29] With a million years of savagery and hostility, ignorance, isolation, and bestial suspicion to keep them divided, it seems that men should have had plenty of time to develop a vast number of separate "denominators" of language, legend, race, and culture. But that is not the picture we get at all.[30]

In religion it is the same. It was not until 1930 that a group of researchers at Cambridge cautiously presented evidence for the prevalence through the ancient world of a single pattern of kingship, an elaborate religious-economic-political structure that could not possibly have been invented independently in many places. We do *not* find, as we have every right to expect, an infinite variety of exotic religious rites and concepts; instead we find a single overall pattern, but one so peculiar and elaborate that it cannot have been the spontaneous production of primitive minds operating in isolation from each other.[31]

When history begins, "let us say c. 5000 B.C.," to follow J. Mellaart, "we find throughout the greater part of the Near East . . . villages, market towns . . . and castles of local rulers" widely in touch with each other as "goods and raw materials were traded over great distances."[32] It is essentially the same picture we find right down to the present; and we find it everywhere—if we go to distant China "the life of the Shang [the oldest known] population can have differed little in essentials from that of the populous city-states of the Bronze Age Mesopotamia,"[33] or from that of the peasants of the Danube or of "the earliest English farming culture."[34] This is what has come out since World War II. Before that, archaeology had made us progressively aware of the oneness of our world with successive discoveries of Amarna, Ugarit, Boghazkeui, Nuzi, and so on, each one tying all the great Near Eastern civilizations closer and closer together while revealing the heretofore unsuspected presence of great nations and empires as active and

intimate participants in a single drama. And the Bible is
right in the center of it: the patriarchs who had been reduced to solar myths by the higher critics suddenly turned
out to be flesh-and-blood people; odd words, concepts and
expressions, and institutions of the Bible started turning up
in records of great antiquity; the Hittites, believed to be a
myth by Bible scholars until 1926, suddenly emerged as
one of the greatest civilizations the world has ever seen.
Since then a dozen almost equally great empires have been
discovered, and the preliminary studies of each of them
have shown in every case that they had more or less intimate ties with the great Classical and Middle Eastern civilizations.[35] The picture of ancient civilization as a whole has
become steadily broader and at the same time more uniform, so that the growing impression is one of monotony
bordering on drabness. Seton Lloyd is depressed by "the
drab impersonality of the 'archaeological ages.' "[36] Archaeology gives us, as M. P. Nilsson puts it, "a picture-
book without a text";[37] or, in the words of Sir Mortimer,
"the archaeologist may find the tub but altogether miss
Diogenes."[38] The eager visitor to a hundred recent diggings
is fated to discover that people once lived in stone or brick
or wooden houses, cooked their food (for they ate food) in
pots of clay or metal over fires, hunted, farmed, fished, had
children, died, and were buried. Wherever we go, it is just
more of the same—all of which we could have assumed in
the first place. The romance of archaeology has always re-
sided not in the known but in the unknown, and enough is
known today to suggest the terrifying verdict that a great
Cambridge scientist pronounced on the physical sciences a
generation ago: "The end is in sight."

And now we come to the crux of the matter. As the tub
without Diogenes has nothing to do with philosophy, so
archaeology without the prophets has nothing to do with
religion. "You cannot," says Piggott, "from archaeological
evidence, inform yourself on man's ideas, beliefs, fears or
aspirations. You cannot understand what his works of art

or craftsmanship signified to him."[39] The ancient patriarchs and prophets ate out of ordinary dishes, sat on ordinary chairs, wore ordinary clothes, spoke the vernacular, wrote on ordinary paper and skins, and were buried in ordinary graves. The illusion of the pilgrims to the holy land, Christian, Moslem and Jewish, that this is not so—that is, that contact with such objects by holy men rendered them holy—gave rise to Biblical archaeology at an early time. The Palestine pilgrims from Origen and Gregory to Robinson and Schaff had all been looking for extra-special things, for miraculous or at least wonderful objects. Men who viewed the idea of *living* prophets as a base superstition turned to the dead stones of the "Holy Land" for heavenly consolation, and enlisted archaeology in the cause of faith.[40] But though archaeology may conceivably confirm the existence of a prophet (though it has never yet done so), it can never prove or disprove the visions that make the prophet a significant figure. Former attempts to explain the scriptures in terms of nature-myths, animism, and psychology had nothing to do with reality.[41] What can archaeology tell me about the council in heaven? Nothing, of course—that all happened in another world. The same holds for the creation, taking place as it did at a time and place and in a manner that we cannot even imagine. Then comes the garden of Eden—a paradise and another world beyond our ken. It is only when Adam and Eve enter this world that they come down to our level. Strangely enough, the biblical image is not that of our first parents entering a wonderful new world, but leaving such to find themselves in a decidedly dreary place of toil and tears. Before long the children of Adam are building cities and are completely launched on the familiar and drab routines of civilized living: "dreary" suggests old and tired, and there is nothing fresh or new about the Adamic Age.

On the archaeological side we have Jericho, by general consensus (as of the moment) the oldest city in the world. It emerges abruptly full-blown, with a sophisticated and stereotyped architecture that remains unchanged for twenty-one successive town-levels, and from the first it displays a way of life substantially the same as that carried on by the inhabitants of the nearby towns right down to the present day. This has come as a great surprise; it is not at all consistent with the official model of the onward and up-ward march of civilization that we all learned about at school. When the civilization of China was rediscovered by European missionaries in the seventeenth century, skep-tics and atheists saw in it a crushing refutation of the Bible—here was a great civilization thousands of years older and far richer, wiser, and more splendid than any-thing Western man had imagined, thriving in complete un-awareness of God's plan of salvation. It was the discovery of such other worlds, such island universes, that was once the concern of archaeology, ever seeking the strange, the marvelous, and the exotic. But now archaeology has found too much; the worlds are there, but they are not isolated—not even China; they are all members of a single community, and by far the best handbook guide to the nature and identity of that community remains the Bible.

NOTES

1. Sloan, Raymond D., "The Future of the Exploration Geolo-gist—Can He Meet the Challenge?" *Geotimes* 3, no. 1 (1958), p. 6. "Only one wildcat well in nine discovers oil or gas: only one in forty-four is profitable." In spite of scientific methods, "the high risks . . . are unusual in the business world." (Sloan, pp. 6, 7.)

2. Wheeler, Sir Robert Eric Mortimer, *Archaeology from the Earth* (Oxford: Clarendon Press, 1954), p. 50.

3. Wheeler, p. 2.

4. Jeremias, Joachim, "The Present Position in the Controversy Concerning the Problem of the Historical Jesus," *Expository Times* 69 (1958): 333.

5. Rapport, Samuel, and Helen Wright, eds., *Archaeology* (New York: New York University Library of Science, 1963), pp. 18-20.

6. Gall, August Freiherrn von, *Basileia tou Theou* (Heidelberg: Winter, 1926), p. 12, discussing the Wellhausen school.

7. Gillespie, Charles Coulston, "Lamarck and Darwin in the History of Science," *American Scientist* 46 (Dec. 1958): 397.

8. Darwin, Charles, *Autobiography* (New York: Harcourt, Brace, 1959), describing the period between 1836 and 1839. Darwin was born in 1809.

9. Green, John C., "Darwin and Religion," *Proceedings of the American Philosophical Society* 103 (1959): 717.

10. Wheeler, p. 23.

11. Piggott, Stuart, ed., *The Dawn of Civilization* (New York: McGraw-Hill, 1961), p. 11.

12. Petrie, William Matthew Flinders, *Social Life in Ancient Egypt* (1923), part 3, pp. 80, 81.

13. Woolley, Leonard, *Digging Up the Past* (New York: Crowell, 1954), p. 119.

14. Bushnell, G.H.S., "The Birth and Growth of New World Civilization," in Piggott, p. 377.

15. Swinnerton, Henry Hurd, *The Earth Beneath Us* (Boston: Little-Brown, 1955), p. 15.

16. Morgan, Jacques Jean Marie de, *La Prehistoire Orientale* (Paris: Paul Geuthner, 1925), II, pp. 4ff., discusses this phenomenon, with pictures of "hatchet-shaped seile chipped by the heat of the sun." (Fig. 2.)

17. Coghlan, H. H., "Some Experiments on the Origin of Early Copper," *Man* 39 (1939): 106-8.

18. Mead, George H., *Movements of Thought in the 19th Century* (Chicago: University of Chicago Press, 1936), p. 508, discussing Bergson.

19. Spieker, Edmund M., "Mountain-Building Chronology and Nature of Geologic Time Scale," *Bulletin of the American Association of Petroleum Geologists* 40 (August 1956): 1803; cf. Norman D. Newell, *Proceedings of the American Philosophical Society* 103 (1959): 265.

20. Piggott, p. 40.

21. Osborn, Henry Fairfield, *The Origin and Evolution of Life* (New York: Scribner's, 1918), p. 24.

22. Lyell, Charles, *Principles of Geology* (New York: John Murray, 1872) 1:318.

23. Friedell, Egon, *Kulturgeschichte Aegyptens und des alten Orients* (München: C.H. Beck, 1953), p. 105.

24. Simpson, George Gaylord, *The Major Features of Evolution* (New York: Columbia University Press, 1953), p. 360.

25. Peters, John, in Rev. Franklin S. Spalding, *Joseph Smith as a Translator* (Salt Lake City: Arrow Press, 1912), p. 28.

26. Peet, Thomas Eric, *A Comparative Study of the Literatures of*

Egypt, Palestine and Mesopotamia (London: British Academy, 1931), pp. 52f., 96f., 127-29, 113-16.

27. Piggott, Stuart, *Prehistoric India* (London: Cassell, 1950), p. 26.

28. Hockett, Charles F., and Robert Ascher, "The Human Revolution," *American Scientist* 52 (1964): 90.

29. Hockett, p. 90.

30. Hockett and Ascher insist not only that man had *already* achieved the essence of language and culture at least a million years ago (p. 89), but that "the crucial developments must have taken place once, and then spread" by that time, since "true diversity is found in more superficial aspects of language" but not in the fundamental aspect (p. 90). That is, all the languages of the world have retained *recognizable* ties to a parent language from which they separated over a million years ago! Since C. S. Coon puts the age of the human race at about 50,000 years, this is quite a thing.

31. Lord Raglan, *The Origins of Religion* (London: Watts and Co., 1949).

32. Mellaart, James, "The Beginning of Village and Urban Life," in Piggott, *Dawn of Civilization*, p. 62.

33. Watson, William, in Piggott, p. 271.

34. Sieveking, Gale, "China: The Civilization of a Single People," in Edward Bacon, *Vanished Civilizations of the Ancient World* (New York: McGraw-Hill, 1963), this being the Windmill Hill site of 2750 B.C.

35. For a good survey, see Sieveking's paper in the preceding footnote, which deals in major civilizations of which we have virtually no history but all of which are definitely tied to the great civilizations of antiquity.

36. Seton, Lloyd, "The Early Settlement of Anatolia," in Piggott, p. 185.

37. Nilsson, Martin Persson, *Minoan and Mycenaean Religion* (Lund: C. W. K. Gleerup, 1950), p. 7.

38. Wheeler, p. 214.

39. Piggott, p. 15.

40. We have discussed this in the *Jewish Quarterly Review* 50 (1959): 99ff., 109ff.

41. Lord Raglan, p. 38.

3

Myths and the Scriptures

A student confronted for the first time by classical and Oriental myths that read like reruns of well-known Bible stories—such as the garden of Eden episode and the Flood—often goes into a sort of shock, emerging from which he announces to family and friends that he has just discovered a fact of life: the Bible is just a lot of mythology.

Such a conclusion may be the result of a faulty approach to the Bible as well as to the myths. The first thing to do in such a case is to apply cold packs and calm the student down, pointing out to him that such deeply religious writers as Dante and Milton not only were aware of many parallels between Christian and pagan lore and imagery, but also freely mingled the two together in constructing their faith-promoting epics.

Some of the earliest religious writers were edified by the Egyptian Phoenix, and the later Fathers of the traditional church diligently catalogued those heathen myths and doctrines that most closely resembled their own beliefs as proof that the gentiles had always pirated the true teachings of the prophets and patriarchs.

The idea was that the Egyptians had picked up a lot of stuff from the Israelites during the latter's sojourn in Egypt, and of course the Egyptians got it all mixed up. Also, since Adam, Enoch, Noah, and Abraham had all left writings behind long before Moses, it was only to be expected that in times of apostasy their teachings, in contaminated form, should fall into profane hands.

There is a good deal to be said for this theory, for the myths and rites of all the ancient world, if traced backward

"Myths and the Scriptures" was published in the October 1971 *New Era*, pp. 34-38.

in time, do show a marked tendency to conform more and more to a few basic themes and to converge on a limited geographical area as their apparent place of origin. But whatever the real explanation, there is a very real relationship between the biblical and the worldwide pagan traditions. There has been no question of proving that such a relationship existed; however, there has always been the neglected task of showing just what that relationship is.

This sensible and promising line of approach to the problem of mythology and the Bible has been vigorously rejected by the modern clergy, by professional scholars, and by the literate. Three points bear elaboration here.

1. The clergy, Christian and Jewish alike, have insisted before all else on the absolute originality and uniqueness of the teachings of Christ and Moses respectively, laboring under the strange illusion that if anything coming from any other source shows a close resemblance to those teachings, the claims of the founders to originality and hence to divinity are in serious jeopardy.

A close resemblance between biblical and nonbiblical teachings and practices is necessarily a "suspicious resemblance." Theologians have worked out their own theory of communication between God and man, which they have strictly limited as to time and place, allowing no latitude whatever for the possibility of anything occurring that is not accounted for in the Bible.

Indeed, the Fathers of the fourth century insist that we may safely assume that whatever is not explicitly mentioned in the Bible could not possibly have occurred—ever or anywhere.

The present-day insistence, especially by the Catholics (though vigorously challenged by the brilliant Jesuit Hugo Rahner), on the absolute originality of Jesus is the result of total rejection of the idea of dispensations. If we know, however, that the gospel has been on the earth from time to time ever since the days of Adam, then it is easily understandable that recognizable fragments of it should be seen floating around in sundry times and places.

But "dispensationism" has long been anathema to the clergy. Hence their hostility to the Apocrypha, their marked coolness to the Dead Sea Scrolls, and their hot denunciation of Joseph Smith for giving the world ancient writings that not only resemble the Bible but also lay claim to the same inspiration while widening the horizon of God's covenant people to include times and places heretofore undreamed of.

2. Professional scholars, who as a matter of course reject the whole idea of inspired writings, have been as reluctant as the clergy to recognize resemblances between the myths and legends of various parts of the world as being anything but the purest coincidence. The reason for this is departmental pride. For example, a Celtic or Semitic scholar may very well know more about Greek than I do; but if Greek is my one and only field, I may still turn up my nose with a great show of scientific skepticism and technical superiority, and categorically refuse to consider even the possibility of a relationship between the documents I can read and the documents I cannot read.

A dazzling demonstration of this type of precious myopia was the century-long refusal of Egyptologists to acknowledge any connection whatever between Israel and Egypt (they used it as an argument against Joseph Smith), though links and ties confronted them at every turn. When Erman finally showed beyond a doubt that an important piece of Egyptian wisdom literature also turned up in the body of Hebrew wisdom literature, he was almost ashamed of his discovery and never followed it up.

Secular scholars, on the other hand, have been quick to take any resemblance between heathen traditions and the Bible as absolute proof that the scriptures are simply ordinary stuff. The classic example of this was the Babylonian flood story, discovered by Layard in the mid-nineteenth century. It resembled the biblical account closely enough to show without doubt that they were connected, but before any search for the source of either version was undertaken, it was joyfully announced that the biblical account was derived from the Babylonian and was, therefore, a fraud. The experts were wrong on both points—the Assurbanipal version is really a late redaction, and the duplication of the flood story, instead of weakening it, actually confirms it. Indeed, if there really were a universal flood, it would be very strange if memories of it did not turn up in many places, as in fact they do.

3. Most students learn about ancient myths from teachers and textbooks of literature by way of the late classic poets to whom the myths were little more than literary playthings. A student cannot understand "A Midsummer Night's Dream" without knowing something about the many myths that cluster about the figure of Theseus, but the teacher's only concern is to put the student in the literary picture, and for that a trip to the handbook suffices.

For the student of literature, the myths are but handy aids to the writer, useful devices for achieving decorative or erudite effects, as they were once the paint and gilt of decadent poetry. Since the day of Augustus, the literati have had neither the desire nor the equipment to look beneath the surface.

Hardly worth mentioning at this date is the nineteenth century *Wissenschaft*, which inevitably explained everything as "nature myth"—primitive man's reaction to his natural environment. The ancient Sophists played around with that idea, naively assuming, as did the scholars and scientists of a hundred years ago, that any reasonable explanation for a phenomenon that they could come up with would necessarily be the true and correct answer—how could it be otherwise if it was a strictly rational conclusion free of all superstition and religion? It was an impressive exhibition of scientific gullibility, but it is not taken seriously today, now that we know a lot more about ancient myths than we did.

In recent years the early myths have acquired a new status and dignity. A steady accumulation of comparative studies tying this to that and these to those now crams the stacks of our libraries. Spread out before the mind's eye, their myriad pages interweave into a grandiose texture, a vast shadowy tapestry in which we begin to discern the common backdrop of all history and religion.

But the books are still sedulously segregated and widely distributed among the floors and alcoves of the library, and to bring them all together into the one organic whole from which they were taken is a task that will yet tax the capacity of the computer. Meanwhile, we must imagine the pieces of this huge jigsaw puzzle as heaped in separate piles, each representing a special field of study or cultural area, from Iceland to Polynesia. To date no one has taken the trouble to integrate the materials in even one of these hundred-odd piles; and as to taking up the whole lot and relating every pile to every other, so far only a few bold suggestions have come from men of genius like G. Santillana, Cyrus Gordon, or Robert Graves, whose proposals get chilly reception from specialized scholars who can only be alarmed by such boldness and appalled by the work entailed in painting the whole picture.

But such study as has been done shows us that the old myths are by no means pure fiction, any more than they are all history. As the Muses told Hesiod, "We know both how to fib and how to tell the truth"; and, as Joseph Smith learned of the Apocrypha, "there are many things contained therein that are true, and there are many things contained therein that are not true" (see D&C 91)—all of which means that we must be very careful in accepting and condemning.

Today, formidable task forces of first-rate scholars and scientists are working on the Atlantis problem, whereas a very few years ago anyone careless enough to express interest in that question was announcing his candidacy for the asylum. The world that "deepbrowed Homer" was supposed to have conjured up out of his own head has in our own day taken on flesh and blood, and today we read the novels of Marie Renault or Robert Graves with a feeling that Theseus or Heracles were probably real persons who did at least something like the deeds attributed to them.

If we attempt to untangle the probably historical from the fanciful, we soon discover the common ground on which they meet and fuse: it is *ritual*. Myths arise at attempts to explain ritual doings, whose meaning has been forgotten—"What mean these stones?" After much discussion back and forth, the consensus now emerges that it is the rites and ordinances that come first. This should have been clear from the outset, since myths and legends are innumerable while the rites and ordinances found throughout the world are surprisingly few and uniform, making it quite apparent that it is the stories that are invented—the rites are always there.

Such indeed has always been the Latter-day Saint position. Adam first performed an ordinance and when asked to give an explanation of it replied that he knew of none "save the Lord commanded me." (Moses 5:6.) Then it was that the true explanation came forth from the mouth of a heavenly instructor.

But if in later times members of some distant tribe, having inherited the rites, were asked to explain them, they would have to come up with some invented stories of their own—and that would be myth. It is in their contact with ritual that history and fantasy share a common ground and mingle with each other.

Take the model heroes Theseus and Heracles, for example. We know that they are ritual figures because they repeatedly get themselves involved in well-known ritual situations. Thus each in his wanderings is not once but often the guest of a king who tries to put him to death, forcing the hero to turn the tables and slay the host or his officiating high priest in the manner intended for himself. The nature of this business is now well understood, thanks to hundreds of similar examples collected from all over the world and from every century, making it clear that we have to do with an established routine practice of inviting a noble, visiting stranger to be the substitute for the king—on the throne, in the favor of the queen, and finally and all too quickly on the sacrificial altar—thus sparing the king himself the discomfort and inconvenience of being ritually put to death at the end of a sacred cycle of years. This exotic little drama was more than a fiction; it was an actual practice, surviving in some parts of the world down to modern times, but flourishing with particular vigor in the Near East around 1400 B.C., the period to which most of the Greek myths belong.

Since, as we have said, myths are invented or adjusted to explain ritual, the two are naturally identified, and hence any event reported in a myth is customarily dismissed as purely mythical. But that won't do any more, because such strange ceremonial events actually did take place, regularly and repeatedly.

Ancient civilization was hierocentric—centered around the temple. The everyday activities of farming, trade, and war were all ritually bound to the cycle of the year and the cosmos. The great periodic rites were of a dramatic nature, but they were none the less real: a coronation is the purest ceremony, yet for all that it is still real recorded history; a war or migration, though only too real to its victims, would be carried out with strict ritual propriety, according to the religious rules of the game. It is hard for us to understand this ritualizing of history, but once it was a very real thing, and one can still find it miraculously surviving among the Hopi.

So when the ancient myths from all over the world show us the same situations and the same adventures and monsters recurring again and again, we may look upon this endless repetition not as discrediting the historicity of those events and situations but as confirming it. These myths tell about such things happening because that was the type of thing that did happen, and the ritual nature of the event guaranteed that it should happen not once but over and over again.

Nothing illustrates this principle better than the long-despised (by scholars and clergy) and neglected book of Abraham. Since we have chosen Theseus and Heracles as our archetypes, we may well consider the most spectacular and celebrated stories of how each escaped from his inhospitable host. The last and worst actor that Theseus had to deal with was Procrustes, whose notorious murder bed has become proverbial. Was there such a bed? A century ago the Egyptologist Lefebure noted that there are quite a number of old traditions around the eastern Mediterranean about kings who built cruelly ingenious altars, sometimes mechanically operated, usually of metal, and shaped like beds, on which they would put to death their noble guests.

In 1859, B. Beer pointed out for the first time that Abraham belongs in the old Procrustes tradition, noting that the wicked Cities of the Plain where Abraham was given a bad time all had in their central marketplaces ritual beds on which they would sacrifice strangers by stretching them out if they were too short and whacking them off if they were too tall to match the exact length of the bed. This, of course, is the celebrated Procrustes technique, and Beer duly notes that Procrustes' other name, Damastes, has exactly the same meaning as Sodom—the "Forcer" or "Violator." Furthermore, Beer reports early traditions telling how Eleazer, when he went to represent Abraham in those cities, appeared there in the exact form and stature of Abraham and narrowly escaped being put to death on such a bed. So we have Abraham on the altar as another Theseus or Heracles, surprisingly sharing the fate of the great patriarch of the Athenians!

But Lefebure also notices that Theseus and the bed of

Procrustes have a close counterpart in the story of Heracles' most famous and sensational escape. This took place not in Greece nor in Asia, but in Egypt, at the court of Pharaoh. The Greeks regarded this as the first and oldest example of the oft-repeated royal sacrifice of an honored visitor, the archetype of them all, and they always located it in Busiris, which actually was from prehistoric times on down, the most celebrated and venerated center of human sacrifice in Egypt.

Egyptologists do not doubt the reality of a periodic sacrifice of the king of Egypt in early times, or the practice of drafting a substitute (preferably a noble, redheaded stranger) to take his place, first on the throne to establish his identity with the king, and then on the altar. So we have a three-way tie-up, and a very firm one, in which Theseus is related to Heracles as an intended victim on the famous "cruel altar" of a desperate and designing king. The same Theseus is also related to Abraham in a like situation by the peculiar name and nature of his evil host Procrustes. And Abraham in turn is tied to Heracles as the intended but miraculously delivered victim on the altar of a pharaoh of Egypt.

What are we to make of these three heroes? Do their stereotyped adventures cancel each other out? On the contrary, they confirm each other as long as we recognize that the reality that lies behind them is a ritual reality. The book of Abraham is particularly strong on this point, making much of the awesome ceremonial nature of the doings in which the patriarch as a young man got himself dangerously involved. We are dealing with well-established routines of which nothing was known a few years ago.

Recently someone has noted that mention of the attempted sacrifice of Abraham is to be found in the once widely read Bayle's "Dictionary" as early as 1732 and suggested that that is where Joseph Smith got the story. But all Bayle says on the subject is that there is a rabbinical tradition "that he was cast by the Chaldeans into a fire, from which he emerged unscathed," with the usual stereo-typed observation that the story arose from a misreading of his escape from "Ur," Ur meaning both "Ur" (the city) and "fire."

And that is the whole story—no mention of any altar, let alone a description of deliverance by the angel accom-panied by the disastrous earthquake and other details that any reader of the book of Abraham knows about. Bayle mentions the rabbis but gives us no references whatever. All this is preserved in early Jewish tradition but was not published to the world before 1859, and the really signifi-cant documents did not first see the light until within the past twenty years or so. Actually, Joseph Smith's account of Abraham is a highly unoriginal story, one that can be documented from a hundred parallel sources. But nobody in Joseph Smith's day knew anything at all about that story or dreamed of putting Abraham in the mythical picture where he fits so nicely. The story is in every detail an au-thentic myth, describing an authentic ritual, and as such is to be considered seriously as authentic history.

Another example. To the Babylonian flood story and the Greek myth of Deucalion (the Greeks made much of their forefather Japetus—Japheth), Joseph Smith added yet another tale of the deluge, which he boldly attributed to the Egyptians. It was the story of a great lady who came to Egypt just after the flood, found the land still under water, and "settled her sons in it," establishing the monarch by matriarchal right. (Abraham 1:24.)

It was not until the second decade of the present cen-tury that H. Junker gathered together the widely scattered Egyptian documents that told the same story preserved by the Egyptians since the beginning of their history by being ritually dramatized every year in a great national water fes-tival. This episode from the book of Abraham is, like the story of Abraham on the altar, a perfect little vignette, placed with unerring accuracy in its proper ancient setting.

In conclusion, like those rare elements in deserted mines and dumps that miners and prospectors have hitherto ignored but that now promise great riches, the riches of mythology, so poorly worked in the past, still await the serious exploitation made possible by new skills and techniques.

There is no telling what wonders may be brought to light simply by bringing together new combinations and associations of documents already in our possession. But from the few hesitating steps that have been made so far, it already appears that the ancient myths, wherever they turn up, have a tendency to fit together into the same picture, supporting and confirming each other due to the solid ground on which they stand—the reality of ritual, by which history becomes a religious phenomenon—as is markedly the case in the annals of the Pharaohs. This leads us to conclude that there is a serious historical reality behind the myths as a whole, in spite of the adjusting and romancing that sometimes effaces them almost beyond recognition.

The myths thus provide us with a new and powerful tool for searching into hitherto inaccessible recesses of the past. Though the use of this tool has barely begun, it has already given us a useful means of checking up on the revelations of Joseph Smith, showing us that what were thought by some of his critics to be his wildest stories, the purest figments of his imagination, turn out to be mythological commonplaces, overlooked by generations of scholars and clergymen.

4

Before Adam

I am often asked by students: What about those people that lived thousands of years before Adam? They usually ask after class and expect me to give a definitive answer before leaving the room. Why don't I bring up the subject *in* class? I did for twenty years, and then gave it up—it was a waste of time. Within the past ten years, however, things have changed so much that it is time to resume the discussion if only to reorient my own thinking on a subject that is impossible to avoid.

The Latter-day Saints are the only Bible-oriented people who have always been taught that things were happening long, long before Adam appeared on the scene. They have never appreciated just how revolutionary that idea is. It does away with *creatio ex nihilo*, which, ever since the triumph of the School of Alexandria, has been for Christian and Jewish theologians alike the only possible definition of the word *creation*. In the April 1980 *National Geographic Magazine* is a reproduction of a heroic relief sculpture on the wall of the so-called National Cathedral in Washington, D.C., showing eight full-grown human beings popping out of a turmoil of cloud.[1] It is entitled *"Creatio ex nihilo—*Out of the Void."* It should not be hard to confound such an absolute concept, since any alternative will do; and long before the time of Christ the ancient Sophists, supplanting religion by naturalism, came up with a scenario very close indeed to what we think of as evolution. And so we get at an early time (at the trial of Socrates, in fact—at which, incidentally, Socrates is the defender of religion—not the other way around!) the sight of an apostate religion squar-

---

"Before Adam" is the edited text of an address given to the BYU community on April 1, 1980.

ing off against an always inadequate science. And the issue is never the merits of the evidence but always the jealous rivalry of the contestants to see which would be the official light unto the world.

Right down to the present day we have been the spectators of a foolish contest between equally vain and bigoted rivals, in which it is a moot question which side heaps the most contempt on God's creatures. For the fundamentalist, to associate man too closely with God's other creatures was the supreme insult to God and man. Man, say the Christian theologians, faithfully following Aristotle, is *the* rational animal—the *only* rational animal. *All* other beings in nature are soulless, speechless, thoughtless automata. Moreover, Adam was not only the only rational, immortal creation of God on earth, but the only intelligent actor on *any* solid world anywhere, being created out of nothing on the only inhabited planet in the entire universe—the solid earth, which was obviously the heavy center of everything, around which all other things revolved and onto which everything fell. Beside that, all was spirit.

The evolutionists took the doctors at their word and had a very easy time showing that man shares so many visible qualities and traits with other animals that if animals are mere "things" then so is man. Since *they* are able to survive and function simply as organisms reacting to an environment and nothing more, then man, being animal, has no more need of a soul than they have. The philosopher Arthur Schopenhauer, in his "Essay on the Christian System," said that the two fatal flaws of Christianity were (1) denying spirit and mind to any other creatures but ourselves (which both fundamentalists and Darwinists do) and (2) allowing life to no other world but our own. Adam in a vacuum—all alone in the society of God's creatures and all alone in the emptiness of space, the only thinking animal on the only inhabited spot in all the the emptiness of space! When it began to appear that the earth was only one among countless possible earths and not the one-and-only center of everything, the discovery was viewed by both sides as the fatal blow to the dignity of man and the integrity of the Bible. This has always amazed me. Why on earth should the idea of life on other worlds lead scientists like G. B. Kistiakowsky, D. N. Michael, Harlow Shapley, Arnold Toynbee, and Otto Struve to assume as a matter of course that such a situation renders God expendable and the Bible unacceptable?[2] Such a conclusion follows only from the all-or-nothing premises of Alexandrian absolutism: the universe and truth and God could not be otherwise by very definition than as the doctors of the fourth century described them; any changes in the scenario would require scrapping the whole thing, including God. It only shows, for Latter-day Saints, how "strongly riveted [were] the creeds of the fathers, who have inherited lies, upon the hearts of the children, and filled the world with confusion!" (D&C 123:7.) Strongly riveted, indeed! Those preconceptions were the very thing that Joseph and Brigham had the most difficulty in coping with among the Saints—who cling to them to this day.[3]

This futile quarrel should be no concern of ours. For one thing, we have a story to tell before Adam. Religion and science have *none*, absolutely none.

For the churchmen, the whole universe comes into existence in the week before Adam's own creation. But for the scientists, too, there is nothing to tell before the history. They set the stage for human history, but until a man with a *book* walks onto the stage there is no story, no play. Science studies the properties and the sets for the play, but the set *is* the play. The medium is the message. There is no more to follow. All around us in the universe, things are just happening. If they didn't happen one way, they would happen another. What difference does it make? The scientists of past decades have been proud of the *erhabene Zwecklosigkeit*, the "majestic meaninglessness" of it all. Since this is not to be my subject, one quotation, the classical remark of Tyndal, will suffice: "In the purely natural and inevitable march of evolution, life . . . is of profound unimportance, . . . a mere eddy in the primeval slime."⁴ The wise men gloried in the strength of mind and character that enabled them to look an utterly indifferent universe in the face without flinching (after all, *they* had tenure), insisting that the rest of us rid ourselves of our infantile longings for more. When we visit the planets and their satellites today, what do we find? Nobody at home! Somewhere the side of a cliff slips and slumps, somewhere dense clouds of dust are blown by super-winds, somewhere gas or magma seeps through cracks in the ground or huge blocks of ice collapse or collide, somewhere a meteor lands without a sound, somewhere. What difference does it make? It is all, as some of my professors used to remind their impressed but unhappy classes with malicious glee, utterly meaningless. Mount St. Helens takes on interest only because *we* are here. Globes on which nothing happens for millions of years are just as interesting as those on which change is taking place all the time. The static condition is in itself a happening, and with nobody around to measure the time, one scenario moves as fast as another.

When science takes us to *human* prehistory, it is just more of the same. Since World War II, an immense lot of digging has been done all over the world, and the result is a great accumulation of properties—but still *no play*. We learn from what is being turned up that people lived in shelters of various kinds, ate food that they gathered or hunted, warmed themselves and cooked with fire, wore clothing as they needed it, had pots to cook and store food in, had children, drank water, breathed air, and so on. And that is the whole story. The table is now set for the banquet, but no live guests ever show up. We sit in the darkened theater waiting for the show that never begins. It won't begin until we get a written record. Listen to the latest word on the subject by one of the foremost prehistorians, A. J. Jelinek (1977): "The overriding impression of the technological evidence in the archaeological record is one of almost unimaginable monotony. . . . The most overwhelming example . . . is . . . Olduvai Gorge where for approximately a million years no significant innovation is discernable." Even the later innovations "take place over hundreds of thousands of years; this means that we are talking about tens of thousands of generations of hominids maintaining patterns of technological traditions without discernable change."[5]

No Adam, no play. These can't be our people. Science promised an exciting new world, a great show, to which H. G. Wells offered to conduct us, but it all went stale in his own lifetime. To paraphrase the eminent biologist René Dubos, existentialist nausea has found its home in the most affluent and technologically advanced parts of the world. The most poignant problem of modern life is probably man's feeling that life has lost its significance. The view that the modern world is absurd is no longer limited to the philosophical or literary avant-garde. It is spreading to all social and economic groups and affects all manifestations of life.[6]

I spend my days in the midst of noise, dirt, ugliness, and absurdity, in order to have easier access to well-equipped laboratories, libraries, museums, and a few sophisticated colleagues whose material existence is as absurd as mine. I doubt that mankind can tolerate our absurd way of life much longer without losing what is best in humanness.[7] It is religion that makes man humble in the face of nature, Dubos infers, and science that makes him arrogant, *not* the other way around.[8]

The humanists have always known that they have no play. Euripides has a little song to that effect, which he repeats no fewer than five times. What it says is, in effect, "I know this play makes no sense, but neither does anything else!" Shakespeare's last word on the subject in his last play, *The Tempest*, was: "Our revels now are ended. These our actors . . . are melted into air, into thin air: and, like the baseless fabric of this vision, the cloud-capp'd towers, the gorgeous palaces, the solemn temples, the great globe itself, yea, all which it inherit, shall dissolve, and, like this insubstantial pageant faded, leave not a rack behind." (Act 4, scene 1, lines 148-56.) That's all there is. No one is going anywhere. Or take the highest achievement of modern theater, a play that won the Nobel Prize, no less. The characters in *Waiting for Godot*, writes an admiring critic, "have nothing to say, nor have they anything to do. Language for them is a means for expressing the meaninglessness of existence. . . . Godot is a symbol of hope that keeps man waiting for something big to happen, but that never happens. On the whole, all that man does centres round his physical needs and devices to kill time."[9]

Now as to the past, when I first joined the army I was sent to weather school and became a weatherman, working with the primitive charts and diagrams of the day. Coordinating the information that came over the teletype from a hundred other weather stations, I tried to report and predict the weather at Godman Field, Kentucky. Wouldn't it be wonderful, I thought in those days, if we had a movie that showed us all the moving storms and fronts. Then instead of having to throw the models together with feverish haste to project the past into future weather, I would only have to look at the moving picture and know exactly what was going to happen tomorrow. Meteorologists can do that today. It is all before our very eyes on the evening news. Seeing is believing. We are going to be hit by a big one tomorrow (which turns out to be a beautiful day), or that big clear spot shows perfectly heavenly weather ahead (so it snows and sleets all day tomorrow). Now imagine that instead of a weather-eye, enabling such brilliant predictions a few hours ahead, we had a satellite picture showing the earth over millions of years. Every time we stop the picture we ask the scientist what is going to happen next. And so he tells us with great confidence. Can we trust him? We can check on the weather day by day and make corrections and adjustments and keep score. But as Professor Campbell, formerly of UCLA, reminds us, the paleontologist cannot do any of that. He cannot observe processes but only results. He has no regular sequence of pictures before his eyes but only a few badly blurred snapshots of the earth over the last three million years. Studying these, the specialists try to tell us just what happened. Am I willing to stake my eternal salvation on their highly conflicting opinions? The little pictures are very few in number, very far apart, and very badly damaged. Every authority today emphasizes that, more than ever before. In the place of connections between the specimens, we have only resemblances, and it is on them that we base our whole story—classification, taxonomy, biosystematics—it is all a question of endlessly debated definitions, not a whit different from the harangues of the ancient Sophists. In the same breath, the experts today emphasize the scarcity and bothersome overabundance of evidence, the paradox resulting from a sudden accumulation of evidence during the past decade.

Upstairs in the old Education Building at Brigham Young University, there stood for many years a tall, thin, glass showcase. On the top shelf was a human skull; below it was the cast of a Cro-Magnon skull; then Neanderthal; and so on until we got to a skull of a gorilla. Here before our very eyes was an unimpeachable sermon on how man came to be. But things have changed now. "As late as 1955," writes Professor B. G. Campbell, fossils "could be fitted into a relatively simple and not very controversial phylogenetic lineage. The numerous fossils now known offer alternative interpretations." Not so compellingly simple as before, but how many alternative interpretations? "The number of possible hypotheses are both theoretically and practically unlimited."[10] J. J. Jerison wrote in 1975, "The simple picture of evolution from an australopithecine to a habiline to a pithecanthropine to a sapient grade is obviously inadequate."[11] He added rather wistfully, almost regretfully, "Things would actually fit together more easily if the dating of the new specimen at 2.8

million years ago were in error."[12] The equally eminent D. Pilbeam comments on the same development: "Until a few years ago relatively simple schemes that viewed past hominoids as foreshadows of living ones functioned very well as organizing paradigms." Today, "classification of past forms on the basis of present-day distinctions may not be very useful. Interconnections among fossil species and between them and the present species are increasingly difficult to draw. Concern with phylogeny . . . is perhaps on the wane."[13] "A great deal of heated debate has occurred over the past ten years or so concerning hominid origins. The last decade has seen a number of significant changes. . . . We are now in a period of uncertainty. This contrasts with the preceding period, during which much seemed so clear-cut and obvious."[14]

The sensational new discoveries in Africa only remind the researchers how much they have been missing and how much they're still missing. "Whence came these late Neogene hominoids?" asks Professor Pilbeam of the Olduvai population. The question remains unanswered because "our knowledge of the fossil record is sparse, and heavily skewed toward representation of jaws and teeth."[15] And Professor Jelinek informs us that "the entire excavated area of occupation surfaces (all over the world) is well under the size of a modern football field." At Olduvai, 80 percent of the material comes from a band of strata representing only 4 percent of the time-span of occupation.[16] As opposed to the certitudes that were the most characteristic—as well as the most obnoxious—trait of past generations of the Darwinian ministry, Campbell reminds us, "We know that we can never do more than present hypotheses on the basis of the presently available evidence. As time-bound creatures, no ultimate truth about the origin and evolution of mankind can ever be known to us."[17] "If nothing else," Professor Pilbeam concludes his study, "perhaps the only thing that is certain is that the next decade will provide us many surprises."[18] If that is certain, we should in all conscience postpone any further discussion or debate on such matters for at least another ten years. I could have saved myself a lot of trouble by simply ignoring the experts for thirty years. It is sad to think how many of those telling points that turned some of our best students away from the gospel have turned out to be dead wrong!

Now it is admitted, in the words of W. W. Howells, that all those years when everybody was sure of the answers, "no scheme was presented that intelligibly interpreted the fossil record."[19] And now the interpretation is far more difficult than ever, because there are just too many types to relate and explain. It is a strange fact, "a paradoxical problem," as Pilbeam puts it, that "the hominids are one of the poorest represented of fossil mammal groups, relative to their apparent past diversity."[20] An astonishing number of different types are running around (there are seven at Olduvai), and yet so very few specimens! What is wrong? It is no longer enough to fall back, as S. Washburn does, on the old chestnut: "Surely as more fossils are found . . . [his tool theory] will be found to have been a major factor."[21] What kind of science is that—basing our theories on evidence not yet discovered?

This is a reminder that those who study the origin of man *begin* with the final answers. The ultimate questions that can only be answered after all the returns are in are the very questions with which Lyell and Hutton and Darwin began their explorations. Our thrilling detective drama begins by telling us who did it and then expects us to wait around with bated breath while the detective brings in the evidence. The premise is stated, for example, by G. G. Simpson: "In the evolutionary pattern of thought there is no longer need or room for the supernatural. The earth was not created: it evolved. So did all the animals and plants that inhabit it, including our human selves, . . . mind and soul, as well as brain and body. So did religion."[22] Well, if we grant that, we already have the answer to the big questions. We know the final score. And as giving the plot away spoils the fun, so Simpson must go back to the Bible whenever he wants to interest an audience.

Here it is important to bring to attention the great number of knowledge banks that must be brought under contribution before we can get it all together. There was a time when the Bible was the only knowledge bank. Some fathers of the church, like Hilary, declared that anything not specifically stated to have happened in the Bible could not possibly have happened anywhere. When Aristotle's only knowledge bank became available, the doctors of the church diligently accommodated the Bible to his teachings. With the study of the heavens, the stars became the next great source of guidance to the real nature of things. Then Bacon opened the book of nature. Next, geology and biology called the tune. Geology took a direct look at the past—we had to believe what *it* told us—while biology examined the active processes that brought about the visible changes. On these two hung all the laws and the prophets.

And why not? Where else could one turn for answers? It is an illusion to look elsewhere, Freud explained in a famous essay, "The Future of an Illusion," for what other science is there except science? Duly impressed, the world failed to ask whether those data, no matter how concrete and precise, were adequate for the immense burden of proof that was needed. The prestige of science rested on shocking oversimplification and elaborate tautologies. "Never mind the details," we were told. "We can fill them in later"—which means, as noted, that the great search for truth begins with the final answers.

Darwin decided at the age of twenty that the Bible was a fraud. He claimed he felt no distress and never doubted for a single second that his conclusion was correct.[23] In a disarming article, T. Dobzhansky admits that his own beliefs are based on anything but exhaustive evidence and that others with competent knowledge of that evidence do not agree with his conclusions.[24] In other words, his model doesn't work, but that is no reason for rejecting it or looking for another model. After all, it is scientific. He has put a great deal of time and study into it. It is based on known facts and sound reasoning. Why should he give it up for gross superstition, mysticism, and ignorant religious ranting? There's always the assumption that there is no other alternative to *my* science but your anti-science. Your knowledge bank does not count if it obfuscates mine. As usual, Dobzhansky rests his case on discoveries yet to be made: "Guessing where new discoveries are likely to be made is a risky venture in science. And yet, a scientist is constantly forced to take this risk."[25] True, and for that very reason, as Karl Popper reminds us, a scientist can never be dogmatic. But Dobzhansky is nothing but dogmatic. Well, again, why not? Here were the sciences which *in time* would give us all the answers. We are quite sure of that, so why not accept their conclusions *now*? That is just what the public has done, and the results have been paralyzing. The Darwinian Sleep has done much more damage than the Newtonian Sleep—a dullness of mind that cripples curiosity with the authority of the Approved School Solution.

The two big questions today, Dobzhansky says, are (1) the mechanisms of evolution—the very question that Darwin was supposed to have answered for all time, and (2) "the biological uniqueness of man," which is the real Adam question. How do you define man? How do you define Adam? There were a lot of creatures running about long ago who looked like men, but for that matter there are a lot of them today; you can go to Hogle Zoo [in Salt Lake City, Utah] and see some of them, but they are not men. Are these zoo critters ancestral to us? No, for they are contemporary. And what about the other creatures who disappeared long ago? Are they ancestral to us? That is just the question, and there is no agreement on it. Since World War I, *homo erectus* has been found all over the Old World, the term including a number of prehistoric types. "Where did Homo Erectus come from?" asks W. W. Howells. "Where did he go? The paths are simply untraced. Above all, the nature of the line leading to living man remains a matter of pure theory."[26] In September 1979, 150 of the world's leading paleontologists met at the Eighth Pan-African Congress of Prehistory and Quaternary Studies in Nairobi. The main issue discussed was, "What is the definition of Homo?"[27] How do you know a true man when you see him? Well, he looks like a man. Again, there are creatures in the zoo that look like men. "In recent years the old concept of a single, steadily evolving lineage from ape to man has been completely replaced by at least three and possibly more different forms of early man evolving simultaneously in Africa." By two million years ago "at least two forms of hominids were living," and one of them "died out perhaps a million years ago."[28] And the other? It was no more manlike than many of the others. What evidence have we that it did not also die out? Pilbeam writes that three hundred individuals found in East Africa represent at least seven hominid species. He also notes, "These species do not resemble any of the living Old World higher primates." In fact, they seem to have been in many ways distinctly different from all later hominids.[29] The tool-using Dryopithecids "disappear around 8 or 9 m[illion] y[ears] ago"; the Rampithecidae about 8 million years ago.[30] Campbell thinks they were related to us "on a personal assessment of very complex and conflicting evidence," but he concedes that Leakey and Napier and others do not think Anthropus africanus was ancestral to H. habilis.[31]

A contemporary theory of great importance is that evolution has been directed and boosted through the ages as various homonid species have fortuitously adopted tools. After the initial innovation, the use of a particular tool could go on by simple imitation, yet Washburn claims that tools have made us what we are. He tells us that the famous chopper tool "remained in day-to-day use as a major element in the human tool kit for about two million years."[32] One would think that 2 million years without a change would show quite remarkable immunity in these creatures to any didactic influence of the *coup de poing,* *Faustkeil,* or hand-ax. Perhaps the nature of the instrument itself is to blame. In 1964, President Barnes, of the American School in Beirut, gave me what is perhaps the first Mousterian artifact ever recognized in Palestine, an excellent example of an Acheulean point, discovered by Fredrick Bliss, the founder of the University, at Buri-el Khadr. What puzzles me is what it could have been used for, for it was of marly chert, and I doubt if it could cut cheese. When I dropped it from a height of about nine inches on the tile floor, the top of the point broke off with the greatest of ease. So I was not surprised to read recently that while "there is virtually no evidence of nonlithic tools" for our pre-Adamites, and that these hand-axes are "the hallmark of most Middle Pleistocene cultures, prehistorians are still without firm evidence relating to the function of these first recognized and most elaborate of Lower Paleolithic stone tools."[33] Hundreds and thousands of them, the standard all-purpose tool of 2 million years of diligent use—but what on earth were they used for? Yet Washburn assures us that thanks to such tools alone "the human way and the brain evolved together to produce ancient man of the *genus Homo* about half a million years ago. Then the brain evolved under the pressure of more complex social life until the species *Homo sapiens* appeared perhaps as recently as 50,000 years ago."[34] Fortuitously discovered tools vigorously pushed man toward his full-blown glory, and yet 2 million years of that exhilarating process left not the slightest effect on their users. Just how powerful is the influence of the gadgets?

"Considerable academic debate surrounds the date for the appearance of modern man," Washburn tells us. "By 35,000 years ago, however, the hunting populations of western Europe were biologically indistinguishable from modern man."[35] Yet he also tells us that "man began when populations of apes, about a million years ago, started the bipedal, tool-using way of life."[36] In the same volume of essays, H. de Lumley reports on the 350,000-year-old village of Terra Amata, with its well-made huts, central heating (a hearth), and a special compartment for tool-making, the oldest known man-made structures.[37] What kind of men? R. G. Klein tells us that "modern man (Homo sapiens) seems to have made his *first* appearance between 45,000 and 35,000 years ago," and then goes on to describe one of some 100 Pleistocene sites in the Ukraine between 80,000 and 75,000 years old, where the people wore furs and beaded garments, buried their dead, and built substantial heated huts.[38] The artifacts were Mousterian and, to quote the same scientist, "Mousterian artifacts invariably belong to Neanderthal man."[39] But didn't Neanderthal man become extinct? Some say he did, some say he didn't. Which is it to be, 2 million years, 1 million years, half a million years, 50,000 years, or 35,000 years? Each one introduces a new species, though all of them used tools.

According to Klein, when "true sapiens" appears, it is with a sudden "quantum advance in human culture evolution."[40] By definition evolution comes only by minute and gradual steps—a quantum advance must be something else. T. Dobzhansky, who lays particular emphasis on the tiny steps of micro-evolution, explains the anomaly by noting that culture brings an entirely new element into the picture: "The cultural evolution of mankind is superimposed on its biological evolution; the causes of the former are non-biological." But once caused, he insists, they contribute to biological changes by natural selection. "Genes determine the possibility of culture but not its content, just as they determine the possibility of human speech but not what is spoken."[41] Whatever is behind it, it is the culture that marks the appearance of man as such, just as by very definition it is the written record that begins his history.

When about twenty years ago it was decided that man himself is the chief conditioner of his evolution, scientists began to view him as outside and independent of the mainstream of organic evolution. Here was a new dimension, an evolution that no longer operated on blind chance. To define true man is to discover the uniqueness of man, that which he does not share with any other creature. It can only be his culture. And when do you get a real culture? Not until you get Adam. Those 100,000-year-old villages have nothing to tell us that we do not know. It is time we got to Adam.

To recapitulate, religion has no plot. Science has no plot. This means that Joseph Smith is the only entry. He, at least, has given us a picture. But is it a convincing picture? The fact is, we have never looked at it closely! We have drawn back from that assignment, preferring to save a lot of trouble and take sides with the traditional schools.

The stories of the garden of Eden and the Flood have always furnished unbelievers with their best ammunition against believers, because they are the easiest to visualize, popularize, and satirize of any Bible accounts. Everyone has seen a garden and been caught in a pouring rain. It requires no effort of imagination for a six-year-old to convert concise and straightforward Sunday-school recitals into the vivid images that will stay with him for the rest of his life. These stories retain the form of the nursery tales they assume in the imaginations of small children, to be defended by grownups who refuse to distinguish between childlike faith and thinking as a child when it is time to "put away childish things." (1 Corinthians 13:11.) It is equally easy and deceptive to fall into adolescent disillusionment and with one's emancipated teachers to smile tolerantly at the simple gullibility of bygone days, while passing stern moral judgment on the savage old God who damns Adam for eating the fruit he put in his way and, overreacting with impetuous violence, wipes out Noah's neighbors simply for making fun of his boat-building on a fine summer's day.

This is another case of what I have called the gentile dilemma or, if you will, the devil's dilemma.

Joseph Smith gave the world something that nobody else could. That is why I say that Joseph Smith, with nothing going for him and everything going against him, simply could not lose. He told us what the play is all about. If you can come up with a better story than his, more power to you, but up until now no one else has had any story at all to place before us. If only for that reason, I believe, the Prophet's story deserves a hearing.

The Latter-day Saints have four basic Adam stories, those found in the Bible, the book of Moses, the book of Abraham, and the temple—each seen from a different angle, like the four Gospels, but not conflicting if each is put into its proper context. And what is that context? One vitally important principle that everyone seems to have ignored until now is the consideration that everything is presented to us in these accounts through the eyes, or from the point of view of, the individual observers who tell the story. Historians long ago came to realize that the boast of German *Geschichtswissenschaft*—to report what happened at all times *"wie es eigentlich geschah,"* the whole truth, the complete event in holistic perfection as it would be seen by the eye of God—is a philosopher's pipe dream. And, indeed, it is from the philosophers that we got it, rooted as the fathers and the doctors are in the sublime absolutes of Alexandria: There is God and God only, and his holy and infallible book was written by his very finger, untouched by the human mind. We must credit the Moslems with carrying this doctrine all the way. Not only is it the crime of *Shirk* to credit the existence of anything besides God, but his book is as divine and ineffable as he is. I have been told that it is presumptuous for mortals, let alone infidels, to pretend to understand anything in it.

The Latter-day Saints, inheritors of the Christian version of this teaching, are constantly converting statements of limited application to universal or at least sweeping generalities. To illustrate, I was told as a child that the Rocky Mountains, the Appalachians, and the Andes all came into existence overnight during the great upheavals of nature that took place at the time of the Crucifixion—an

absurdity that plays into the hands of critics of the Book of
Mormon. But what we find in the 3 Nephi account when
we read it carefully is a few sober, factual, eyewitness reports describing an earthquake of 8-plus on the Richter
scale in a very limited area. Things that appear unlikely,
impossible, or paradoxical from one point of view often
make perfectly good sense from another. The *Nautical Al-
manac* gives the exact time of sunrise and sunset for every
day of the year, yet astronauts know that the sun neither
rises nor sets except from a particular point of view, the
time of the event being strictly dependent on the exact location. From that point of view and that only, it is strictly correct and scientific to say that the sun does rise and set. Just
so, the apparently strange and extravagant phenomena
described in the scriptures are often correct descriptions of
what would have appeared to a person in a particular situation. You and I have never been in those situations. To
describe what he sees to people who have never seen anything like it, the writer must reach for metaphors and
similes: "His eyes were *as* a flame of fire; the hair of his
head was white *like* the pure snow; . . . his voice was *as* the
sound of the rushing of great waters." (D&C 110:3; italics
added.) There was no fire, no snow, no rushing waters, but that is as near as Joseph Smith and Sidney Ridgon
could come to telling us what they experienced when "the
veil was taken from [their] minds, and the eyes of [their]
understanding were opened!" (D&C 110:1.) They were reporting as well as they could what they had seen from a
vantage point on which we have never stood.

A recent study points out that the charge that Abraham's story in the Bible must be fictitious because no one
could know the highly intimate things reported there—nobody, Hamming admits, unless it were Abraham himself.
The earliest Abraham books are supposed to be autobiog-
raphies, and the story told from his point of view makes
perfectly good sense. So with Noah in the ark. From where
he was, "the whole earth" (Genesis 8:9) was covered with

water as far as he could see; after things had quieted down for 150 days and the ark ground to a halt, it was still three months before he could see any mountaintops. But what were conditions in other parts of the world? If Noah knew that, he would not have sent forth messenger birds to explore. The flood as he described it is what he saw of it. "He sent forth a dove from him, to see if the waters were abated from off the face of the ground." (Genesis 8:8.) Couldn't he see for himself? Not where the dove went. It was not until seven days later that he sent it out again; and after flying all day, the bird came back with a green leaf fetched from afar; "so Noah knew that the waters were abated from off the earth." (Genesis 8:11.) Still he waited another seven days. When the dove did not return, Noah had his answer. In some distant place, trees were bearing and there was bird-food to be found. But not where Noah was. All that time he had not dared to open up.

Note that the author does not fall into the literary trap of telling where the birds went and what they saw. That became a standard theme of early Oriental literature, faithfully reflected in the classical stories of the sea-eagle and the hoopoe. All Noah tells us is what *he* saw of the birds and the flood. The rain continued at least in spots, for there was that magnificent rainbow. Why do Christians insist on calling it the *first* rainbow, just because it is the first mentioned? Who says that water drops did not refract light until that day? Well, my old Sunday School teacher, for one, used to say it. The rainbow, like the sunrise, is strictly the product of a point of view, for which the beholder must stand in a particular place while it is raining in another particular place and the sun is in a third particular place, if he is to see it at all. It is a lesson in relativity.

This principle is recognized today as "the anthropic cosmological principle." I refer you to the April 1980 *Scientific American*. It specifies that what an observer is able to see of the universe actually makes a difference in the real nature of that universe: "Man's experience is a constraint on the kinds of universe he could observe. Many features of the universe that are remarkable to ponder are inevitable prerequisites of the existence of observers."[42] Though the authors say it is a mystery why this should be so, still "the principle overcomes the traditional barrier between the observer and the observed. It makes the observer an indispensable part of the macrophysical world."[43]

Nowhere is the principle of this relativity more clearly proclaimed than in the cosmologies of the book of Moses and the book of Abraham. Both epics begin in realms above, far from the earth (which has not yet come into existence). At each step it is made perfectly clear who is speaking and from what vantage point. "I dwell in the midst of them all; . . . I came *down* in the beginning in the midst of all the intelligences *thou* hast seen." (Abraham 3:21; italics added.) First, second, and third persons appear in a large cast of characters leaving one place for another. "*We* will go down, for there is space *there*, and *we* will take of *these* materials, and we will make *an* earth whereon *these* may dwell." (Abraham 3:24; italics added.) What a world of inference opens up as we are launched into the mighty drama! Yet we immediately begin to feel ourselves into the situation. Those to whom the speaker refers (and there is no doubt who *he* is!) are known to Abraham from aforetime—they are "all the intelligences *thine eyes* have seen from the beginning." (Abraham 3:21; italics added.)

Before being introduced to his home planet, Abraham is given a view of the cosmos, in the which he is reminded again and again that all distances, directions, and motions are to be measured with respect to his own position only. From another position, the picture might well look very different.

Kolob, as we noted, is not the center of the universe but governs only one class of stars: "I have set this one to govern all those which belong to the *same* order as that upon which *thou standest*." (Abraham 3:3; italics added.) In the apocryphal Abraham literature, which has very recently and very suddenly taken on extreme importance in the eyes of the learned world, this point of vantage is a place in the heavens to which Abraham has been taken. There he is at first terrified because he finds no place on which to stand, until the angel who is with him gives him a correct orientation by drawing a round diagram of things. This is reflected in Facsimile No. 2 of the Book of Abraham, but we cannot discuss that here.

Time also is not reckoned in absolutes but is limited to Abraham's system; "the reckoning of the Lord's time" is not reckoned absolutely but "according to the reckoning of Kolob"—an in-between element to gear Abraham's time to a larger but not necessarily the largest system. There is also reckoning by sun and moon, relative to "the earth upon which thou standest." (Abraham 3:4-5.)

In verse 6 the expression "set time" is used four times, reminding us that there is more than one frame of time reference. One must in the "times of reckoning" take into account that "two facts" can exist, the one not excluding the other. This is one of the mysteries of cosmology today. The Doctrine and Covenants explains it by the necessity of limiting all "existence" to closed systems, for "otherwise there is no existence." (D&C 93:30.)

Kolob's influence and time governs "all those planets which belong to the *same order* as that upon which *thou* standest"—the expression here used for the seventh time. (Abraham 3:9; italics added.)

After being apprised, like Moses, of the endless nature of God's works—"I could not see the end thereof"—Abraham is reminded of the glory elsewhere "before the world was." (Abraham 3:22.) Then, at the beginning of chapter 4, we see a delegation going "down" to organize this earth and its heaven. To begin with, we see bare rock, "empty and desolate," as the other planets and satellites of the system seem to be today, "because they had not formed anything but the earth." (Abraham 4:2.) Then the whole thing is water-covered beneath a dense envelope of cloud—

"darkness reigned upon the face of the deep." But things
were already being prepared for what was to follow, for
"the Spirit of the Gods was brooding upon the face of the
waters." Dictionaries define *brooding* as "to sit or incubate
(eggs) for the purpose of hatching." As Milton puts it—
"dovelike sat'st brooding on the vast Abyss and mad'st it
pregnant." Also, "to dwell continuously on a subject."
Brooding is just the right word—a quite long quiet period
of preparation in which apparently nothing was happening. Something was to come out of the water, incubating,
waiting—a long, long time.

Next, in verse 3, "there was light." Where? It is an exercise in point of view again. All this time the Gods had been
dwelling in light and glory, but the earth was dark. It was
to where "darkness reigned," according to our text, that
the light came. (Abraham 4:2.) This was not the first creation of light. Wherever light comes into darkness, "there
is light."

The next verse reminds us that light itself is relative, a
part of the energy spectrum seen by some being with the
capacity to be aware of it: "They . . . comprehended the
light, for it was bright" (Abraham 4:4), that is, visible. Basic
chemicals react to light, but are they aware of it—do they
comprehend it? In verse 5 we are introduced to the dualism
of night and day, land and water, which is peculiar to the
earth and conditions of all life upon it.

The creation process as described in the Pearl of Great
Price is open ended and ongoing, entailing careful planning
based on vast experience, long consultations, models, tests,
and even trial runs for a complicated system requiring a
vast scale of participation by the creatures concerned. The
whole operation is dominated by the overriding principle
of love. You may accept the Big Bang, with its potential for
producing all that came thereafter, but by any reckoning
the earth was definitely *not* among the instantaneous pro-
ductions of the first millisecond or even of the first fifteen
minutes. No matter how you figure, it came along much,

much later after a great deal had happened. "Worlds without number" had already come into existence and gone their ways: "And as one earth shall pass away, and the heavens thereof even so shall another come; and there is no end to my works, neither to my words." (Moses 1:38.)

Consider how it was done: "And the Gods said: We will do everything that we have said, and organize them." (Abraham 4:31.) "And the Gods saw that they would be obeyed, and that their plan was good." (Abraham 4:21.) "We will end our work, which we have counseled. . . . And thus were their decisions at the time that they counseled among themselves to form the heavens and the earth." (Abraham 5:2-3.) After the talk they got down to work. "The Gods came down and formed these the generations of the heavens and of the earth, . . . according to all that which they had said . . . before." (Abraham 5:4-5.) They worked through agents: "The Gods ordered, saying: Let [such-and-such happen] . . . ; and it was so, even as they ordered." (Abraham 4:9, 11.)

What they ordered was not the completed product, but the process to bring it about, providing a scheme under which life might expand: "Let us *prepare* the earth to bring forth grass" (Abraham 4:11; italics added), not "Let us *create* grass."

"Let us prepare the waters to bring forth abundantly. . . . And the Gods prepared the waters that they might bring forth great whales, and every living creature that moveth." (Abraham 4:20.) Note the future tense: the waters are so treated that they will have the capacity. The Gods did not make whales on the spot but arranged it so that in time they might appear. They created the potential. "And the Gods saw that they would be obeyed, and that their plan was good" (Abraham 4:21), that is, it was working, not because they were doing it all themselves—there were other agents at work: they were being obeyed. By whom? Well, the land animals, we are told, which "would obey." (Abraham 4:25.) "And the Gods watched those things which they had ordered until they obeyed." (Abraham 4:18.)

"They obeyed" is the active voice, introducing a teaching that, in my opinion, is by far the most significant and distinct aspect of Mormonism. It is the principle of maximum participation, of the active cooperation of all of God's creatures in the working out of his plans, which, in fact, are devised for their benefit: "This is my work and my glory. . . . " (Moses 1:39.) Everybody gets into the act. Every creature, to the limit of its competence, is given the supreme compliment of being left on its own, so that the word "obey" is correctly applied. "We will go down, for there is space there, and we will take of these materials, and we will make an earth whereon these may dwell." (Abraham 3:24.) Why? "And we will prove them herewith, to see if they will do all things whatsoever the Lord their God shall command them." (Abraham 3:25.) What he commands is what will best fulfill the measure of their existence, but they are not forced to do it—they are not automata. Adam was advised not to eat the fruit but was told at the same time that he was permitted to do it. It was up to him whether he would obey or not. If he did obey, he would qualify for a higher trust.

Abraham 4:11-12 continues: "Let us prepare the earth to bring forth grass. . . . And the Gods organized the earth to bring forth grass from its own seed, . . . yielding fruit [the fruit is the seed], whose seed could only bring forth the same . . . after his kind; and the Gods saw that they were obeyed." Here are levels of independence down to a complete programming by which the "seed could only bring forth the same." It reminds us of DNA, but nothing is completely automatic, for the Gods watched those things which they had ordered "until they obeyed," that is, until they could be trusted to carry on on their own. This is not Deism, the prearranged harmony of Leibniz, for the Gods keep up an active interest in the operation in which indeed things often go awry: "We shall go away now," they say, "but we shall visit you again," which they do from time to time, keeping up an active interest. The most important provision of all is, "We will bless them," and "cause them to be fruitful and multiply." (Abraham 4:28.) That blessing of everything makes all the difference. The Darwinists might say, "You people are simply describing a natural process in humanized terms," for they have always made much of the completely natural, inevitable, mindless, undirected, spontaneous, mechanical aspect of natural selection necessary for its operation as a purely and completely physical law. They ever gloated on the unfeeling cruelty of the whole thing—"nature red in tooth and claw," as Kipling put it. The *blessing* is the whole difference between a play and no play.

After the earth is set up we are shown everything from Adam's point of view. In Genesis 2:5, we are definitely referred to a pre-temporal creation, then (2:8) we see a garden planted, and (2:15) a man put into the garden, where he is wonderfully at home. He can eat of every tree in the garden (2:16). He lives on terms of greatest intimacy with other creatures, naming and classifying them as he takes his place among them, in the manner of Claude Levi-Strauss's "primitives." (Genesis 2:19-20.) When Adam eats the fruit his eyes are opened—he is a *piqqeah*, one who sees things as they were not seen before, who sees things which he in another condition could not see. He is in a new ambience. Cast out of the garden, he finds himself in a dry climate and changes his diet from fruit to grains, which he must work hard to cultivate.

The book of Abraham is more specific. After the great cycles of creation come the smaller cycles, starting with a very dry planet followed by a very wet phase. (Abraham 5:5-6.) Man is formed of the elements of the earth like any other creature, and he lives in a very lush period, a garden, which is however reduced to an oasis in an encroaching desert. (Abraham 5:7-10.) To this limited terrain he is per-

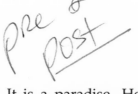

fectly adapted. It is a paradise. How long does he live there? No one knows, for this was still "after the Lord's time," not ours. (Abraham 5:13.) It was only when he was forced out of this timeless, changeless paradise that he began to count the hours and days, moving into a hard semi-arid world of thorns, thistles, and briars, where he had to toil and sweat in the heat just to stay alive and lost his old intimacy with the animals. (Genesis 3:17-19.)

The questions most commonly asked are: When did it happen? How long did it take? Our texts make it very clear that we are not to measure the time and periods involved by our chronometers and calendars. Until Adam underwent that fatal change of habitat, body chemistry, diet, and psyche that went with the Fall, nothing is to be measured in our years, "for . . . the Gods had not appointed unto Adam his reckoning." (Abraham 5:13.) Until then, time is measured from their point of view, not ours. As far as we are concerned it can be any time, and there would be no point to insisting on this again and again if all we had to do to convert their time to our time was multiply our years by 365,000. Theirs was a different time. The only numbers we are given designated the phases of periods of creation: "and this was the second time" (Abraham 4:8), "and it was the third time" (4:13), and so on. The periods are numbered but never measured. The Gods called them "days," but the text is at great pains to make clear that it was day and night from their point of view, when our time had not yet been appointed. "And the Gods called the light Day, and the darkness they called Night. And . . . from the evening until morning they called night; . . . and this was the first, or the beginning, of that which they called day and night." (Abraham 4:5.) Doctrine and Covenants 130:4-5 explains that "the reckoning of God's time, angel's time, prophet's time, and man's time [is] according to the planet on which they reside." That implies different time schemes at least. In moving from one system to another one also changes one's timing. "There are no angels who minister to this earth but those who do belong or have belonged to it." (D&C 130:5.)

"It was from morning until evening that they called day; and it was the fifth time." (Abraham 4:23.) How long is such a time? In the "fourth time," we read, "the Gods watched those things which they had ordered until they obeyed." (Abraham 4:19, 18.) That important word "until" tells us two things: (1) that they took all the time that was necessary, no matter how long it might have been, measuring the period in terms not of a terminal date but in terms of the requirements of the task; (2) "until" means up till a certain time, but not thereafter. When things were running smoothly, they were left on their own, which implies a shift from one time-scale to another. When, for example, "the Gods prepared the earth to bring forth" (Abraham 4:24), after they had prepared the waters to do the same long before, how long do you think that took? Again, the record is deliberately vague.

The relative times are clearly shown when "the Gods organized the lights in the expanse of the heaven." From our position that is just what they are—lights, nothing more. "And caused them to divide the day from the night. . . ." Such a division had already taken place at the beginning, but this was a new time-system for this earth. " . . . And organized them to be for signs and for seasons, and for days and for years." (Abraham 4:14.) A sign is a symbol, a mark, an arbitrary indicator, a means of measuring. It is only a sign relative to a particular observer. These lights were not originally created as markers of time, but they could be used as such, they could be "organized for" such. The moon was not created for my convenience; but just the same, from where I stand it can be made to serve a number of special purposes. Aside from measuring time, those heavenly bodies do "give light upon the earth . . . , the greater light to rule the day, and the lesser light to rule the night; with the lesser light they set the stars also." (Abraham 4:15-16.)

Here we get what is perhaps the most striking instance of "anthrocentric cosmology." An astronomer (I think at Notre Dame) recently calculated the probability of a planet in the solar system having a moon (just one moon, at that) that subtended exactly the same arc in the sky as does the sun from the surface of the same planet. The chances are astronomically remote, so remote, indeed, that there seems to be something deliberate about what is otherwise a stunning coincidence. From no other point of view in all the universe will the sun and the moon have exactly the same size. It is also arranged that the stars come out with the moon—though the ancients knew perfectly well that they were there in the daytime too; yet for us, again—from our point of view only—they are simply not there. The North Star does not really stand still while the other stars circle around it (move away from the earth and all your calculations will be spoiled). Hence the repeated insistence on specifying, according to the time appointed as that "upon which thou standest." (Abraham 3:3.)

What the book of Abraham shows me is that we are in the midst of eternity, surrounded by evidence of the fact. Every morning on the way to work, I behold those very old rocks at the base of Rock Canyon and think how everywhere around us in space float masses of rock like that, that never, never want to change and really never need to. What does a million years mean to them? For that matter, what does ten minutes? If they were blasted tomorrow, reduced to powder or vapor, nothing would be lost. That is the First Law: The stuff is there. In whatever form it may take, it is always all there. That is the first point scored by the book of Abraham, the first great mystery. Don't ask why it is there. Nobody can tell you. In 1951, the Pope officially declared for the Big Bang theory, because it looked to some like a *creatio ex nihilo*. Actually, it is just the opposite: the Big Bang took place precisely because all that the universe contains was already compressed within that primal singularity so tightly that it had to explode. It was all there, always. So we begin with an imponderable given quantity: "See, yonder is matter unorganized," or as the Book of Abraham puts it, "We will go down, for there is space there, and we will take of these materials, and we will make an earth whereon these may dwell." (Abraham 3:24.)

Mystery No. 2: Why should it be so organized? Its natural state calls for progressive *dis*organization—the Second Law. But organizing is the exact reversal of that law. Whose idea was it to build this elaborate organization— which we can see for ourselves exists, however contrary to natural law? Many scientists are puzzling over that just now. Trust the book of Abraham to anticipate such problems; this sort of thing has been going on for a long, long time. It is planned, programmed, and tested. The "anthropic cosmological principle" recognized that the state of organization depends on the observer. He reads order into the chaos. We may be looking at total chaos or at nothing, but to *us* it makes sense. Not just to me but to us. If it were only to me it could be an illusion, so we check with each other. Many find the whole thing absurd. Eminent scientists tell us that we are living in an absurd world. But that only means that we know that it should be different. When I say it is absurd, I am complaining that what I see is "not the way it really is." And who are we? Abraham sees that as the ultimate question and meets it handily: intelligence—awareness—is the beginning and ending of it all. You start out with "intelligences," beyond which nothing is to be said. You can doubt everything else, but that much you must grant—there were those intelligences, because they still are. What the book of Abraham tells me is that, if this moment of consciousness is real, then it is all real. I can bear unshakable testimony to one thing: I am here. I am under no obligation to explain it or prove it before it can be believed.

Let us consider our Adam. What kind of being is he? The same kind as ourselves—but what is that? He plays a surprising number of roles, each with a different persona, a different name, a different environment, a different office and calling: (1) he was a member of the presidency when the earth project was being discussed; (2) he was on the committee of inspection that came down from time to time to check up on the operation; (3) then he changed his name and nature to live upon the earth, but it was a very different earth from any we know; it had to be a garden place specially prepared for him. (4) When he left that paradise, he changed his nature again and for the first time began to reckon the passing of time by our measurements, becoming a short-lived creature subject to death. (5) In this condition, he began to receive instructions from heavenly mentors on how to go about changing his condition and status, entering into a covenant that completely changed his mentality and way of life. "The first man Adam was made a living soul; the last Adam was made a quickening spirit," when "that which is natural" became spiritual. (1 Corinthians 15:45-46.) The man Adam passes from one state of being to another, and so do we: "as we have borne the image of the earthly, we shall also bear the image of the heavenly." (1 Corinthians 15:49.) (6) In time he died and became a spirit being, the head of all his spirit children in the waiting-place, according to common Christian tradition as well as our own. (7) Then he became, after Christ, the firstfruits of the resurrection and returned triumphantly to his first and second estates (8) to go on to glory and eternal lives.

In these seven or eight Adams, we have another fundamental teaching that sets Mormonism off from all contemporary religion and science. The one views man's life on earth as a one-act drama: Adam fell, Christ redeemed us, and that is the story. Before Adam, there was nothing. Science tells us that the drama is pointless, because there is really nothing after it. We, on the other hand, see an ongoing epic of many episodes, each one a play in itself—a dispensation.

The fifth chapter of Genesis begins with a very important episode—the formal establishment of Adam's family
organization. It begins with a book, a book of remembrance
or genealogy, entitled "The Book of the Generations of
Adam." It begins, "In the day the Gods set apart [*bara*—we
are being very literal here] Adam in the likeness of the
Gods [*bi-dmuth elohim*] he made him. Male and female he
set them apart, and gave them a blessing, and gave them
their names as Adam, in the day he set them apart." (See
Genesis 5:1-3.) Next comes Seth in the proper line of
Adam, and the patriarchal line follows. The preceding
chapter tells of the division into Cainites and Sethites, and
it is significant that the line of Cain is omitted from the
genealogy of Adam. The book of Moses tells of multitudes
of Adam's children born before Cain and Abel (Moses 5:12,
16). They had followed Satan by choice and were disqual-
ified as sons of God. We read in Moses: "And unto thy brethren have I . . . given commandment, that they . . . should
choose me, their Father. . . . But behold, their sins shall be
upon the heads of their fathers; Satan shall be their father."
(Moses 7:33, 37.) Those who accepted the covenant were
called sons of God and also the sons of Adam: "And this is
the genealogy of the sons of Adam, who was the son of
God." (Moses 6:22.) Only those qualify as *Bene-Adam* who
are still in the covenant. *Bene-Adam*, however, is the normal
Jewish word for human beings. The Septuagint considers
Adam a proper noun from Genesis 2:16 on; the Vulgate
from 2:19 on; Adam appears for the first time as a proper
noun in the standard Hebrew Bible only after Genesis 4:25.
In that text *twenty-two* of the twenty-seven occurrences of
the name are accompanied by the article: "the man." They
are not proper names. In Genesis, E. Lussier concludes
that *Adam* has four senses:

1. "Man," a particular man, the first man (sixteen
times).
2. The first husband (nine times).
3. Generic, "mankind" (two times).

4. As a proper name—once![44]

So we might well ask: What about those people who lived before Cain and Abel? What about those who disappeared from sight? What about those who were not even warned of the Flood? What about those many, many who visited the earth as resurrected beings? What about the Watchers? What about the sons of God who should not marry the daughters of men, and vice versa? And what about the giants they begot when they did marry? What about the comings and goings of Enoch's day between the worlds? What about his own status as "a wild man, . . . a strange thing in the land"? (Moses 6:38.) Who were his people, living in a distant land of righteousness, who never appear on the scene? What about the Three Nephites, whose condition so puzzles Moroni, until he is told that they are neither mortal nor immortal? (Mormon 8:10-11.) What about the creatures we do not see around us? What about the Cainites? What about the nations among whom Noah will have surviving progeny?

Speaking of Noah, God promised Enoch "that he [God] would call upon the children of Noah; and he sent forth an unalterable decree, that a remnant of his seed [Enoch's through Noah] should always be found among all nations, while the earth should stand; and the Lord said: Blessed is he through whose seed Messiah shall come." (Moses 7:51-53.) Methuselah boasted about his line as something special. (Moses 8:2-3.) Why special if it included the whole human race? These blessings have no meaning if all the people of the earth and all the nations are the seed of Noah and Enoch. What other line could the Messiah come through? Well, there were humans who were not invited by Enoch's preaching—not included among the residue of people not entering Enoch's city. They were "the residue of the people which were the sons of Adam; and they were a mixture of all the seed of Adam save it was the seed of Cain, for the seed of Cain . . . had not place among them." (Moses 7:32.)

One thing we should understand is that the image of the pre-hominid is not a discovery of modern science any more than the idea of evolution is. Primitive man is the easiest thing in the world to imagine. Just look at your neighbor. The Greeks were fascinated with him, and so were the Middle Ages. Albrecht Altdorfer's painting "Der Wilde Mann," done in the early sixteenth century, showing a real ape-man at home with his family, is as good as anything H. F. Osborne ever turned out. Albrecht Dürer also was intrigued by the subject. Herbert Spencer had only to lean back in his armchair to turn out the First Principles. I have never found students the least hesitant to write papers on "A Day in the Life of Primitive Man." They know all about it. They don't have to look up a thing.

This is a natural product of the silliest doctrine of all— that of cultural evolution. Taking one's own, contemporary civilization as the very latest civilization (which it is) and therefore the best (which it is not), it is the easiest thing in the world to classify all other civilizations on a scale of proximity to your own in time and spirit. Chrétien de Troyes in the twelfth century begins his famous work with such a classification. This is just as sound and scientific as textbooks on cultural anthropology used for years.

But is it logical to begin at the top, as our Adam does? The Adam tradition has it that Adam was the best and greatest, the most perfect of all men. Isn't that getting the normal process of things backwards? Not at all, in some things. If you want to found a university, do you begin by gathering a colony of very stupid and ignorant people and wait for it to evolve into an increasingly glorious institution? Does a university evolve? It accumulates books and buildings and staff; and if size is what makes a university, then we do indeed progress. But as often as not the big problem is to keep it from deteriorating!

So it is with Adam. Must modern man be an improvement on him? Such is that absurd doctrine of cultural evolution with which the schools have been saddled for a century. I well remember my old music teacher, Mr. Seyler, shaking his head with wonder at how Mozart could possibly have written such wonderful music two hundred years ago!

Those soporific words "gradually" and "step by step," repeated incessantly, are aimed at covering an ignorance that is both vast and surprising. One is lulled, over-whelmed, and stupefied by the gradualness of it all, which is at best a platitude, only good for pacifying the mind. The lazy word "evolution" has blinded us to the real com-plexities of the past. It raises an appalling number of ques-tions to which we have no answer. Our ignorance not only remained vast, but became pretentious as well.[45]

Are we superior to the ancients? "If man had originally inhabited a world as blankly uniform as a high-rise housing development, as featureless as a parking lot, as destitute of life as an automated factory, it is doubtful that he would have had a sufficiently varied experience to retain images, mold languages, or acquire ideas."[46]

If unused organs atrophy, we are losing rather than gaining brain-power. A. R. Wallace sorely offended Dar-win by asking him, If every organ represents that minimal response to which it has been pressured by the need for survival, whence the brain, that marvelous organ endowed with a hundred times more power than any primitive has ever needed for survival or any modern man ever makes use of? What possible environment could, as a requirement for survival or any other purpose, have called forth such a prodigal reservoir of intellect? We can only look to a "first primeval childhood" far different from anything we know and conclude that Adam's background reaches into a past more marvelous than any we can imagine.

That is another thing the most recent studies are bring-ing to light more clearly all the time: uniformitarianism is assumed in all calculations, but now it begins to look to the naturalists as well as the physicists that things were far, far different back there than we can ever imagine them, recalling H. R. Haldane's famous remark that the universe is not only stranger than we think it is but stranger than we ever *can* think it to be.

One of those innumerable hypotheses that Professor Campbell mentions, now released for serious discussion by recent discoveries, is that human life may have been transplanted directly from some other planet. Speculating on the subject, we have the romantic Carl Sagan; Leslie E. Orgel of the Salk Institute; Francis H. C. Crick, a Nobel laureate; and others. One eminent scientist, Albert Rosenfeld, confesses, "I'm somehow not surprised at the idea that someone out there put us here. And if such a magical, mysterious, and powerful intelligence exists that is utterly beyond human imagining, can you give me a good reason why I shouldn't call it God?"[47]

Which takes us back to the issue with which the Adam question began and which has always been the central issue of human paleontology: a matter of definitions. They may seem trivial, secondary, naive—but the experts have never been able to get away from it. Evolution and natural selection were never defined to Darwin's satisfaction. Today all the specialists are trying to agree on a clear definition for man: when is a *homo* a *homo*, and how much? And one of our biggest stumbling blocks is not knowing how Adam relates to other beings, earthly and heavenly. That is the root of the Adam-God misunderstanding. (Until we care to look into the matter seriously, I will keep my opinions in a low profile.)

Do not begrudge existence to creatures that looked like men long, long ago, nor deny them a place in God's affection or even a right to exaltation—for our scriptures allow them such. Nor am I overly concerned as to just when they might have lived, for their world is not our world. They have all gone away long before our people ever appeared. God assigned them their proper times and functions, as he has given me mine—a full-time job that admonishes me to remember his words to the overly eager Moses: "For mine own purpose have I made these things. Here is wisdom and it remaineth in me." (Moses 1:31.) It is Adam as my own parent who concerns me. When he walks onto the stage, then and only then the play begins. He opens a book and starts calling out names. They are the sons of Adam, who also qualify as sons of God, Adam himself being a son of God. This is the book of remembrance from which many have been blotted out. They have fallen away, refused to choose God as their father, and by so doing were registered in Satan's camp. "Satan shall be their father, and misery shall be their doom." (Moses 7:37.) Can we call them sons of Adam, *bene-Adam*, human beings proper? The representative Egyptians, Babylonians, Greeks, and Romans, to name only the classic civilizations of old, each fancied themselves to be beings of a higher nature, nearer to gods than others who inhabited the land with them (and before them), or who dwelt in other lands. And yet they did not deny humanity to them.

Adam becomes Adam, a hominid becomes a man, when he starts keeping a record. What kind of record? A record of his ancestors—the family line that sets him off from all other creatures. Such records begin very early, to judge by the fabulous genealogic knowledge of the Australian aborigines (A.P. Elkin) or the most "primitive" Africans (L. Frobenius). Even written records go back to ages lost in the mists of time—the Azilian pebbles, the marking of arrows, and the identity of individuals in their relationships with each other.[48] Whether former speculation about life *on* other worlds is now to be upgraded to life *from* other worlds remains to be seen, but Adam is wonderful enough without that. That gap between the record keeper and all the other creatures we know anything about is so unimaginably enormous and yet so neat and abrupt that we can only be dealing with another sort of being, a quantum leap from one world to another. Here is something not derivative from anything that has gone before on the local scene, even though they all share the same atoms.

NOTES

1. Jordan, Robert Paul, "Washington Cathedral, 'House of Prayer for All People'," *National Geographic Magazine*, April 1980, pp. 566-67.

2. *Life on Other Worlds*, Symposium (CBS), sponsored by Jos. E. Seagram & Sons, Mar. 1, 1961.

3. Smith, Joseph, *History of The Church of Jesus Christ of Latter-day Saints*, 7 vols., 2nd ed. rev., edited by B. H. Roberts (Salt Lake City: The Church of Jesus Christ of Latter-day Saints, 1932-51), 5:362; *Journal of Discourses*, 26 vols. (London: Latter-day Saints' Book Depot, 1854-86), 10:147.

4. Cited in Joad, Cyril Edwin Mitchinson, *Guide to Philosophy* (New York: Dover, 1946), p. 524.

5. Jelinek, Arthur J., "The Lower Paleolithic: Current Evidence and Interpretations," *Annual Review of Anthropology* 6 (1977): 28.

6. Dubos, René, *So Human an Animal* (New York: Scribners, 1968), pp. 14, 15.

7. Dubos, p. 195.

8. Dubos, p. 209.

9. Singh, R. S., *Absurd Drama* 1945-1956 (Delhi: Hariyana Press, 1973), p. 5.

10. Campbell, Bernard G., "Conceptual Progress in Physical Anthropology: Fossil Man," *Annual Review of Anthropology* 1 (1972): 27.

11. Jerison, Harry J., "Fossil Evidence of the Evolution of the Human Brain," *Annual Review of Anthropology* 4 (1975): 46.

12. Jerison, p. 46.

13. Jerison, p. 46.

14. Pilbeam, D., "Recent Finds and Interpretations of Miocene Hominoids," *Annual Review of Anthropology* 8 (1979): 339f.

15. Pilbeam, p. 339f.

16. Jelinek, p. 20.

17. Campbell, p. 27.

18. Pilbeam, p. 350.

19. Howells, William W., "Homo Erectus," in B. M. Fagan, ed., *Avenues to Antiquity, Readings from the Scientific American* (San Francisco: W. H. Freeman and Company, 1976), p. 30.

20. Pilbeam, p. 350.

21. Washburn, Sherwood L., "Tools and Human Evolution," in Fagan, p. 27.

22. Simpson, G. G., quoted by John C. Whitcomb and Henry M. Morris, *The Genesis Flood* (Philadelphia: Baker Book, 1961), p. 443.

23. Darwin, Charles, *The Autobiography of Charles Darwin and Selected Letters* (New York: Dover, 1958), p. 62.

24. Dobzhansky, Theodosius, "Evolution at Work," *Science* 127 (May 9, 1958): 1092.

25. Dobzhansky, p. 1092.

26. Howells, p. 35.

27. B. Rensberger, in *New York Times*, Sept. 10, 1979.

28. Rensberger.

29. Pilbeam, p. 343.

30. Pilbeam, p. 341.

31. Campbell, pp. 43, 44.

32. Washburn, p. 5.

33. Jelinek, pp. 16, 19.

34. Washburn, p. 15.

35. Washburn, p. 6.

36. Washburn, p. 15.

37. Lumley, Henry de, "A Paleolithic Camp at Nice," in Fagan, p. 39f.

38. Klein, Richard G., "Ice-Age Hunters of the Ukraine," in Fagan, pp. 66, 71.

39. Klein, p. 73.

40. Klein, p. 75.

41. Dobzhansky, p. 1097.

42. Barrow, John D., and Joseph Silk, "The Structure of the Early Universe," *Scientific American* 424 (April 1980): 127.

43. Barrow, p. 128.

44. Lussier, Ernest, "Adam in Genesis 1, 1-4, 24," *Catholic Biblical Quarterly* 18 (1956): 137-38.

45. Santillana, Giorgio de, *Hamlet's Mill* (Boston: David R. Godine, 1969), pp. 68-71.

46. Cited in Dubos, p. 174.

47. Discussed in Rosenfeld, Albert, "Did Someone Out There Put Us Here?" *Saturday Review*, Nov. 20, 1973, p. 59.

48. Nibley, Hugh, "The Arrow, the Hunter, and the State," *Western Political Quarterly* 2 (1949): 328-44.

5

Patriarchy and Matriarchy

My story begins with Adam and Eve, the archetypal man and woman, in whom each of us is represented. From the most ancient times their thrilling confrontation has been dramatized in rites and ceremonies throughout the world, as part of a great creation-drama rehearsed at the new year to celebrate the establishment of divine authority on earth in the person of the king and his companion. There is a perfect unity between these two mortals; they are "one flesh." The word *rib* expresses the ultimate in proximity, intimacy, and identity. When Jeremiah speaks of "keepers of my *tsela* (rib)" (Jeremiah 20:10), he means bosom friends, inseparable companions. Such things are to be taken figuratively, as in Moses 3:22 and Genesis 2:22, when we are told not that the woman was made out of the rib or from the rib, but that she *was* the rib, a powerful metaphor. So likewise "bone of my bones, and flesh of my flesh" (Genesis 2:23), "and they shall cleave together as one flesh"—the condition is that of total identity. "Woman, because she *was* taken out of man" (Moses 3:23; italics added) is interesting because the word *woman* is here mysteriously an extension of man, a form peculiar to English; what the element *wo-* or *wif-* means or where it came from remains a mystery, according to the *Oxford English Dictionary*. Equally mysterious is the idea of the man and woman as the apple of each other's eye. Philological dictionaries tell us that it is a moot question whether the word *apple* began with the eye or the fruit. The Greek word is *kora* or *korasion,* meaning a little girl or little woman you see in the eye of the beloved; the Latin equivalent is *pupilla,* from *pupa* or *little doll,* from

"Patriarchy and Matriarchy" was first delivered on February 1, 1980, to the annual women's conference at Brigham Young University.

which we get our word *pupil*. What has diverted me to this is the high degree to which this concept developed in Egypt in the earliest times. The Eye of Re is his daughter, sister, and wife—he sees himself when he looks into her eye, and the other way around. It is the image in the eye that is the ideal, the *wdjat*, that which is whole and perfect. For "it is not good that man should be alone"; he is incomplete by himself—the man is not without the woman in the Lord. (See 1 Corinthians 11:11.)

The perfect and beautiful union of Adam and Eve excited the envy and jealousy of the Evil One, who made it his prime objective to break it up. He began by making both parties self-conscious and uncomfortable. "Ho, ho," said he, "you are naked. You had better run and hide, or at least put something on. How do you think you look to your Father?" They had reason to be ashamed, because their nakedness betrayed their disobedience. They had eaten of the forbidden fruit. But Satan wanted to shock them with his pious show of prudish alarm—he had made them ashamed of being seen together, and that was one wedge driven between them.

His first step (or wedge) had been to get one of them to make an important decision without consulting the other. He approached Adam in the absence of Eve with a proposition to make him wise, and being turned down he sought out the woman to find her alone and thus undermine her resistance more easily. It is important that he was able to find them both alone, a point about which the old Jewish legends have a good deal to say. The tradition is that the two were often apart in the Garden engaged in separate tasks to which each was best fitted. In other words, being one flesh did not deprive either of them of individuality or separate interests and activities.

After Eve had eaten the fruit and Satan had won his round, the two were now drastically separated, for they were of different natures. But Eve, who in ancient lore is the one who outwits the serpent and trips him up with his own smartness, defeated this trick by a clever argument. First she asked Adam if he intended to keep all of God's commandments. Of course he did! *All* of them? Naturally! And what, pray, was the first and foremost of those commandments? Was it not to multiply and replenish the earth, the universal commandment given to all God's creatures? And how could they keep that commandment if they were separated? It had undeniable priority over the commandment not to eat the fruit. So Adam could only admit that she was right and go along: "I see that it *must* be so," he said, but it was she who made him see it. This is much more than a smart way of winning her point, however. It is the clear declaration that man and woman were put on the earth to stay together and have a family—that is their first obligation and must supersede everything else.

Now a curse was placed on Eve, and it looked as if she would have to pay a high price for taking the initiative in the search for knowledge. To our surprise the *identical* curse was placed on Adam also. For Eve, God "will greatly multiply thy sorrow and thy conception. In sorrow shalt thou bring forth children." (Genesis 3:16.) The key is the word for sorrow, *atsav*, meaning to labor, to toil, to sweat, to do something very hard. To *multiply* does not mean to add or increase but to repeat over and over again; the word in the Septuagint is *plethynomai*, as in the multiplying of words in the repetitious prayers of the ancients. Both the conception and the labor of Eve will be multiple; she will have many children. Then the Lord says to Adam, "In *sorrow* shalt thou eat of it all the days of thy life" (that is, the bread that his labor must bring forth from the earth). The identical word is used in both cases; the root meaning is to work hard at cutting or digging; both the man and the woman must sorrow and both must labor. (The Septuagint word is *lype*, meaning bodily or mental strain, discomfort, or affliction.) It means not to be sorry, but to have a hard time. If Eve must labor to bring forth, so too must Adam labor (Genesis 3:17; Moses 4:23) to quicken the earth so it shall bring forth. Both of them bring forth life with sweat and tears, and Adam is not the favored party. If his labor is not as severe as hers, it is more protracted. For Eve's life will be spared long after her childbearing—"nevertheless thy life shall be spared"—while Adam's toil must go on to the end of his days: "In sorrow shalt thou eat of it *all* the days of thy life!" Even retirement is no escape from that sorrow. The thing to notice is that Adam is not let off lightly as a privileged character; he is as bound to Mother Eve as she is to the law of her husband. And why not? If he was willing to follow her, he was also willing to suffer with her, for this affliction was imposed on Adam expressly "because thou hast hearkened unto . . . thy wife and, hast eaten of the fruit."

And both their names mean the same thing. For one thing they are both called Adam: "And [he] called *their* name Adam" (Genesis 5:2; italics added). We are told in the book of Moses that *Adam* means "many," a claim confirmed by recent studies of the Egyptian name of Atum, Tem, Adamu. The same applies to Eve, whose epithet is "the mother of *all* living."

And what a woman! In the Eden story she holds her own as a lone woman in the midst of an all-male cast of no less than seven supermen and angels. Seven males to one lone woman! Interestingly enough, in the lost and fallen world that reverses the celestial order, the ratio is also reversed, when seven women cling to one righteous man. This calls for an explanation: God commanded his creatures to go into the world "two and two," and yet we presently find the ancient patriarchs with huge families and many wives. What had happened? To anticipate our story, it so happened that when the first great apostasy took place in the days of Adam and Eve, the women, being wise after the nature of Mother Eve, were less prone to be taken in by the enticements of the Cainite world. For one thing they couldn't—they were too busy having children to get into all that elaborate nonsensical mischief. Seven women could see the light when only one man could.

The numerical imbalance in the Garden is caused by the presence of all the male heavenly visitors on the scene. Why are all the angels male? Some very early Christian writings suggest an interesting explanation. In the earliest Christian poem, "The Pearl," and in recently discovered Mandaean manuscripts (the Berlin Kephalia), the Christian comes to earth from his heavenly home, leaving his royal parents behind, for a period of testing upon the earth. Then, having overcome the dragon, he returns to the heavenly place, where he is given a rousing welcome. The first person to greet him on his return is his heavenly mother, who was the last one to embrace him as he left to go down to earth. "The first embrace is that which the Mother of Life gave to the First Man as he separated himself from her in order to come down to earth to his testing." So we have a division of labor. The angels are male because they are missionaries, as the Church on the earth is essentially a missionary organization; the women are engaged in another, but equally important, task: preserving the establishment while the men are away. This relationship is pervasive in the tradition of the race—what the geographer Jean Bruhnes called "the wise force of the earth and the mad force of the sun." It is beautifully expressed in an ode by Sappho:

> The evening brings back all the things that the bright
> sun of morning has scattered
> You bring back the sheep, and the goat and the little
> boy back to his mother.

Odysseus must wander and have his adventures—it is his nature. But life would be nothing to him if he did not know all the time that he had his faithful Penelope waiting for him at home. She is no stick-in-the-mud, however, as things are just as exciting, dangerous, and demanding at home as on the road. (In fact, letters from home to missionary husbands are usually more exciting than their letters from the field.)

So who was the more important? Eve is the first on the scene, not Adam, who woke up only long enough to turn over to fall asleep again; and then when he really woke up he saw the woman standing there, ahead of him, waiting for him. What could he assume but that she had set it all up—she must be the mother of all living! In all that follows she takes the initiative, pursuing the search for ever greater light and knowledge while Adam cautiously holds back. Who was the wiser for that? The first daring step had to be taken, and if in her enthusiasm she let herself be tricked by the persuasive talk of a kindly "brother," it was no fault of hers. Still it was an act of disobedience for which someone had to pay, and she accepted the responsibility. And had she been so foolish? It is she who perceives and points out to Adam that they have done the right thing after all. Sorrow, yes, but she is willing to pass through it for the sake of knowledge—knowledge of good and evil that will provide the test and the victory for working out their salvation as God intends. It is better this way than the old way; she is the progressive one. She had not led him astray, for God had specifically commanded her to stick to Adam no matter what: "The woman thou gavest me and commanded that *she* should stay with me: she gave me the fruit, and I did eat." She takes the initiative, and he *hearkens to her*—"because thou hast hearkened to thy wife." She led and he followed. Here Adam comes to her defense as well as his own; if she twisted his arm, she had no choice either. "Don't you see?" he says to the Lord. "You commanded her to stay with me. What else could she do but take me along with her?"

Next it is the woman who sees through Satan's disguise of clever hypocrisy, identifies him, and exposes him for what he is. She discovers the principle of opposites by which the world is governed and views it with high-spirited optimism: it is not wrong that there is opposition in everything, it is a constructive principle making it possible for people to be intelligently happy. It is better to know the score than not to know it. Finally, it is the "seed of the woman" that repels the serpent and embraces the gospel: she it is who first accepts the gospel of repentance. There is no patriarchy or matriarchy in the Garden; the two supervise each other. Adam is given no arbitary power; Eve is to heed him only insofar as he obeys their Father—and who decides that? She must keep check on him as much as he does on her. It is, if you will, a system of checks and balances in which each party is as distinct and independent in its sphere as are the departments of government under the Constitution—and just as dependent on each other.

The Dispensation of Adam ended as all great dispensations have ended—in a great apostasy. Adam and Eve brought up their children diligently in the gospel, but the adversary was not idle in his continued attempts to drive wedges between them. He had first to overcome the healthy revulsion, "the enmity," between his followers and "the seed of the woman," and he began with Cain, who went all the way with him "for the sake of getting gain." "And Adam and Eve blessed the name of God, and they made all things known unto their sons and their daughters. And Satan came among them, saying: Believe it not. . . . And men began from that time forth to be carnal, sensual, and devilish." (Moses 5:12-13.) Even in the garden mankind were subject to temptation; but they were not evil by nature—they had to work at that. All have fallen, but how *far* we fall depends on us. From Cain and Lamech through the Watchers and Enoch to the mandatory cleansing of the Flood, the corruption spread and enveloped all the earth. Central to the drama was a never-ending tension and conflict between the matriarchal and patriarchal orders, both of which were perversions. Each has its peculiar brand of corruption.

The *matriarchal* cultures are sedentary (remember that the mother stays home either as Penelope or as the princess confined in the tower), that is, agricultural, chthonian, centering around the Earth Mother. The rites are mostly nocturnal, lunar, voluptuous, and licentious. The classic image is that of the great, rich, corrupt, age-old, and oppressive city Babylon, queen of the world, metropolis, fashion center, the super mall, the scarlet woman, the whore of all the earth, whose merchants and bankers are the oppressors of all people. Though the matriarchy makes for softness and decay, beneath the gentle or beguiling or glittering exterior is the fierce toughness, cunning, and ambition of Miss Piggy, Becky Sharp, or Scarlett O'Hara.

The *patriarchal* order lends itself to equally impressive abuses. It is nomadic. The hero is the wandering Odysseus or knight errant, the *miles gloriosus,* the pirate, condottière, the free enterpriser—not the farmer tied to wife and soil, but the hunter and soldier out for adventure, glory, and loot; not the city, but the golden horde, the *feralis exercitus* that sweeps down upon the soft and sedentary cultures of the coast and the river valley. Its gods are sky gods with the raging sun at their head. Its depradations are not by decay but by fire and sword. As predatory and greedy as the matriarchy, it cumulates its wealth not by unquestioned immemorial custom but by sacred and self-serving laws. The perennial routine calls for the patriarchal tribes of the mountains and the steppes to overrun the wealthy and corrupt cities of the plain only to be absorbed and corrupted by them in turn, so that what we end up with in the long run is the worst of both cultures.

In this great apostasy a new relationship of men and women is the keynote. Lamech got the same degree of Master Mahan as Cain did. These dire operations entail great secrecy, and Lamech's wives "rebelled against him, and declared these things abroad, and had not compassion; wherefore Lamech was despised, and cast out, and came not among the sons of men, lest he should die. *And thus the works of darkness began to prevail among all the sons of men."* (Moses 5:53-55; italics added.) Thus with infallible insight the book of Moses introduces us into the perennial year-drama, which in the past fifty years has become a central theme of comparative world religion and literature. We cannot pursue this fascinating subject here,[1] except to note that from now on the king in his ambition has to cope with equally ambitious females. Robert Graves takes us through all the primal myths of the Greeks, where this deadly rivalry is the name of the game. "In this archaic religious system," he begins, "there were as yet neither gods nor priests, but only a universal goddess and her priestesses, woman being the dominant sex and man her frightened victim."[2] Not a healthy relationship; but matriarchy and patriarchy *must* always be mortal enemies. Why? Because of the last part of the word, the -*archy*. In Bailly's dictionary, the first definition given for the word -*arche* is "beginning, specifically the origin of a quarrel or 'a murder'"; the second definition is "command, power, authority," which is what the quarrel is about. The suffix *archy* means always to be *first* in order, whether in time or eminence; the point is that there can only be *one* first. To be first is Satan's first principle: "Better to reign in Hell, than serve in Heav'n." Whatever the game, the object is to be Number One.

Why do we lay more emphasis on the patriarchal order than the matriarchy in our world today? That is unavoidable if we would maintain a balance between the two, for the matriarchal succession enjoys a great natural advantage that, where it prevails, renders the other all but helpless. There is rarely any doubt as to who a baby's mother is, but paternity may always be challenged. In the end the only assurance we have of a true patriarchal succession is the word not of the father but of the mother, as the Egyptians well knew—Maat is the official approval of the mother, without which no dynasty could be secure. To assure a true patriarchal succession therefore requires something in the way of checks and controls on the women, a stricter moral code than that required by the matriarchy, which, as we have noted, tends to become lax and promiscuous with the passing of time. With close rules, safeguards, and vigilant surveillance it was only too easy for the patriarchs to become arrogant, dictatorial, self-righteous, and oppressive. The gospel sets absolute limitations beyond which patriarchal authority may not be exercised—the least hint of unkindness acts as a circuit-breaker. "Amen to the priesthood or the authority of that man." (D&C 121:37.) Without that sacred restraint, patriarchal supremacy has ever tended to become abusive.

A wonderful insight into the archaic order in the bad days after the flood is found in the book of Ether:

> Now Jared became exceedingly sorrowful because of the loss of the kingdom, for he had set his heart upon the kingdom and upon the glory of the world.
>
> Now the daughter of Jared being exceedingly expert, . . . thought to devise a plan whereby *she* could redeem the kingdom. . . .
>
> Now the daughter of Jared was exceedingly fair. And . . . she did talk with her father, and said unto him: Whereby hath my father so much sorrow? Hath he not read the record which our fathers brought across the great deep? . . . an account concerning *them of old*, that they by their secret plans did obtain kingdoms and great glory?
>
> And now, therefore, let my father send for Akish, . . . and behold, I am fair, and I will dance before him, . . . he will desire me to wife, . . . then shall ye say: I will give her if ye will bring unto me *the head of my father*, the king. [Here the younger king, at the instigation of the princess, a daughter of Jared, seeks the head of the old king, following the ancient practice.] . . .

And Akish did administer unto them the oaths which were given *by them of old who also sought power,* which had been handed down even from Cain. . . .

And they were kept up by the *power* of the devil . . . to help such as sought *power* to gain *power,* and to murder, and to plunder, and to . . . commit . . . whoredoms. (Ether 8:7-10, 13, 15-16; italics added.)

And . . . *Jared* was anointed king . . . and he gave unto Akish his daughter to wife.

[Akish is now next in line.] And . . . Akish sought the life of [Jared] . . . and [he] obtained the head of his father-in-law, as he sat upon his throne. . . .

And . . . Akish began to be jealous of *his* son [and so starved him to death in prison]. . . .

Now the people of Akish were desirous for *gain,* even as Akish was desirous for *power;* wherefore, the sons of Akish did offer them money. . . .

And there began to be a war between the sons of Akish and Akish . . . unto the destruction of nearly all the people of the kingdom. (Ether 9:4-5, 7, 11-12; italics added.)

And it all began with a woman: *Dux femina facti.*

According to the oldest mythologies, all the troubles of the race are but a perennial feud between the matriarchy and patriarchy; between men and women seeking power and gain at each other's expense.

With infallible instinct Shakespeare takes us into a timeless world of elemental spirits where a fairy king and queen are found shamelessly bickering over a piece of property—a little slave. *Proud* Titania and *jealous* Oberon are playing a silly game of one-upmanship—silly, but with appalling results. All nature is blasted and blighted, and the only progeny of the squabbling pair is universal sterility, described in harrowing detail by the queen: "And this progeny of evil comes of us, we are its parent and original!" What dismal parenthood! And it all comes of ambition and greed, to which gods and goddesses as well as kings and queens are prone.

As a sampling of what goes on and on and on, take the Olympian creation myth: "At the beginning of all things Mother Earth emerged from chaos and bore her son Uranus as she slept"; the two of them united to beget a race of monsters as "earth and sky parted in deadly strife," which, according to Graves, "must refer to the clash between the patriarchal and matriarchal principles." The giant children revolted against their father, Uranus, who threw them into Tartarus; in revenge the mother persuaded their leader, Cronus, to murder his father; upon coming to the throne, Cronus in turn imprisoned his own sons and married his sister Rhea. Jealous of his children, he destroyed them to keep them from deposing him until their mother conspired with her son, Zeus, to dispatch Cronus exactly as he had his father, Uranus. Prometheus became chief advisor to Zeus, the new king, who chained him to a mountain for being "too philanthropic." On the mountain Prometheus had a conversation with the girl Io, who was fleeing for her life; Zeus had brutally attacked her in his lust, and his jealous wife, Hera, to avenge herself on him, ordered that Io should be pursued forever by a gadfly. Prometheus prophesied to her, however, that Zeus, the supermacho tyrant, would fall in turn before a hero descended from Io herself. And so it goes, on and on. There must be a better way, and there is.

It was Abraham and Sarah who restored the state of our primal parents, she as well as he, for in the perfect balance they maintained, he is as dependent on her as she on him. With them were restored the covenants and promises of our first parents. The world did everything to force them apart, and if they had thought in terms of power and gain it would certainly have succeeded. What was it that kept them together? The patriarchal narratives bring a new and surprising element into world literature. In the most brutal of worlds they are unique as *romantic* love stories, in which the female lead enjoys a billing equal if not superior to that of the male, with her own name, genealogy, royalty, and fortune, and as much bargaining power as the man. True, all the marriage brokerage is carried on by families and dynasties, with ambitious parents and arrogant monarchs trying to spoil the love match, but God approves of the romance, and for once the dire attempts at substituting family and dynastic business interests for affection are frustrated. From Abraham and Sarah down through Isaac and Jacob and to Joseph and Asenath, that is the plot of the story.

Thus Pharaoh (Nimrod) feared Abraham's power and priesthood (as predicted by Nimrod's astrologers) and so first attempted to prevent Abraham's birth by putting to death all the male infants born in the kingdom and then by imprisoning him as a child and finally by putting him on an altar from which he was delivered by an angel. Finally the proud monarch surrendered and conceded that the God of Abraham had all the power after all.

It was also a pharaoh who sought the hand of Sarah, the true princess, in order to raise up a royal progeny by her. Upon a royal bed identical in form with the altar of Abraham, she too prayed for deliverance and was rescued by an angel while the king was constrained to recognize Sarah's true marriage and heritage, bestowing upon her regal insignia and a royal escort. At God's command, Abraham humbled himself to ask Sarah as a favor to declare herself to be his sister, eligible to marry another and thus save his life. This is only part of the deference that Abraham had to make to his wife, and it left no place for his male pride. Sarah, on the other hand, with equal humility, went to Abraham confessing God's hand in her childlessness and actually begging him to have children by another woman. Can one imagine a greater test of her pride? When both sides of the equation are reduced, the remainder on both sides is only a great love.

Again the apostasy. Recently scholars have compared

Sarah with Helen of Troy, and the latter can show us as well
as anyone how the romantic tradition of the patriarchs went
sour. It begins with attempts at seduction—wanton perver-
sion of the forbidden fruit. Queenly Hera offers Paris power
and gain to get the golden apple from him while Aphrodite
promises him the ultimate—sex and prestige, the world's
most beautiful woman for a wife; as for Athena, she is a
freak, invented by the patriarchal interests to expedite their
takeover of the matriarchal claims: she was not of woman
born, but sprang in full masculine armor from the head (not
the heart) of the All-Father Zeus—a very masculine damsel,
indeed, who always votes with the male contingency; and of
course she is ever-virgin and never a mother. Aphrodite got
the award—the golden apple—and procured Paris his beautiful wife, who was already married to an obnoxious male
chauvinist, who was a king and a serious business rival to her
new husband (for the Achaeans and Trojans had long waged
old war for the control of the rich grain trade that passed
through the straits from Russia). It was Menelaus' brother
Agamemnon, head of the whole vast conglomerate, who led
the expedition against Troy. The opening lines of the *Iliad*
show this bully-boy insisting that the hero Achilles turn over
to him the fair daughter of the priest Chyses, whom Achilles
has won in battle. Agamemnon's claim to the girl is very simple: he is the boss, and he wants her. To the girl's father, who
comes to ransom her, he bawls out: "No, I am not going to let
her go! She's going to get old and gray in my house, far from
her home in the weaving department, and she's going to bed
with me whenever I feel like it. Now you get out of here;
don't bug me—if you want to leave in one piece!" That is the
kind of a great leader Agamemnon is. Note here that Greek
women were treated like captives because originally they
were captives; when the warrior hordes overran the ancient
people of the coast, they subjected their matriarchal society
to perpetual suppression, though from time to time the smol-
dering fires broke out fiercely. It is not surprising that

Agamemnon, to expedite his journey to Troy, sacrifices his young daughter Iphigenia to Poseidon. But this gave a moral pretext to his wife, Clytemnestra, as ambitious and unscrupulous as he, to connive with her lover in murdering her husband on the day of his return. For which the son, Orestes, murdered *his* mother and the king who ruled by her sufferance. While the avenging Furies pursued Orestes, the gods took a vote to decide whether his avenging of his father justified the killing of his mother. Not surprisingly, the vote split on party lines, *every* god voting to acquit the defendant and *every* goddess voting to convict him—another showdown between male and female. The tie was broken by the vote of Athena, invented for the express purpose, it is believed, of tipping the scales for the patriarchy. She also holds the balance between imperious Zeus and relentless Hera in their ceaseless feuding at the expense of poor Odysseus and Penelope. "Zeus and Hera bickered constantly. Vexed by his infidelities, she often humiliated him by her scheming ways. . . . He never fully trusted Hera. . . . She therefore resorted to ruthless intrigue." (Iliad 1,53.)

In Egypt, Israel lived under a matriarchal monarchy from which they were delivered under Moses. Moses' romantic career parallels that of Abraham to a remarkable degree. The tension between matriarchy and patriarchy begins with the Hebrew midwives refusing Pharaoh's command to put to death all the *male* babies, an order which the Egyptians carry out with a will. Moses is rescued by his *mother*, placed in a reed float, and rescued and brought up in the rushes of the Delta swamp by two women, a nurse and a princess-mother (exactly like the infant Horus, protected and raised by Isis and Nephthys in the same swamp of Chemmis). Then Moses marries one of seven water-drawing maidens, who declares her independence and to whose father (not his own father, but his wife's) the hero always defers. He balks at assuming the role of the pharaoh he has overcome in the sea—and indeed it was not he but

Miriam who celebrated the victory over the waters and the rival king. When he turns Nile water into blood, he is performing an age-old rite reserved to the women of Egypt celebrating the founding of the nation by a woman who discovered the land. He leads the people to a place of twelve wells and seventy palms, the symbolic number reminding us that Sarah figures as a palm tree in Abraham's dream in the Genesis Apocryphon, as Nausicaa does in Odysseus' fantasy. When the tables are turned against the Egyptians, it is their *male* first born who perish—another blow at male succession. Surprisingly, it is not Moses but his wife Zipporah who circumcises their first born son and proceeds to rebuke her husband with stinging contempt. Plainly the attempt at patriarchal assertion met tough resistance. The people rejected Moses as their leader even after he had saved them (Exodus 16:2; 32:23) and plunged with a will into the licentious matriarchal rites led by the wives and daughters and their sons under their influence (there is no mention of husbands or brothers), who contributed their gold earrings to make the golden calf. That was Ka Mutef, "Bull of His Mother," who represented to the Egyptians the youthful pharaoh's submission to his mother. While they were singing and dancing in the best matriarchal tradition, Moses ordered the death of every *male* participating in the rites; they were to "slay every man his brother" if he caught him at the party. (This third liquidation of males was followed by a solemn rededication to the patriarchal order: "*Consecrate* yourselves . . . even every man upon his *son*, and upon his *brother*; that he may bestow upon you a blessing this day." [Exodus 32:29; italics added.])

This apostasy had been one of the fastest yet: "They have turned aside *quickly* out of the way which I commanded them," said the Lord to Moses. (Exodus 32:8; italics added.) "My people have *sold* themselves for gold and silver." That, along with total depravity, completes the picture and brings the world order back to normal.

After Moses, the romantic David had his women-trouble, as we all know. Like Aaron, he danced in the manner of Pharaoh before the altar, and the queen, looking on, "despised him in her heart." What need be said of Solomon and the ladies? That supermacho male chauvinist met his match in the Shulamite woman, who outwitted the all-wise Solomon and thoroughly humiliated him. A whole epic cycle revolves around Solomon's Benedict-and-Beatrice, Petrucchio-and-Catherine game with the Queen of Sheba, who, as Bilqis (the name designates her as a ritual hierodule), matches wits with him for throne and empire, in which he cheats shamelessly but is beaten just the same.

Years ago I collected some hundred versions of the story. Beginning with the account of how Jacob took advantage of the helpless Tamara, who turned his sin against him and came out winner, I was struck to find a whole line of ancient queens doing the same sort of thing—and usually going under the same name. Thus when Cyprus, having conquered all the world but one country, that of the Amazon Massagtae, ignored the wise counsel of his advisor Croesus and invaded that land, its queen Tomyris trapped him at a banquet, where she cut off his head and sloshed it around in a bag of blood. I do not talk about such things for their sensationalism but for their extreme frequency in myth and history—they form a regular pattern, a constant groundwork for history. (In the long line of tragicomic *Odi et amo* ["I can't live with you and I can't live without you!"] confrontations, man and woman stage an endless tournament of dirty events with survival as the prize, in all of which there is something very wrong, however much we have come to relish it in novels and TV programs. Can this be the purpose of the marvelous providence that brings men and women together? If we must all live together in the eternities, it can never be in such a spirit.)

And so we find the celestial order of marriage resorted

to again in the meridian of time. From the earliest writings both defending and attacking Christianity, it is clear that the relationship between the sexes was something very special with them. Outsiders were shocked and scandalized, for example, by the promiscuity implied in the Christian practice of calling each other brother and sister. A more-than-ordinary emphasis on family life is apparent in the warnings of First Clement to the leaders of the church that they are neglecting to pay sufficient attention to their own families and the bringing up of their children in the church. The more recent discoveries of early Christian documents allow us insights into the nature of the teaching that incurred the wrathful criticism of an immoral age that did not understand it at all. Thus we learn in the Gospel of Philip and the Apocalypse of Adam how Adam and Eve were united in celestial union before the creation of the world but, upon descending to the earth, became separated, with death entering into the scene. Christ came to earth, says the Gospel of Philip, "for the express purpose of bringing them together in eternal life. Thanks to him those who are united in the Bridal Chamber will never more be separated." The ordinances here are symbolic, but the images are important models to be followed. Let us recall how often the Lord refers to himself as the Bridegroom. The symbols we have here are indeed meager compared with the perfect glory. The things we do in symbols merely hint at things as they are, "for there is glory above glory and power upon power. . . . The Holy of Holies and the Bridal Chamber, these are the ultimate. . . . Though sin still enslaves us, when the truth is revealed the perfect life will flow for everyone . . . that those who were separated may be united and fulfilled. . . . All who enter the Bridal Chamber may beget in the light—not after the manner of nocturnal mating. . . . Whoever becomes a Son of the Bridal Chamber will receive the light . . . and when he goes out of the world he shall already have received the true instruction through types and images."

That early Christian ideas of marriage were far from the conventional ones is plain enough from the difficult solution to the problem arrived at in the fourth century, when the ceremonies of the church were widely accommodated to those of the world: "Was the church conquering the world," asks the great Catholic historian Duchesne, "or was not the world rather conquering the church?" The solution was to accommodate a difficult concept of marriage with the practices of the world and to accept that ancient and established cop-out, celibacy. In the Christian literature of the early centuries, when Christianity was splitting up into many sects, each claiming to possess alone the *gnosis*, the secret teaching of the Lord to the apostles after his resurrection, one reads much of the tribulations of Sophia, who is equated with Zoa or Eve. Once long ago, she tried to become perfectly independent and go it alone. She was Wisdom, as her name signifies (the Hebrew *Hokhma*), who is almost a person in the scriptures, but not quite. If the woman is life she is also Wisdom. Well, Sophia thought that she, as the mother of all, could not only produce but govern the universe all by herself; the result was a ghastly abortion. Chastened and terrified, she was rescued by Jesus Christ, the Bridegroom, who reached out his hand to her and took her back again, for he needed her too, and only when the two worked together in perfect accord could God's purpose go forward in the universe. Jesus was born when Caesar Augustus was inaugurating the long line of emperors while his wife Livia was initiating the long and fateful line of imperial wives and mistresses. She poisoned right and left to get her son Tiberius on the throne, not because she loved him, but because that was the way of preserving and increasing her own power—and wealth. (Nobody knew better than the Romans that when the treasury was empty the emperor was finished.) Most of the Roman emperors were murdered by their successors, who in turn were murdered by their successors. Rome's one original contribution to letters was a brilliant and per-

ceptive line of satirists telling us all about life in the Roman
world: the theme, of course, was money and sex.

From the confused jumble of traditions and beliefs of
late antiquity (the heritage of very ancient times indeed),
there emerged at the beginning of the Middle Ages such
mysteries as the Round Table, in which we find rejuve-
nated the romantic ideal of the hero who is never ambitious
for himself, and the lady pure and holy whom he serves. A
more dramatic contrast to the reality of the times (as we see
in the ten books of Gregory of Tours' *Frankish History*)
would be hard to imagine. What put a quietus to the Round
Table was partly the stress and tension of perpetual dal-
liance under the code of chivalry—if Lynette snobbishly
humiliated her knight, so Galahad prudishly denied his favors to the ladies—but mostly the failure was brought on
by the jealousy and ambition (personified by the sinister
Mordred) that poisoned the minds of true lovers.

Shakespeare has given us a classic study in sex and
power in *Macbeth*. There is a beautiful relationship between
the lord and his lady, until they both start reaching for
power. The moral of the play is that the lust for power and
gain inevitably destroys the true and proper nature of the
sexes. It begins with the archaic matriarchy—dark, chthonian *Hecate*, no less—who sets three women (the witches)
to trap and destroy the hero. But they are unnatural
women: "You should be women," says the hero's companion when he sees them. But what can these bearded creatures be? Full of confidence, the hero brushes them aside,
and yet he is fascinated by them—"Speak then to me, who
neither *beg* nor *fear* your favors or your hate." Proudly independent, he has already taken the bait and is in the trap.
Their prophecies get him all excited, and he writes to his
wife, who reads his letter and sees right off that in order to
promote themselves she and her husband will have to
forget all about their natural roles as man and woman:

> Yet do I fear thy nature.
> It is too full the *milk* of human kindness. . . .

For Macbeth was a *kind* man to begin with (the spark of his former self flashes through from time to time during the play), and the lady was known as a sweet and gentle woman. But now she must get down to business:

> Hie thee hither,
> That I may pour my spirits in thine ear,
> And chastise with the valor of *my* tongue,
> All that impedes thee from the golden round.

It is the crown they are after. Why settle for less? In view of such a prospect, all their former values are violently wrenched in a new direction as a messenger comes in and tells the lady that they are about to have a royal guest—the king is already in power:

> Come you spirits
> That tend on mortal thoughts, unsex me here. . . .
> [She must be unsexed to follow her ambition.]
> Come to my woman's breasts
> And take my *milk* for gall, you murdering ministers.

Already milk again: that is the human side of them; both of them share the milk of human kindness—but they must get rid of it to get ahead. Next, flinching from the murder, Macbeth shows his old human self when he is stopped short by the thought of "pity, like a naked newborn babe." But Lady Macbeth pushes him on by telling him to become a *man*. He doesn't like that; a man is one thing, a monster is another: "I dare do all that may become a man. Who dares do *more* is *none*."

You are wrong, she says; I am trying to make a man of you now. That means going all the way:

> When durst do it, then you were a man, And to be more . . . would
> Be so much more the man.

Then she gets back to *milk* again, and says a terrible thing:

> I have given suck, and know
> How tender 'tis to love the babe that milks me.

I would, while it was smiling in my face,
Have plucked my nipple from his boneless gums and
dashed the
brains out, had I so sworn as you
Have done to this.

Unsexed as a woman, unnatural as a mother—if that's
what it takes to get what she wants. And what does she
want? Power. She wins the argument.

Bring forth men-children only,
For thy undaunted mettle should compose
Nothing but *males*.
[She is too good to be a woman! Women are weak.]

But Lady Macbeth has her moment of weakness: "Had
he not resembled my father as he slept, I had done 't." The
next words she cries out are, "My husband!" Later she
takes him to task: "My hands are of your color, but I shame
to wear a heart so white."

Macduff tells Lady Macbeth he cannot tell her what has
happened:

O gentle lady . . .
The repetition, in a woman's ear,
Would murder as it fell.
[It should, but she is no longer a woman.]

In fact, someone describes the stormy night as "unnatural."
So the old matriarchs gave Macbeth the crown, but the
whole thing is wrong.

Upon my head they placed a *fruitless* crown
And put a *barren scepter* in my grip.

(The words are significant, this sort of success is fruitless and barren.) Macbeth does have a conscience: "Oh,
full of scorpions is my mind, dear wife!" He does not want
to involve her in any more murders: "Be innocent of the
knowledge, *dearest chuck*" (an almost comical betrayal of
how he wanted to think of her still). But at the banquet she

is at him again: "Are you a man?" "Proper stuff!" "These flaws and starts . . . would well become a *woman's story* at a winter's fire, authorized by her *grandam*. Shame itself." "What, quite *unmanned* in folly? Fie, for shame!"

The ultimate humiliation is now that he should be like a woman—a silly, superstitious woman, a feeble, helpless old woman.

To the ghost he says: "What man dare, I dare." "Protest me the *baby of the girl* [this is as low as self-contempt can get]." "Why, so. Being gone, I am a *man again*."

In his rage and frustration he orders the extermination of Macduff's family:

> His wife, his babes, and all unfortunate souls
> That trace him in his line.

"He has no children," is Macduff's reaction when he hears the news. Lady Macduff says when the murderer approaches,

> I remember now I am in this world, where to do harm is often laudable, to do good sometime accounted dangerous folly [an utter perversion of values]. Why, then, alas, do I put up that womanly defense?

The young and sensitive Malcolm has had more than he can take and raves:

> Nay, had I power, I should
> Pour the sweet *milk* of concord into Hell,
> Uproar the universal peace, confound
> All *unity* on earth.

At this point Shakespeare introduces an important but often neglected interlude. To check his raving, Macduff replies to Malcolm that his father and mother were a "most sainted" royal pair.

Malcolm then says: "I am yet unknown to woman, never was forsworn, scarcely have *coveted* what was my own" (neither sex nor greed had spoiled him).

The doctor then introduces talk of Edward the Confessor, the reigning king of England: "At his touch, such *sanctity* hath heaven given his hand, [those with maladies] presently amend."

Malcolm follows with this observation:

A most miraculous work in this good king. . . .
to the succeeding royalty he leaves
The healing benediction, With this strange virtue
He hath the heavenly gift of prophecy,
And sundry blessings hang about his throne
That speak him *full of grace*.

This scene sets forth the conditions upon which power may be enjoyed without satanic corruption—only by those who are totally unworldly; for one in a position of power the only alternative to becoming devilish in this world is to be *holy*.

In the same scene, when Macduff learns the news, Malcolm says, "Dispute it like a *man*."
Macduff replies:

I shall do so,
But must also *feel it as a man*.

For the Macbeths, on the other hand, to be a man was to have no feelings. What does the lady care about such things?

Fie, my lord! A soldier, and afeard? What need we fear
who knows it, when none can our power to account?

Get enough power and you can forget about things like feelings and conscience—what can anybody do to you?

As it turns out, Macbeth's undoing is his contempt of women; the witches, "lying like truth," have told him to do whatever he pleases "since none of *woman* born can harm Macbeth." What's humanity to him? And he keeps harping on that: no mere *woman's* sons can get the best of him!

What's the boy Malcolm?
Was he not born of *woman*? What's he

> That was not born of *woman*? Such a one . . .
> Am I to fear, or none.
> But swords I smile at, weapons laugh to scorn,
> Brandished by man that's of a *woman* born.

So everything collapses when it is plain that the sisters have played him a rare trick:

> Accursed be the tongue that tells me so,
> For it hath *cowed* my better part of *man*!

In the last scene the new king calls for punishing "the cruel ministers of this dead butcher and his fiendlike Queen." A woman unsexed as she was can no longer be called human.

With the rise of commercialism at the end of the Middle Ages came a feeling of liberation—a romantic release for love, and a free field for acquisition. The relationship of the sexes became both romantic and calculating.

From Shakespeare's and Moliere's comedies down to Agatha Christie, there is nothing wrong with the beloved's expectations of ten thousand dollars a year. Gilbert and Sullivan got away with exposing the deep and pious Victorian situation by making great fun of its absurdity: "I'd laugh my pride to scorn in union holy," says the fair maid, perfectly willing to forget rank and wealth and marry a poor sailor for love alone—on one condition: "Were he more highly born, or I more lowly." For inevitably it was *not* true love that triumphed, as sentimental audiences made themselves think, but the ten thousand a year.

Actually the situation had not changed for thousands of years. The standard plot of modern comedy was that of the New Comedy, which Plautus and Terence got from Menander, where the obstacle to true love is overcome not by sacrifice, but by the manipulation of a clever servant who gulls a rich old man or woman, or, even more delightfully, by the discovery of a token that proves after many years that the poor youth or maiden was nobly born after all and is the heir to a handsome fortune: so now they can get married because they are *both* rich!

And so we come down to the present-day sitcom (where we can laugh freely at everything but the money) and the heavy prime-time show (crime, of course, with single-minded dedication to really *big* money heavily spiced with the super status symbol: plenty of expensive sex).

One of my daughters has a little book with these words on the cover: "The College Survival Kit: Fifty-One Proven Strategies for Success in Today's Competitive College World. Survive and succeed—Don't take chances with your college career." Survival, success, competitive, career—the dictionary defines *strategy* as "deception practiced on an enemy." The word is well chosen. No deception is too shameful to use against an enemy, and whatever the game, your competitor—even the reluctant customer—is the enemy. What a seedbed of mischief this is! The result of this philosophy in terms of human values has recently been the subject of numerous studies. One of the pioneer studies was S. Whyte's *Organization Man*, which told us how the company man would never think of wooing or marrying anyone not approved of by his superiors. So much for true love.

A recent summary of many of these investigations is Michael Maccoby's *The Gamesman*. The section called "The Head and the Heart" is relevant to our discussion: "A corporate president remarked that if he thought of one word to describe his experience with managers over a period of thirty-five years, that word would be *fear*." (There is the cloven hoof again!) "Why are corporate managers fearful?" Mr. Maccoby asks, and he discovers that if the corporate individual could penetrate to the causes of this paralyzing fear and anxiety, he would find *careerism*. (Can we improve on Satan's formula as a definition for that? Careerism is the determination to reign in hell rather than serve in heaven.) "From the moment a person starts treating his life as a career, worry is his constant companion. . . . Careerism results not only in constant anxiety, but also in an underdeveloped heart. . . . The careerist constantly betrays himself, since he must ignore idealistic, compassionate, and courageous impulses that might jeopardize his career."

"Perfect love casts out all fear," said the Lord, but who wants that if it jeopardizes one's career? Satan's promise to split Adam and Eve was accomplished when God declared, "My people have sold themselves for gold and silver."

The few scattered case studies introduced here are merely straws—but they show where the fatal wind is ever blowing. Thinking back, what was Satan's express purpose in inaugurating a rule of blood and horror, power and gain on this earth? It was to breach that wall of enmity that protected "the seed of the woman" from his direct attack. Only the covenants of Adam and Abraham and the church of God can overcome it. Though nothing is to be gained by men and women in fighting for the whip handle, that disgraceful tussle will continue until God cuts it short in righteousness.

So one must choose between patriarchy and matriarchy until the Zion of God is truly established upon the earth. It is that old Devil's dilemma, in which we are asked to take sides with Gog or Magog as his means of decoying us away from our true dedication to that celestial order established in the beginning.

NOTES

1. Nibley, Hugh, *The Roman Games as the Survival of an Archaic Year-Cult* (Berkeley: University of California, 1939).

2. Graves, Robert, *The Greek Myths* (Baltimore: Penguin Books, 1955) 1:28.

6

Unrolling the Scrolls—
Some Forgotten Witnesses

Yesterday I was in Disneyland, and that gives you different views of things. One thing was very impressive: all these exhibits you see about the structure of the universe and their accompanying historical views are drawn from just one source. We have but two sources: written and unwritten. By unwritten I mean the "facts" of science, whether reported in writing or not. By written records, I mean the accumulation of human written records that has been going on for thousands of years. It's immense, it's very valuable, and the contents are quite as "factual" as the other, whether intentionally or not; but would you believe it, nobody ever considers the written record in that light. I'm not talking about special historical studies, these very interesting things done on early American history—the frontier and so forth—or glimpses back into the Middle Ages and the like. How can you consider the whole vast body of historical and literary material as a single writing? What will it tell us about the world we live in? We are all guilty of underestimating and largely ignoring the larger written record. This collection of written documents is one of the great spectacles the world has to offer. It would be a wonderful thing if Walt Disney were alive now to do something with it, and I am sure he would leap at the chance.

The documents first started coming out in great numbers with the Council of Constance (1414-1418) and finally

---

This is a transcript of a talk given in 1967 in Glendale, California, where Hugh Nibley lived during his teenage years. The informal style typical of his talks has been preserved. Nibley himself says he speaks much too fast, and the frequent repetitions are to make sure he is understood. The reader who seeks documentation for statements made in this talk is referred to "*Treasures in the Heavens*," of which this is a more popular and Church-related presentation.

with the fall of Constantinople in 1453. Vast numbers of ancient documents that had been reposing in the East and in various places for a long time suddenly poured into Europe. They were collected and organized in great ducal, royal, and imperial libraries, sometimes by very rich individuals. They captured the imagination of the age. Owners would have them organized in great rotundas, tier upon tier of knowledge, organized chronologically and topically so that you would be completely surrounded with books on all sides, round and round, mounting gallery after gallery almost out of sight, in the form of a huge planetarium of written human knowledge. But unfortunately for the books, about this same time the Book of Nature was discovered.

Bacon, Galileo, and Scaliger are strictly contemporaries. They all at the same time discovered the Book of Nature, which is much easier to read, in a way. The men who could read it would become the great geniuses of the world—the Galileos, the Keplers, the Copernicuses, Toracellis, and so on. But the average man could read it just as well as anybody else. After all, the beginnings of geology were simply by a Scotch farmer, James Sutton, who went out and started guessing about the rocks on the beach near his home. And anyone could play that game. On the other hand, the written records were read mostly by dunderheads. You didn't have to have any genius at all to read them, but you had to have training. You had to know or pretend to know the languages, and while that didn't take any brains, it did take patience and a body, as the saying goes, to read the things. The result was that everybody wanted to play the game of reading the Book of Nature, because everyone's guess was as good as anybody else's; and you can guess like mad. So they completely ignored the written record from then on.

Joseph Justus Scaliger, who died in 1608, was the last man ever to make a serious attempt to read what the written human record said. It covers thousands of years. The human race has documented its doings for a long time, and no one pays any attention to the record. Nobody in the world does that anymore. Oh, it's a librarian's paradise: we classify, we photograph, we reproduce, we store and preserve, and we transfer. We can do all the tricks electronics can do today, but nobody reads the records. Nobody knows what is actually in these books. I mean this literally. A few specialists may consider documents in one area or in another, but who knows what the record as a whole has to tell us? It's a most interesting thing the way these records have been shamefully pushed aside. It would take a man of Walt Disney's genius to dramatize that, to bring it to our attention. (I wish there were someone who could do it.) The actual written record is terrific.

Every book imparts information on two levels—what the author intends to tell you, and what he tells you unintentionally. The unintentional is the interesting thing—it is more important. For example, Cicero wrote hundreds of letters that we still have—all sorts of things about himself, telling us he was the greatest man in the world. In fact, he was really telling us that he was one of the greatest nincompoops who ever lived—a fool! This is what he tells us unintentionally. Intentionally he gives us one story, unintentionally another.

Now any document can be treated just like a fossil—just as impersonally, just as scientifically as anything else. Books fell into disrepute for this reason: people would say, "Look, these are just the musty superstitions of a past age; let's forget them." These were actually a drag on the market, very unscientific. It's true, people who wrote them were usually not very scientific, though sometimes they were. But in many cases, they knew a great deal more than we credit them with. Giorgio de Santillana is writing a great deal on that. He shows that the Egyptians knew more than we have ever given them credit for. Levi-Strauss, an anthropologist, has written an astonishing book on that quite recently—how much more our "primitives" have really known all along than we've been giving them credit for. We had the idea that since people lived long ago and before our science, their ideas must be superstitious. We don't read the books for the ideas that people intended to convey, but for what they tell us unintentionally all over the place.

Any page of any letter will give you all sorts of things about the times, circumstances, the person who wrote it—whether the person intends to tell you that or not. And that's why we want to read these books. If we view all the books in the world as fossils, they can tell us much. As fossils, they're astoundingly perfect. In them we have not just boney, broken structures, but also the flesh; we even have the life, the very thoughts of the creature, left imprinted for our inspection. We don't have to fill in the whole story from our own imaginations. It's because scientists are denied that privilege that they are impatient with our books. They want a situation in which they can pretty well call the tune. But books hamper and confine freedom of invention. (You see, what I could do, what I have done before, is to show a lot of slides of these documents. They would mean nothing to you. I could show you rocks; I could show you pictures of star spectrums; I could show you ferns and other plants and fossils, and you could guess about them as well as I. A person who really knew something about them could be very instructive, couldn't he? But I show you a picture of a document—it means nothing. It wouldn't take too much study for it to begin to mean something, but if you haven't tried that we might just as well be showing nothing at all. So there's no point in showing slides with this sort of thing, is there?) This is one of the reasons why the books have been shoved aside and ignored. People can't get at them, can't "open" them. As a spectacle, they are quite a thing. But what is in them? What do they actually say? I tell you again, nobody knows, because nobody reads them; nobody knows what is in the records of the past, though they are enormous today. Someone in Europe is now making a microfilm card catalog of all of the books that have been printed since the invention of printing. There are only twelve and a half million. There are almost that many books inside the Widener Library today. You don't have to read them all, but it's astonishing how little has been read of certain areas.

Now comes an interesting question: If you were to read these written records, would they give you the same picture of the world that the scientific transcripts give us? In the scientific fields the Book of Nature has been read; it gives us one picture, and these written books give us another picture. Remember, reading them both impersonally, we're viewing them both as phenomena: do they tell us the same things? No they don't. They give a totally different picture of what was going on in the past, the so-called scientific view. This is very good news, because until now we have been told there is only one possible valid picture of the world—the picture science gives us at the moment. Many scientists are getting over that now—men like Karl Popper and Thomas Kuhn. People like that are giving us a very different picture, showing us that it's always changing—which we should have known all along anyway. We shouldn't be stuck with just one picture at one image, even if we are laymen and can't understand the scientists. They say, "Well, you have to take it, this is it; this is it." That's the voice of authority speaking: "I'm sorry we'll just have to settle for that." But it hasn't been particularly good news, because in recent years the picture's become a rather dismal one, and many scientists have been talking about that. Quite a number say the picture's not only dismal but false in many respects. There's something radically wrong with it. It doesn't match the real world we live in, certainly not in all points. Then why do we accept it? Because, as I say, we've been told there's no alternative. Many scientists have said that about evolution. It's a very defective tool, but they must use it because it's the only one they have. So we've been left with but one picture of the world, and all the time there's the other one from the books. I don't say it will give you a true picture of things or anything like that;

I will say there might be something very wonderful if you went and looked. Yet nobody goes and looks. It's just too much trouble.

Since World War II, some very new and important additions have been made to the library. We are now buried under an avalanche of manuscripts. We don't even pretend to read them anymore. We have given up trying. We have reached the saturation point and don't even know what's in the books. They could be full of great surprises. I'm sure we all know about the Dead Sea Scrolls and the Khenoboskeion (that is, the Nag Hammadi) texts, found in Egypt at the same time and forming the earliest Christian library; the Bodmer Papyri; the Mandaean and Manichaean texts discovered recently; before them, slightly, the Chester Beatty Papyri, the Odes of Solomon, and the Oxyrhynchus Papyri. We can go back to the great library collections of the Nineteenth Century—from Babylonian, Assyrian, and Egyptian libraries.

What can we do with all these? We try different approaches. Simply to describe them, when they were found, and under what circumstances, would take many hours. You would then know the books were there, but you wouldn't know what was in them. We can make some generalizations about them. They're not found as separate documents but in batches—whole libraries turn up. You don't just find a document here and a document there. There's a great flood of them, found in great collections, and their value and significance can be gradually appreciated only because what they contain is quite radically different from what we have thought about certain things before. Remember, people haven't been studying the document picture, so when some of these were found just after World War II, they left everybody rather embarrassed. Only a handful of people in the world could read the Dead Sea Scrolls or the Nag Hammadi texts on sight. Then these documents called for a reevaluation of all the other stuff. The entire library has to be reevaluated. When we go back and look, we find many things we'd overlooked, many things we didn't even know were there. We had got the whole thing wrong in the first place anyway and are going to have to do the whole thing over, because of these new discoveries. This has been very embarrassing. We could describe the contents of one or two, we could take one or two really good examples, such as the Serekh Scroll or the Apocryphon of John or of James, and go into them in some detail. But then we miss the cumulative impact. There are not one or two but hundreds of these documents, and they match each other. So what do we do? Well, the best thing is to look at some of the teachings found in all of these documents that are very different from anything that anybody expected.

Why are we able to accept these? Why haven't we been able to sweep them under the rug, as we've done before? Because of the circumstances of their discovery. Because these sources are so new and unspoiled, men have been willing to accept from them what they have refused in the past to accept from the other sources. The earlier discoveries were just as sensational when they were discovered, but they came one by one, and people were able to sort of push them aside. You can't do that now, because the documents are very old, they've been preserved in their purity and nobody had got at them, and they're not copies of copies of copies, as everything else is. (All of our classical literature was copied so many times that we don't have a manuscript that's anywhere near the original.) But these new finds are the originals, and we've never had anything like this happen before. These are libraries that were hidden to come forth in their purity in the due time of the Lord. In fact, the people who hid them were aware that they were hiding them for a long term, a long rest, to come forth at a later time, so that when they would come forth they would not be distorted and changed.

Now they've come forth, and we've been willing to accept things from them that we'd never have taken from anybody else before. Heretofore, conventional Christianity and Judaism have exercised strict control over documents as they've been discovered. They have decided what's to be admitted as orthodox and what's to be rejected—"This is Gnostic," or something else suspect. You can't do that anymore. We have only to let the Jews and Christians speak for themselves, because their documents are much older, much purer. We cannot force them to say what they don't want to say, as we've always been able to do before.

A good example of a teaching propounded in early Christian and Jewish documents, a teaching we've been forced to accept against our will, is cosmism. Cosmism was an idea always present in these early sources, and it made them rather offensive. It is the hallmark of early Christianity, of what Jerome calls primitive Christianity—the kind he didn't like. He said the church had to get rid of it. "I will admit this is the teaching of the early church," he confessed, but "it's rather embarrassing to us. We've outgrown that. We're much too intelligent for this sort of thing now." The doctrine accepted in early Christianity was the literal interpretation of things, which Carl Schmidt, the greatest documents student of the last century, has labeled cosmism.

The idea is that somehow or other the physical cosmos is involved in the plan of salvation. It has been there all the time, and because we are living in it, we are part of it. It was the prevailing doctrine of the University of Alexandria, and it prevailed with tremendous authority. At that time, everybody was "spiritual," everything allegorical. The influence of neo-Platonism was very strong. The idea was that anything spiritual or anything divine had nothing to do with the physical world whatever, because God is pure spirit, and matter is vile; any matter, anything that is physical, is vile, a mistake that shouldn't exist at all. It was a natural reflection of the moral feelings of the people of the time. People couldn't even conceive of a normal existence that wasn't grossly immoral. Because things got very bad, they thought of the flesh as necessarily vicious; therefore, God could have nothing to do with it. The idea that the physical cosmos could have anything whatsoever to do with our existence before we came here and hereafter was regarded with the utmost abhorrence. But whether they liked it or not, the early doctors faced certain basic doctrines that embarrassed them greatly and confused them, so that as Origen says, it made him so ashamed of himself that he almost died with humiliation when he thought of the idea that Jesus was born as a person, a human being, a little baby that cried and fussed and had to be changed, and all that sort of thing. He said it was a mystery that was beyond the apostles, beyond even the angels; no one could understand how such a thing was possible: the idea that here we are in a physical universe, a physical world, and physical bodies—a physical creation that God created.

When those church fathers talked about God to the pagans or anyone else, the great epithet was that he was the Creator. The creator of what? This physical world. What an awful thought! It actually sickened the doctors of Alexandria to have to face up to the fact that God created the physical world, that Jesus came, that God came and was incarnated in the physical body and then hereafter provides a physical resurrection, because there is no other kind of resurrection (Jerome did say there is a spiritual resurrection—the only one that counts). But they couldn't get around the fact that there is physical concomitance in things. It greatly embarrassed them. Now these early documents being discovered are full of the doctrine. They tell us a lot about it.

The doctrine of creation from nothing is one example. God supposedly made the world out of nothing—*ex nihilo*. This was a necessary premise, to avoid the taint of cosmism, the idea that God worked with matter, processed it, adapted it, and used it as a workman, as an artisan, as a super scientist, or something like that. The popular idea was that God merely has a thought, merely utters a word, and it is.

That's that. Something completely and fully organized. H. A. Brongers, a great Jesuit writing now, says that God just thinks and all is there at once, organized, complete in all its forms. The idea of God working matter, using something already there, is utterly horrifying, because that deprives him of all his divinity. It involves him with the physical world.

Moslems got on the same track too. But they have not got very far because, as Fred Hoyle says, "I challenge you to make three meaningful statements about anything without some reference to the Physical Universe." When you start out with these basic principles of Christianity—the creation, the incarnation, the resurrection—which are all physical—how are you going to get around them? There's really nothing wrong, but Justin Martyr, the earliest Christian apologist, writing three hundred years before Origen, emphatically says, in the *Apology,* the early Christians did *not* believe in creation out of nothing, but believed that when God created the world, He organized matter. This is the theme these new documents have a great deal to say about. Scholars have recently been writing articles on this theme. Richter and H. F. Weiss, for example, in a number of recent studies, point out that it is not until we get to the doctrines of the church in the Fourth Century, wholly committed to the prevailing teachings of the school, that we hear of creation out of nothing. Before that century the early Christians didn't believe in that at all. They believed that God created the universe out of stuff, and that he organized it. How he did this is one of the most intriguing aspects of the documents we are talking about.

There are the Nag Hammadi manuscripts (*Nag Hammadi* is Arabic for the old monastery the Greeks called Khenoboskeion, about sixty miles north of Thebes where the Nile takes a big bend, about ten miles off the river in the eastern desert). In the same year and under very much the same circumstances in which the Dead Sea Scrolls were found, a peasant, while digging for fertilizer, found a special cache just like the Dead Sea Scrolls. It contained thirteen volumes, beautifully bound in leather. They weren't scrolls at all, but volumes, marvelously preserved, as if they had been written yesterday. They were regular books with pages, whose wrappings and bindings we still have. These leather bindings contained forty-nine different works, five of them repeated works. One of these thirteen volumes is in the Jung Museum in Zürich. (The museum may have to give it back to the Egyptian government. There's a big fuss going on about it now.) The other twelve are in the Old Cairo Coptic Museum in Cairo. These contain forty-nine works, written and preserved and put away in an early church, many of them going back to the First Century A.D., others to the Fourth Century A.D. Most of them are Coptic translations of Greek documents that are lost today. They have started to come out now. As with the Dead Sea Scrolls, there was a lot of political and other pressure to keep them from coming out.

This library is a marvelous thing. Van Unnik says that the books were written in a little local country church in Egypt before the apostasy ever took place—before there was any Gnosticism. They represent in certain ways the pure teachings of the Early Church. (We won't discuss this problem here.) These documents are very numerous and can be correlated with others—for example, the Mandaean texts.

Especially through the efforts of a woman called Ethel Drower (who's in her eighties now), who spent many years among the Mandaeans of southern Mesopotamia, we know something about the very secretive Mandaean religion, a last holdover of the people who came from the Dead Sea. Their traditions and their ancient writings describe them as possibly leaving the Qumran people (the Dead Sea Scroll group) at the fall of Jerusalem. They first went up to Haran, then down the river. Some two thousand or so Mandaean people remain today. They have their own language and preserve the marvelous records they've kept for all this time. The Mandaeans went down to Qumran in the time of Joseph ben Rekha (they call themselves Rekha-bites). He arrived just before Lehi went out into the desert. People were doing this sort of thing in Book of Mormon days, going out into the desert to live the gospel in its purity, setting up their own churches and communities—"the church in the wilderness"—then practicing their baptisms. These doctrines were taught in those communities. The Mandaean writings relate very closely to the Nag Hammadi, and to the Dead Sea Scrolls people, too, because the Mandaeans came from there.

Up on the Tigris, quite far north, were found in 1906 the forty-two Odes of Solomon, viewed as the earliest, most valuable Christian collection of writings known. Lo and behold, one of the Odes turns up in the Dead Sea Scrolls and in the Nag Hammadi collection way down in Egypt, up the Nile at Thebes.

The point is that all these writings come together. We have a large collection from the East, a large collection from Qumran, from Palestine, and a huge collection from southern Mesopotamia—all discovered since World War II, all sitting together, showing early isolated Christian and Jewish communities, all teaching very much the same thing.

For all of these people, matter was important; they weren't ashamed of it at all. Peter says in the Clementine Recognitions, "There's absolutely no evil in matter as such." As Eusebius's Preparation for the Gospel explains, "Matter is not the cause of evil." And the great Origen, the earliest and by far the greatest Christian theologian, who lived in the Third Century, says, "I cannot explain it, but it is important nonetheless to understand that this world is not pure incorporeal ideas." (That was a tremendous concession, a shocking thing, for a man of Alexandria to make. He had been born and brought up at the University of Alexandria. His father was a professor there, and full of incorporeal notions. All his life Origen fought with these two doctrines because he was very honest and upright, yet he was completely indoctrinated in the teachings of Alexandria.)

One of the very recently discovered documents says, "God the Father of all our eternal bodies, brings about the resurrection of the flesh through members of the Godhead; do not be afraid of the world of the *physis*. The living spirit clothes itself with the body of elements, through which it is enabled to carry out its works in the worlds." The creation means matter and organization: men are to accept matter and not be ashamed of it. (There are dozens of such quotations from different writings, all on the same subject.) Creation means organization of the elements, as the so-called Codex Brucianus explains. Manuscript No. 96 says that first, there is matter. So what do you do with it? You organize it to create things. God is aware of it and makes good use of it. His activity and concern are everywhere evident in number and measure, because if you are going to get any kind of creation, any kind of life at all, you're going to have consistent patterns—number and measure. This is taken as evidence of an organizing mind, an organizing activity. Regular divisions of time and place mark an ordered universe. *Cosmos* means order. The Pistis Sophia, a very important early work, says, "There is a place afforded for everything, a *topos*." (Some Coptics use Greek words every once in a while because they don't have any that express exactly the idea of *topos*, a place for a certain thing to be performed.) There is a numbering of souls for each world, and a dispensation is not completed until that number has been fulfilled. Every soul stays in its appointed *topos* until it has fulfilled the mission and task appointed for it in that place. "God's plan sets times and seasons," says the Apocryphon of John. The Dead Sea Scrolls are obsessed with the idea of the times of iniquity, a time allotted for Satan to tempt mankind, and times of suffering of various kinds. And there is the cycle: you mustn't hasten the time and you mustn't delay the time—it is always a warning to us. There are times of suffering and times of punishment. All times are exactly prescribed from the beginning: they belong to a plan. Time and matter and space are all organized. It's well understood that all this setting of times is for our nature and for the purpose of our testing in this world. (It's only a temporary arrangement.) It is a characteristic of this particular world. For God there is no time; at least He doesn't use our time at all. The documents make this very, very clear.

The Manichaean Psalm Book, a very early and important writing, says on the Creation that if you ever set yourself to build, let the measuring come first, for if you build without a measuring device in your hand, your building will be crooked. Measurement is the very essence of creation.

The whole Creation, says Clement of Alexandria, who was the teacher of Origen, the first Christian philosopher, is to be understood as the imposing of an inner order on outer material—a progressive organizing of material from the center out. You build the structure inside; what you have outside is background material that you take into the structure as you build. And this is the way even Clement of Alexandria, in the *Stromata 2*, describes creation: It is the imposing of an inner order on outer material, progressively built out this way. It is all organization and synthesis.

The Apocalypse of Abraham, a very early Jewish work and one that has most interesting stories of Abraham, matches remarkably our book of Abraham in many points. God is hailed as the one who brings order out of confusion whenever worlds are demolished, ever preparing and renewing worlds for the righteous. Codex Brucianus says, "Creation is organization." But God is, by definition, the one who brings order into the confusion of the universe, ever preparing and renewing worlds for the righteous. But it is not enough to arrange matter. The matter is here, and when you create, you organize it. But that isn't enough. You merely produce an inert structure, and structure in itself isn't divine. Structure can't produce anything in itself. You can organize your molecules or your electrons and change them into any order you want, but, according to these people, there must be something else.

Incidentally, these authors sound very much like our science fiction writers. While looking up some science fiction books in the bookstore the other day, I jotted down some titles, and you'll notice they all have certain things in common. "Now wait a minute," you may object. "Aren't you getting rather close to science fiction here?" Yes, this does get remarkably close to science fiction. These include all sorts of theorizing on how the physical cosmos was organized, and some of these suggestions are extremely ingenious. They show remarkable insight, astonishing knowledge. Consider a few recent titles: *Bow Down to Nul*, the worship of Satan; *Ten Years to Doomsday*, the doomsday motif; *The End of Eternity*, *Second Foundation*, worlds founded again; *Billennium*, obviously from the notion of millennium; *The Burning World*, destruction by fire; *Passport to Eternity*, *Worlds for the Taking*, *Boodry's Inferno*, *Beyond the Galactic Rim*, *Possible Worlds*, *Three Stigmata of Palmer Eldritch*, *Trans Finite Man*, *Stranger in a Strange Land*, *Bowman's World*, *Earth Abides*, *Those Who Watch*, *Recalled to Life*. What do all these have in common? These ideas are basically scriptural and apocryphal, taken from the traditions of the Bible. This is surprising, isn't it? Why should these derivatives be more interesting than the originals? Why don't we read the apocrypha and the Bible instead? Look what the Christian world has done. It has emasculated the whole thing, denatured it. Till now these themes have been just spiritual or symbolic things. We find the literal view more interesting. Why? They're fiction, but they're science fiction. There's a possibility that such things could be true. When you bring the word "science" in, things become conceivable, and as long as there is a slight, remote possibility that such a world could exist, it rather interests you. But you read the Bible and say, "Oh, yes, but that's an abstraction. That's not even fourth dimensional." See what they have done to the scriptures?

How do you know these scriptures were originally meant to be taken literally? Any history, any scientific structure, can be interpreted allegorically, but no one goes to the trouble to invent really good history to have it dena- tured as allegory or symbolism. Most Bible stories weren't made up; scripture wasn't composed for the purpose of being allegorized, and it was certainly not invented as an allegory or as a symbol. That was read into it later. Until the theologians of the schools came along, it never occurred to anyone to do that. Remember what the doctors of the Fourth Century called the early Christians: "primitive," and that has a note of contempt in it. They call their stories old wives' tales, because the Christians really believed in these things. They called the Christians "literalists" and made great fun of them. (That is the word Jerome used.) The new interpreters became the "spiritualizers." They un- derstood all these things in a spiritual sense, uncontami- nated by the idea of a physical world. But if you go back to the early Christians, you find they accepted things phys- ically, and that puts everything on a different footing. It makes the real thing more interesting than science fiction. Science fiction is only rather a horrible aberration, but it's much more optimistic, and you might even say more con- vincing, than a dematerialized future.

Let's see what people have to say about the question now. They now admit that matter is there, and that it's or- ganized; but it's not enough to arrange matter with order and system. Such matter remains, for all its pretty patterns, inert, background stuff. Without life, matter is inert and helpless, these early writers say. It must be improved by the action of light. (The creators have a special force which the early writers call light, not light exactly as we under- stand it.) Structure is not enough. Whenever the active principle is withdrawn, matter at once falls back into its original, lifeless, inert condition. We think of the inert gases, like argon and xenon and helium and so forth. When they are activated, they glow. As soon as you take the activating away, they are nothing. It is the same with all matter. It must be touched by some activating force, according to the ancients.

The records call it the "spark," (*spinther*) a word that occurs numerous times. The spark is mentioned throughout, and it is what makes the difference. Whether you are in the Mandaean or the Manichean, whether in the Dead Sea Scrolls or in the Coptic Documents from Egypt, all take up the idea of the spark, because the spark can leap the gap. The spark is that which comes from one world to another. The spark is also that which animates at a distance. This vitalizing principle is everywhere referred to as the "spark," without which, says the so-called Second Coptic Work, "there is no awareness." It's all right to have an electric eye in the supermarket open the door for you. You say, "Thank you very much," but there is no consciousness there. It hasn't been polite or anything else. Without this spark, the mechanism doesn't work, but still there is no awareness. You have to be aware of something. Unless the electric eye is actually aware of you, there is no mind at all. It's a gadget.

There is a lot of this theme in the Cabala. The Jews adopted it. In the Cabalistic literature are the Hasidic forms that preserve the old teachings among the Jews, just as certain out-of-the-way Christian sects preserve, sort of in the dark, secretly, underground, many of these teachings well into the Middle Ages. Some of them emerged only lately. But the Cabalistic teachings about how God's intelligence unites with matter to form life, to form a unity, is depicted in the Cabala as "God is in everything." The Gospel of Truth, a very important writing (published at great expense), the first of the Coptic documents to come out in 1956, says much the same thing: "Unity engulfs matter within itself like a flame." It isn't enough to build your structure from the center out; you must engulf it with a life

principle, engulf it like a flame. Instead of an absolute separation of matter and spirit, an all-or-nothing arrangement
like that of the Gnostics and Neoplatonists whom the
church fathers followed, the earliest Christian apologist,
Aristides, explained that everything is a mixture of the
two. To produce a new thing, you must have the original
matter, and you must have the spirit to infuse it. Otherwise, you won't get results, because structure alone won't
do it.

Melito, one of the early Christian fathers, says the same
thing, that all the world is moved as a body is moved by the
spirit, so all the world must be moved by some animating
spirit itself, not just our bodies, but everything. When this
vitalizing principle touches matter, according to the Psalm
of Thomas, one of the new Syriac manuscripts, "consciousness" is expanded. "The worlds of darkness gathered and
beheld his brightness. They breathed his fragrance. They
orbited about him, and bowed and knew him and worshipped him." It is this implanting of the mind with the
thought of life that works within the elements to bring
about the Creation. The Berlin (Mandaean) Papyrus says,
"At the same time, the great thought came to the elements
in united wisdom, spirit joining with matter."

But this animating principle still isn't enough. Though
joined with spirit, matter is not spirit; it constantly undergoes processing. The matter itself is just part of the story. It
can be imbued with the spirit, but it will always change. It
is always undergoing processing and changing. Only progeny is eternal, only sons go on forever, says the Gospel of
Philip. That was the plan of heaven. Part of Satan's plan
was to have a static world that would not change. It would
not only be perfect, it would be static in its physical structure as well. But the plan agreed on was that worlds would
constantly come into existence and pass away, and that the
process would never cease. Matter would always be processed again and again, and this would go on, whereas this
same writing says that only sons are eternal. Sonship,

progeny, goes on forever. So that while the other elements become serviceable to the needs of the spirit, as the Gospel of Philip puts it, there is no permanence in matter; it always undergoes change as worlds come into existence and pass away. Only progeny is eternal. All the *physis*, all physical nature, all plasm, all organized things, all structure, is interdependent and will return to its old roots, but the root is not destroyed.

A passage in the Apocalypse of Abraham is very good on this point. Abraham sees what's going on inside of a star. A very exciting picture is displayed. (Like the process of conversion from one element to another—helium to hydrogen, then to the carbons; the cycle goes on.) Here is how he describes it. He's taken there by an angel. Abraham has been praying, wanting to know how the stars were made, so the angel actually takes him. He says his spirit left his body. He didn't go there physically, but he saw it all, and he was completely bowled over. He saw an indescribably mighty light, and within the light was a tremendous fire, and within that was a host of mighty forms that are constantly seething and exchanging with each other; they constantly change their shape as they move, altering themselves, one exchanging with another.

Abraham frankly doesn't know what's going on, so he says to the angel, "Why have you brought me here? I can't see a thing. I've become weak. I think I'm out of my mind." (I think we would too if we got too near to a star! A red giant, a white giant, even a white dwarf, would scare you enough!) The angel tells him to stick close and not be afraid. But when later they were both wrapped in something like flame and heard a voice like many rushing waters, even the angel took precaution. Abraham wanted to fall on his face, but he could not, because "there was no ground or earth anywhere to fall on." He couldn't even fall on his face. (He was awfully glad to get back home again.)

Abraham was taken to see the chemical changes going on inside the stars. The most useful property of matter is its plasticity. According to these writings, it can be adapted. It submits to handling. Eusebius points that out in his Preparation, "You can't make everybody in the church responsible for sinful man in his sinful nature." Physical matter is just a tool we use, something we just put to our purposes. Matter can't help itself—it's inert. Remember, man is to act and not to be acted upon. (2 Nephi 2:26.) Eusebius says, "Matter submits to handling. It can't by itself be the cause of evil." We simply put it to use—the uses we want. It's always being reformed, reorganized, renewed, in accordance with the law of plenitude. Nothing is wasted. There's no space where there isn't something. And if you're not using it for one thing, you can use it for another. And then there's the principle of multiple use, so that worlds can be used by spirits of various levels at the same time. All this is very nicely explained in these writings.

And if it is to be reused, so to speak, it must be melted down. I have left out some of the interesting quotations that talk about the "trough," the process in which matter melts down. It seems that the users have to get it orbiting in the trough. And in this trough it is selected out, certain elements being drawn out when and where they are needed. At certain temperatures they do this or that, and so forth. Here's what the Pistis Sophia says about it: It has to be decontaminated, melted down, then purified. There's a lot about decontamination. The action of the light on matter always has a purifying effect, whether for the first time or whether it's being reused. Indeed, there's no such thing as used or old matter, since by the action of the spark or of the light upon it, the matter always becomes renewed. "Let matter rejoice in the light, for the light will leave no matter unpurified." The "treasure," or the physical substance used in making anything, must be taken from some other treasure. You don't create it out of nothing. (This principle is also mentioned in Codex Brucianus 96, chapter 45.) The various elements must first be separated, cleansed, and reclassified. "When the flame engulfs substance to form a

new unity," the Gospel of Truth says, "then obscurity becomes light, death becomes life. And the old jars are broken to become new." In the Clementine Recognitions,
Peter explains the heavens to Clement: "The perfect form,"
says the philosopher, "is the egg. But the eggshell exists
only to be thrown away, to be crushed, to be used up. It is
just a step to using it in something else. So it is in the physical universe, in the world." As things go on and on, all the
worlds pass away to make way for new ones. The egg, this
perfect form, instead of being contemplated with utter
satisfaction forever after, exists merely to be crushed,
stomped upon, and used again—eaten by the chickens to
make good egg shells the next time. The figure of breaking
up the old jars to make new ones is common. Another like
figure exists: "God took dead bones," the Odes of Solomon
says, "and covered them with bodies." They were inert. He
gave them energy for life. Things were brought to corruption by God, but the cycle of corruption is not disaster.
Death isn't a terrible mistake, but rather a part of the eternal
plan. Everything physical must go through this change.
Nothing is to be permanent, nothing fixed. There are other
aspects of permanence in our life, but not this one. And so
corruption was brought about by God, something the doctors of the church would never consider. Things were
brought to corruption by God that everything might be dissolved and then renewed, thus founded on a rock!

So, we're founded on a firm principle of continuing
existence, but it must be corrupted first to be dissolved,
and then renewed. This corruption shall put on incorrup-
tion, as Paul says. Accordingly, every new creation leaves
behind the matter of its old aeon, its old age, its old period,
its old cycle.

From the beginning, the elements were purified by the
holy living bearers of life, and from the first contest they
were mixed with a background material and have remained so ever since. Also, when the poison or contamination of old matter has been removed, the stuff becomes

sterile. It's pure, but sterile. Again, you have to do something to make it live again. It has to be re-energized, and Peter actually uses the word *energia*. Matter has to have more energy put back into it again, now that it has been purified. It's ready to be used again. It's sterile. You have got the poison and the contamination out of it, but now it has to be energized all over again. When old worlds pass away, a general state of confusion is passed through, so you can organize a new world. Consider passages 13 and 17 in the Apocalypse of Abraham, where Abraham, addressing God, says, "O Thou, who abolishest the confusion, the mixing up of the universe, the confusion that follows that disintegration of the world of evil and of righteous alike, thou renewest the world of the righteous." This approach requires real space.

This idea of space and matter that we have been talking about so far has not been universally recognized by everybody who studies these things. One thing some students have recognized is the concern with real space. Actually, the scriptures are quite taken up with time and space. These ideas weren't recognized until we read the old books and the scriptures again. Sure enough, they are there, large as life. "How could we have missed them all these years?" we ask. We missed them because we have been warped and prejudiced by the accepted schools of thought that took over in the Fourth Century.

The Bible talks a lot about going and coming. Things must be going to somewhere and coming from somewhere. A recent work by a Lutheran scholar says that expressions such as "to visit the earth" and "he went and preached to the spirits in prison" cannot be taken in any but the most literal sense. Early church members really thought they had to go somewhere. All don't think so now. After all, as St. Augustine says, God is everywhere. He can't go anywhere. He is perfect. He can't do anything. To do is the act of an unsatisfied being for whom something has to be done that hasn't been done. Since God has done everything, He can't do anything, can't go anywhere. That's the way scholars used to think, in terms of absolutes. But that's not recognized today. A Catholic writer, writing very recently in *Verbum Domini*, says, "We are never allowed to forget that heaven is not only a state, but a place." Aquinas said that heaven is not a place; that's an absurd, crude, old idea. Heaven is a state, the state of bliss, the beatific vision.

The Pistis Sophia says that it is the nature of every creation to seek a more roomy space. It's an expanding universe that these people described; every creation has its tendency to seek a more roomy place. Every kingdom requires space: "We will go down, for there is space there." (Abraham 3:24.) By the law of plenitude or perfect economy, no space should be wasted and none should be crowded: "There is abundant room in thy paradise," says the 11th Ode of Solomon, "and nothing is useless therein." There is no waste, neither is there crowding. In the Ginza, a very important and very old work of the Mandaeans, Jesus is told, "Go down to that place where there are no *skenas*." (*Skena* is a *topos*, a dwelling place; the same word as the Greek *skenē*, "tent," the same as a *shekinah*, the dwelling of the Holy Spirit of the Jews. In Syriac it means an occupied place.) The Father says, in effect, "Go down to that place where there are no *skenēs* and no worlds. Create there for us another world after the fashion of the sons of salvation." The same writing explains that when the mass and number of the worlds are filled, a squeeze begins, and it's time for expansion. "All spaces come forth from the Father," says the Gospel of Truth, "but at first, they have neither form nor name." He organizes and supervises and sees that a place is properly and economically used; everything is controlled. But the idea of pure space, of absolute emptiness, is abhorrent to these people. There is no point to it. A total void without even chaotic matter is utterly abhorrent.

The ultimate form of damnation is to be with Satan, and

Paul says that Satan is the prince of the air. Demons have no place for their foot, no sure footing; they don't have a place, an establishment, no base of operations anywhere. To be deprived of the ordinances of the gospel, says the Pistis Sophia, is to be like one suspended in the air. The theme is common in the "Forty Day Literature." The apostles ask the Lord, during the forty days after the resurrection, to show them what it is like before the Creation and when the creation arose. He tells them, "Don't ask for that"; people can't remain in their right minds after seeing that sort of thing. (Abraham saw the star. He says you won't like it. It is terrifying.) "My Father worked out his kingdom in fear and trembling, and I must do the same." When these apostles asked to see the spaces, in quite a number of these writings the Lord warned, "No, it's better for you not to, because it is more frightening than anything else if you don't know what is going on." "Only the Lord," says the Gospel of Truth, "has penetrated the terrors of empty space."

All spaces are broken and confused, especially during periods of transition from old worlds to new, for they have no fixity or stability at that time. In 1 Enoch, the ultimate horror is being in a place without a firmament, without a foundation beneath, a place kept as a prison for those who transgress. This is why the idea of the rock, the foundation, or the cornerstone is so important; before you can begin any structure, before you can begin any plan, any life, any building, you must have some point on which you can fix yourself firmly. And what is that? I use the image of the rock to answer that.

There must be a rock, or whatever supports the rock. This, of course, was a main problem with the ancient cosmology, beginning with the philosophers of Melitus. They said the earth is on the back of a tortoise. And what supports the tortoise? He stands on the back of the great water that surrounds it. And what supports the water? Now you have to think fast, because something always supports it.

Our texts are very fond of the word *topos*. A topos is not just a space; it's a special space marked off and set apart for a particular purpose or activity. A *topos* is useful space, just as a *chairos* is a period of time set apart for the carrying out of some specific task. Thus we are often told that the Lord, having accomplished his mission on earth, returned to the *topos* from which he came. We find this in the Gospel of John, and also in the Gospel of Peter, and others.

God started out the Creation by making a *topos* for his children, that they might settle there, and there recognize and serve him as their father. In the Ginza, he tells Adam, "Adam, this is the place in which you are going to live. Your wife, Eve, will come and join you here [notice the pre-existence], and here your progeny will thrive." Then there is the concept of distance, which leads naturally to the idea of multiplicity of worlds. (This has been implicit in all that we have been saying, and on the subject all these writings have a good deal to say.) After the plan of creation was accepted, it was communicated to all the other worlds. All the other worlds contributed something to the making of this one, because they rejoiced in such a project. For the worlds exist, we are told in the Askew Manuscript, so that intelligent spirits might come and inhabit them. Not only are the worlds countless, according to Philip, but they have been going on forever. Adam's holy angels inhabit many worlds. "Thou light of our worlds, come and be king of our land and our city," they say as the Lord goes from one to another. "No words could describe thy power over all thy worlds," says the Ginza. "The Father taught me about the worlds of the Lord and the glory that abides therein. The atom of light treads upon the earth's trembling foundation that is laid in the midst of the worlds." Even Justin Martyr says that the Christian is promised boundless cosmoses. This is our promise that we shall inherit. Maimonides said, "This world is but a speck among the worlds and man is as nothing. Man is nothing in the midst of the worlds." It was the degenerate Minaean Jews who first taught that ours was the only world, says the Talmud. "To correct this we say in our prayers today, Mi-'olamim l-olamim, worlds without end, using the plural." Origen believed, says Jerome, that there are countless worlds. He did not believe, like the pagan Epicurus, that they existed all at once, but that they were constantly coming into existence and passing away. This was the old Christian teaching.

"O Father which art in the heavens"—"heavens" is always plural in any ancient Lord's Prayer you can find anywhere. It is to be understood in the most literal sense: the heavens are plural, and our Father is in the heavens. This has been recognized recently. Both a Roman Catholic and a Protestant have recently written articles on this point. The Protestant says that the idea that this is the only world is not an early Christian but a heathen Greek conception taken over by the Church from Aristotle. And the Catholic writer, in *The New Scholastic,* wrote recently that "the idea that the earth is the heavy center of everything and therefore the only world [this the sluggish earth, the center of everything] is from Aristotle. This is not from the Bible. It was not held by the early Church." Aristotle's concept was the science of the time, not the Bible of the time. The early Christians believed in this multiplicity of worlds. It's only later that the Christian world, following Aristotle, a good scientist, went the other way. Over against this, our older Christian sources also remind us that in the great scheme of things, everything is in the plural: worlds, universes, plans, gods, spaces, saviors, and so forth. A multiplicity of worlds are organized on a common pattern. For example, a newly found Apocryphon of James (also the Askew Manuscript, the Second Coptic work, and the Apocryphon of John) notes that in all the worlds there is a common pattern, and its base is a monad rule—there is one rule everywhere; but God always rules through a presidency of three and through a council of twelve, no matter what the world is. This is a law that exists throughout all the worlds. A number of these sources talk about that. These repetitions are infinite in number and scope.

Carl Schmidt believed that the Second Jeu was the most important of all early Christian writings. It is the best expression of early Christian teachings. And this tells us that a person who is sent to take charge of a new world, as Adam was sent to take charge of this world, is called a *Jeu*, a form of the word *Jehovah*. Then he says, "As *Jeus* become fathers [once you have become established, you become a father], then you will appoint *Jeus* for new worlds, who will in time become fathers, and so on, ad infinitum." So you have the Jeus promoted to fathers, who then send out other sons as Jeus, and so forth. Each aeon has created for its own host ten thousand times ten thousand. They like to talk about these things. In every individual world God made three hundred and sixty thousand agents, in every dwelling place three hundred and sixty thousand other dwelling places. The earth and the planets are but atoms in an infinity of like systems. That's from the Sefer Yetzirah, a very old Jewish work, widely recognized by the Jews.

Origen repeatedly quoted from writers of the early Church. "This is not my opinion; this is what the elders used to teach," he would say. "There will be another world after this one. And in the same way, there were other worlds before this one. We thus share a common nature with other worlds." Or as Methodius, the last man to organize this material and bring it together, in the eighteenth volume of the Patrologiae Graecae wrote, "Christ came down from his vast rule and kingdoms and other worlds to save one percent of those on this evil earth, and to enroll the human race in the heavenly register." For this work goes on in a vast scale, and it involves many other worlds. But what does this do to the oneness of God, and so forth? It does no harm at all, because all is going according to the same system, and before anyone can be entrusted to take charge of a world, he must be trusted.

We are here for the purpose of being saved, and we must also be safe. Exaltation is something more. All will be saved in the kingdom of God, but who is safe? Who can be trusted? With reference to man's responsibilities, we are here to be tested whether we can be trusted to take charge on our own, because if you can be trusted completely, you'd do the very same thing God would do. You'd represent him completely. So there is only one God, only one ruling mind, and only one pattern after all. The oneness of God is never jeopardized here. The Askew Manuscript says, "There are many mansions, many regions, degrees, worlds, spaces, and heavens, but all have but one law. If you keep that law, you, too, can become creators of worlds," an astonishing statement.

The Gospel of Truth says, "It is the perfect Father who produced the all, in whom the all is, in whom all are in need always." We are never free from needing him. He is still in charge. Others are put in charge in whom he can trust, but always it goes back to him. "Out of the one come the countless multitudes, but yet they remain in the One." "All the other worlds look to the same God as to a common sun." The crucifixion is effective in worlds other than this one. Another says, "All the cosmoses follow the pattern of a single world, which is called the type, the archetype. Ever since the beginning this has been so, keeping the entire physis in the state of joy and rejoicing." (Because it has been organized, it's the same.) "The worlds exchange wisdom with each other because they are equally dependent on the Most High." They have the same common source. "They are the heralds of His thought," says the famous 12th Ode of Solomon; "by His word they communicate with each other. They know Him who made them because they are in concord. They have a common ruler, a common lord, so they are in concord with each other, and they communicate with Him and through Him with each other, for the mouth of the Most High has spoken to them." Another

Ode: "The worlds were made by His word and by the thought of His heart, so they are all as one. There is no rivalry or competition among them, but they are glorious in their firmaments and agree among themselves, fitting together like the lashes of an eye. All rejoice in each other, each being more glorious and bright than the other." There is a hierarchy of brightness, the range going on forever, each more glorious than the next.

The Ginza says that when beings from different worlds meet, they exchange garments and treasures as a sign of mutual esteem and identification. "For the creation of endless worlds follows the single pattern laid down by the Creator." The planets then say, "Lord, come, Lord of the Gods, Lord of the entire cosmos." They rejoice and say, "Come, be our Head. Be our head of the whole world." This is the *parousia*—when the Lord visits us for a while, and we want him to stay with us. "The worlds will come before Him in order and in shining hosts," says one of the new homilies. "God is the Father of all the worlds," says 1 Clement, which virtually everybody recognizes as an authentic writing of the early Church. "He knows them; they keep their courses and covenants with Him; He calls them by name, and they answer him from eternity to eternity. As the Father of greatness is in the glorious world, so his Son rules among those cosmoses as first chief lord of all the powers." Thus, as one recent study observes, "The multiplicity of successive worlds tends towards unity." "The cosmos is not simply a oneness of self, of nothing and nothing else," writes the great fourth century Bishop Synesius, "but rather a multiplicity comprised in a oneness."

This is the terror of science fiction today: "If you could only escape from this little confining world of ours and go out into the vastness of space, wouldn't that be a wonderful adventure?" So you go out there and what do you find? The same thing you find here. It's like landing in one airport—it's just like the airport you got on in. And so it becomes rather depressing, and finally it becomes actually terrifying—always just more of the same. It's a horrible trap from which you can't escape.

The universe of the Middle Ages was not small—when thought of in terms of billions of miles, it was tremendous. But it was closed. It makes no difference how big it is as long as it is closed. You see, you can't escape. There's just more of the same. You've seen it all. You're not going anywhere. That is the message of science fiction. That is why writers like Bradbury and Heinlein are turning away from it. They've rather got soured on it now, because once they've gone through all the places they can think of, that's it.

This is the nice thing about the teaching we are talking about. You don't get stuck in that groove. Sir Isaac Newton says, "Only little minds are impressed by size and numbers." What's the point to endless repetitions of the same? (I don't want more of the same.) One of the nicest things about early Christian cosmology is that it is not the repetition of sameness. The types are there, but they are always expressed in individuals who never express the type in exactly the same way—just as no two snowflakes are alike, yet they all have to have six points, no more and no less.

The first thing to get clear, when we start talking about other worlds, is that we know nothing about them. It comes only by revelation. These things are not the extent or the projection of our own scientific world or literary experience, and not the production of our own imagination. Those who have seen other worlds in vision tell us that we simply cannot imagine what they are like.

Remember what Paul said after he talked about going to the third heaven: I can talk about one who was caught up. I've seen those things. And what about it? "Eye has not seen, nor ear heard, neither has entered into the heart of man." Nobody has seen anything like it. Nobody has heard anything like it. You can't imagine what it is like—it has not "entered into the heart of man." So you shouldn't try to make yourself a picture of what heaven is like. You'll be completely wrong. And that's good, because I don't want it to be more of the same, more of this. It would be an awful bore, wouldn't it?

The Pistis Sophia: "Other worlds cannot possibly be described in terms of this world. Not only is there less in common between other worlds and this world, they differ as widely among themselves as any of them does from us." "In the limited confines of the flesh," the new and valuable writing of James explains, "which condition all our thinking, we can't possibly grasp the nature of other existences or even begin to count the number of other worlds." We are necessarily prone to think in terms of our world. Of course we can't think in any other terms. We haven't the remotest idea of what it's like. We use the words we do because we don't have any others. As St. Augustine says, "This is the wrong picture I have given you, but at least it's a picture." *(Impar imago, sed imago.)*

"When we say Light," says the Sophia Christi, "we think of our kind of light." But that's wrong. When we say marriage, for example, in the other world, it'll be entirely different from what it is here, though of course we must designate earthly and heavenly marriage by the same name. Even though spirits may be eternal and thus equal in age, this writing explains, they differ in intelligence, in appearance, and in other things. And these differences are primary, as unbegotten as the spirits themselves. It is not something that's acquired. We are just different, primary and unbegotten, and no two alike.

The Lord tells the Apostles in the Epistle of the Apostles, "Where my Father is, it's entirely different from this world. There you will see lights that are nobler than your kind of light. In the millions of worlds that God has made for his son, every world is different from the others and wonderful in its own radiance." Quoting the Odes of Solomon: "Hence, one of the joys of existence is that the worlds constantly exchange with each other what they have, each possessing something different and peculiar to itself. There is nothing superfluous anywhere, which means that nothing is a mere duplication of something else."

You may wonder why we are not sharing the fun here on earth. That's because we have been quarantined. We've been isolated for a special testing situation. Remember, that's what the Lord told Enoch when he was talking about the world. He had created "worlds without number," and yet he told Enoch, "Among all the workmanship of my hands there has not been so great wickedness as among thy brethren." (Moses 7:36.) So when you are here, you are getting a real test. They talk a lot about that—this test being so much harder. We may mention that when we get to Adam.

This is one of the joys of cosmic contemplation. The Berlin Papyrus tells us how every world breaks up into various types. There are five worlds, five spirits, five bodies, five tastes—the senses. Although the inhabitants have the same senses there that we have here, they are not alike. They don't respond on the same scale. Again, you think of the spectrum—of all the things we are missing that we might be experiencing. There are all kinds of strange beasts on other worlds that we can't even imagine. In some worlds reproduction is carried out differently from here. The Zohar, perhaps the oldest Jewish writing known, says, "There are all sorts of creatures for all sorts of environments. Only man is the same everywhere and yet he's the most individual of all." That's wonderful, isn't it? All these creatures adapt themselves to different worlds, like the monsters of the past—dinosaurs, the stegosaurus, and various creatures living in other geologic ages. They had to adapt themselves, and in other worlds it could be the same thing—the most fantastic forms of life. Man is the only one that is the same everywhere, because he adapts himself in a different way. He's the most different of all. For as Brigham Young used to say, looking out over the Tabernacle, "I don't see two faces alike here." Isn't it marvelous. No two alike. "Vive la différence!"

"In the Hebrew Universe," writes Pederson, "the world consists of a number of lives that are intermixed but can never become merged because each has its special character. Individuals remain forever themselves." Among ten thousand times ten thousand worlds, says the Ginza, you will find no two alike. A prayer from the Mandaean Prayer Book reads, "Before this world there were already a thousand thousand mysteries and a myriad myriad planets, each with its own mysteries." The multiplicity of worlds, as taught by the Early Church, formed a perfect unity as do the strings of a lyre. Each plays a different note; together they make marvelous harmony. If two strings play the same note, there is not much point to that. There must be a great orchestration. This is a common idea among the ancients. Plotinus taught that each star existed for the sake of the whole, to which it contributed its individuality. Each has its particular part to play; by being uniquely itself it can make a contribution of maximum value.

There is the great difference, and among the differences there is a hierarchy. Some are greater than others. That is the concept of the three degrees of glory. The one thing they all have in common is that there are three main degrees. "You can visit the orders below you," says the Pistis Sophia, "but not the level or orders above you." The three degrees are described in a great number of manuscripts. Ignatius, writing to the Trallians, says the same thing. Ignatius was the last church father who knew the mysteries of the church; the Saints have asked him to tell them about some of these mysteries and the levels of other worlds. And this is what he says in reply: "I could write to you about the mysteries of the heavens, but I am afraid to do so. It would do you harm. I am able to understand the orders of the heavens, the degrees of the angels, the variations among them, and the differences of dominions, of thrones and powers, and of the elevation of the Holy Ghost and of the kingdom of the Lord, and the highest of all rules of God over everything else. There is an infinity of hierarchy in the world." But he died and took his knowledge with him. "You're not ready for it yet," he said, "and the Church is not going to have it."

An early hymn says, "Christ rules in second place. His rule exactly duplicates the Father's but over a more limited number of cosmoses." Methodius explains this, he being in my opinion the last church father to correlate what stuff remained of the concept. He says, "If other stars are greater than our world, then it is necessary that they contain life greater than ours, and greater peace, and greater justice, and greater virtue than ours." (Remember, the Lord tells Abraham that as there is one above another, there must be another higher than they. Then he adds, "I am more intelligent than they all." This is the principle set forth in the Pearl of Great Price.) "The spirits," says the Sophia Christi, a newly found manuscript, "are equal in age but different in power, intelligence and appearance, and have been so throughout all time." Origen was greatly intrigued by this diversity, and especially the inequality among God's creatures. How do you explain that inequality? If it is arbitrary then God is unjust. So he concludes that the levels on which we find ourselves in this world must somehow have been merited in a former life. He in fact goes further than this. In this world we not only have a hierarchy, but all things are moving forward, not moving backward. It was a dynamic concept of Origen's in which all things are moving forward: "Until Christ came and opened the way, it was impossible to go from one *taxis*, one level, to another. He is the great opener of the way." The reason we call Christ the Way is that he opened the way by which we can progress.

Being the Way, the Lord himself also advances. Thus, the Word of the Father advances in the All, being the fruit of his heart and the expression of his will. (See the Gospel of Truth.) Through the ordinances, we are told, one makes progress in knowledge, and these ordinances go on and on. There are mysteries so much greater than the ordinances of this world that they make loaves look like a grain of flour, just as the sun looks like a grain of flour from those distant worlds. When we go to our heavenly homes, some of us will be in a world quite remote where we could still see the sun, but it would look so tiny that it would be like a grain of flour. On this earth everyone descends, as it were, to the dregs and shares the common substance with all living things. From here we begin to work our way up step by step to a knowledge of all things, ever seeking for instruction and carrying out the required ordinances that will lead us to more. Thus we move from truth to truth, and the further advanced one is, the faster one moves forward. This is the principle: "To them that have shall be given." With exaltation comes an increase, an acceleration of exaltation, and the further advanced one is, the faster one moves forward. So the further you get ahead, the faster you get ahead. The example is Adam.

Quoting from the Sophia: "Adam, having been established with Christ and God (the Great Three) next established his son Seth in second order which was to follow him on up." "He who has fulfilled all the ordinances and done good works cannot be held back." Another passage says, "We are taught the principles of salvation so that we cannot be held back in this world." A Manichaean text: "Those who shut the doors against me will be held back in the abode of darkness. Those who open the door will advance to the place of light."

It was the ancient Jewish teaching, according to Professor Goodenough, that the patriarchs advanced to the spiritual stage where they assumed the garments of light and became saviors, saviors of their fellows. And R. H. Charles, commenting on the Book of Enoch, says, "For the righteous Jew, hereafter, life will be a constant progress from light to light as we become companions to the hosts of heaven." So the idea of eternal progress is an old Jewish concept and an early Christian concept, too. "To be true and faithful," says the very early Father Papias, "God gave dominion over the arrangement of the universe to the true and faithful. Their rule and their advancement go on forever and ever."

"Because of the Plan," says Codex Brucianus 96, "we are always to look upward"; from time to time there is a great coronation day, a cosmic commencement day in which all who are worthy take over their new position and receive the spaces assigned them with their crowns of advancement. Clement of Alexandria and Origen, those two earliest fathers, each having one foot in the old church and one in the new, characteristically accepted the doctrine of eternal progression at first, then rejected it when the schoolmen finally talked them out of it. In Origen's universe there are more exalted beings who leave the less exalted beings further and further behind. He compares their advancements to a series of examinations and makes much of the three degrees of glory—"three celestial levels, like the sun, the moon, and the stars." According to him, the visible world is only a small fraction of the invisible world, which in turn is only a small fraction of the potential world that is to become reality in the aeons ahead. All this from Origen, the greatest of Christian theologians before he joined the doctors, when he still spoke as an early Christian. "After death," he says, "I think the saints go to Paradise, a place of teaching, a school of the spirits in which everything they saw on earth will be made clear to them. Those who were pure in heart will progress more rapidly, reaching the kingdom of heaven by definite steps or degrees." For Origen, according to Father Danielou, evil is nothing else than refusal to accept progress. This recalls a statement from the Pistis Sophia that hell is what lies in the opposite direction from that of progress, a state of inert and helpless being. Hell is not lively; it is the opposite of action, energy, purpose, and motion. The devil has no real purpose; all he is trying to do is thwart someone else's purpose. He has no principle of action within himself. He is *apolyon*, the destroyer; *satan* or *diabolos*, the accuser.

It is undeniable that this doctrine of eternal progression points inescapably in the direction of becoming like God. There are many mansions, regions, degrees, worlds, spaces, and heavens, but all have but one law. If you keep this law, you will become creators of worlds. The worlds are so that intelligent spirits might come and inhabit them and in the process and in due time become gods, since they are literally the children of God. "The sign of Divinity," says the Ginza, "is that one's glory expands." It is always increasing. It's an expanding universe, isn't it? This reminds me of a statement in the Gospel of Philip: "A dog begets a dog, a horse begets a horse." And you call yourselves the children of God? What does that mean? How can you avoid the conclusion in that case? What does a god beget? What *does* a god beget? Like begets like. You call yourselves the children of God. These people liked to call themselves that—the Children of Light and the Children of God.

Conspicuously lacking in the divine hierarchy is any sense of rank or class. Obedience and subordination in nowise jeopardize individual freedom and leadership and command, and in no way impose dictatorship as long as the whole concern of those above is to reach down in love to those below, and those below strive to rise in love to those above. (Moses 1:38-39.) This sense of equality pervades everything here. Every spirit, says the Apocryphon of John, is a *"monarchia,"* a rule unto itself, and subject to no one, having been in the very beginning with God. There is thus that about it that can never be forced. (One of President Heber J. Grant's favorite expressions was "Never force the human mind.") Some people consider the Apocryphon of John one of the most important discoveries in the last ten years.

"In this world all creatures are of the same material," says the Pistis Sophia, and we should never forget it. God is testing us here to see if we can be trusted to rule over other creatures in love and not in arrogance. If we destroy the things placed under our dominion, just because we have power to destroy, we will never be trusted with real dominion, worlds without end.

Now to examples of the ordinances these writings talk about. God operates through agents. He sends people. They are the "sent ones." In fact, a Swede by the name of Widengren has recently written a book about the "Sent One." Instead of coming personally and giving his messages, God gives others a chance to share in his activities by sending them as messengers with various duties. That is the thing that always stops the Muslims. They think that our plan of salvation is much too complicated. "Why make it so complicated?" They ask, "Why can't you say that God does it, and that is that? He does everything. He'll forgive us in the end, and everything will be all right. We don't need anything but God. And you bring a son in, the Holy Ghost, and all this sort of thing." And you say to the Muslim, "What's the Creed? What's your *shahadah?*" "Well, I testify that I believe in God, in his angels, in his prophets, in his apostles, and in his books." "Hey wait a minute. What are all these angels doing? I thought you believed in a just God. Isn't that enough? What does he need angels for? Why can't he deliver his message directly? Why does he need prophets to come down and speak for him? Why does he need books for you to consult?" God uses agents; he uses agents; he uses "sent ones" all the way through. Don't complain to us about complications!

God sends his agents to other worlds to engage in this operation. We all have a share in this sort of thing. We meet with the "sent one" most frequently and most dramatically in the story of Adam. "After the physical Adam was created, a messenger was sent to the head of all generations (that is, Adam), and at his call, Adam awoke and said, 'How the precious, beautiful life has been planted in this place. But it's hard for me to be down here.'" The "sent one" then reminded Adam, "But your beautiful throne still awaits you, Adam. Why then do you, the image of God, sit here complaining? All of this is being done for your good. I have been sent down to teach you, Adam, and to free you from this world. Listen and return to the light."

The Ginza (488) tells how when Adam stood praying for light and knowledge, a helper came to him and gave him a garment and said to him, "Those men who gave you the garment will assist you throughout your life until you are ready to leave the earth." The commonest account of these visitors, also found in the Ginza, is that when Adam was created he was found in a deep sleep from which he was awakened by the helper who forthwith began to instruct him. And at his death also the "sent one" came to take Adam back to the great, first parental house and to the places in which he formerly dwelt.

First he was taken to a place of detention, the *shomai*, the place in which to be instructed. Here he learns the signs of the nail of glory and the keys of the *Kushta* on both arms. The *Kushta* is a hand grip of some type. A messenger from the House of Light was sent to fetch Adam farther when he was ready. The reason that so often the Adam of light comes down (the preexistent Adam, that is, the Adam of Light that comes down to help us) is that he was the first one who needed help; he as our Father sympathizes with us, and he wants to see that we get through. So he is our great helper. He is the sent one. Of course Jesus Christ is the Sent One of all. When Adam faced the Light and called for help, the Lord himself approached him in glory and took him by the palm of the right hand and calmed him and instructed him. Then he comforted Eve, and in this way he brought joy and aid to his descendants. The Lord came to bring hope to Adam, who was in the image of God. This is repeated also in the case of Abraham. In the vast majority of accounts, it's the three sent ones who instruct Adam. There is no conflict. There are simply two great teams of three. There is the Creation team: Adam and Jesus and the

Father; and there are the three that instruct Adam, who are later of the twelve, the three pillars of the Church, Peter, James, and John. We have references to them in some of the writings, and the passages are rather interesting.

In the Berlin Papyrus, "The first man, Adam, was really the third sent one at the Creation." (There were three sent ones, and he was the third one.) According to the Apocryphon of Adam, Adam was awakened from his deep sleep by three men from on high, who said to him, "Adam awake, arise and hear the teachings of the Savior." It was through a team of three, according to the Sophia Christi, that God created everything, employing them as his agents. As the Abbaton puts it, "The Father instructed the Son, who in turn instructed the great angel to go down and form a new world." But they didn't merely delegate the work, they worked together. "The three," says our source, "stretched forth their hands, took clay and made man." And many expeditions were sent to the earth before things were ready to receive him. Codex Brucianus 96 says, "Whenever that life-giving spark is sent, it is always followed up by three Sent Ones to give instruction." So in any world, those who receive the spark will also find three helpers ready to instruct them. The three are always there to supervise, and the evil spirits resent it. Here is a very interesting passage from the Ginza where the evil spirits say, "They claim this world for their own." They have been cast down here, this is theirs, and they don't like people intruding. "These three men," they say, "are in the world. They are not really men. They are light and glory, and they have come down to this little *enush* [Adam—he's little *enush* now because he has taken on flesh, and he's very susceptible to ills of the world], who is helpless and alone in the world. They are intruding in our world. The children of men have taken over the earth. They are really strangers who speak the language of the three men, and they have accepted the teachings of the three men and rejected us in our own world and refused to acknowledge our kingdom and our glory." And thus the evil ones plotted to overthrow Adam, who was hoping for the Savior, the Teacher of Life, to come down later and teach him—give him aid and support.

"At the creation," says the Ginza, "God gave an order that the angel should come and keep Adam company." And at the beginning, it was the Lord himself and two companions who instructed Adam and Eve in everything. "When Adam was placed on the earth, three *Uthras* were sent to oversee him, with myself at their head. I taught Adam and Eve the hymns and the order of prayer and the *Masagases* (that is, the Mounting Up or Returning to Heaven) and the pattern of the universe." "In sending three," God said to the Pure Sent One, "go call Adam and Eve and all of their descendants and teach them concerning everything, about the kingdom of Light and the worlds of Light. Be friendly with Adam and keep him company, you and the two angels that will be with you, and warn them against Satan." That's the Berlin Papyrus. Another one says, "Also teach them chastity."

We read of another team of three when Adam called upon God; the Great Spirit sent to him from the land of greatness the three who belonged to the twelve who were hidden in the veil of light (and those were later Peter, James, and John). Elohim, Jehovah, and Michael and all the angels come down. "I will come, and my Father and Michael," Jehovah says; "we are the great three who have visited the earth." They are also matched by the three violent ones and the Watchers.

All this implies, of course, preexistence. Adam coming down to earth is a theme you find frequently now. Throughout early Christian literature, in fact, going to heaven is constantly being described as a return to an old home, and that's the way the present Pope describes it: man is an outcast in this world, yearning for his home. If he was created here, and this was the only world he ever knew, that wouldn't be his position at all. He would not be an outcast or a stranger. He'd be in his own world. The implication of preexistence is very strong; these writings talk about it frequently. In the Apocryphon of James, for example, the Lord tells the apostles, "They will ask you where are you going." The answer, "To the place from which I came. I return to that place." And the elect are those individuals, according to the Gospel of Thomas, who shall find the kingdom because they came from it in the first place. The Gospel of Truth dwells at length on the theme of the return: "Whoever has this knowledge is a being from on high. When he is called, he hears and answers and turns toward him who calls him and re-ascends to him. He knows what he is called; he knows whence he has come and where he is going. He has turned many from error and preceded them to the places which belong to them but from which they have strayed. Joy to the man who has rediscovered himself and has awakened and helped others to wake up."

Just so, in the great old Manichaean Song Book, Adam is received by a happy family on his return. On the other side, they have awaited him in high expectation, or the return of the first man with news from him. They have eagerly awaited news of Adam's victory, of the success of his mission; and they want to hear it from his own lips when he returns. On his part, Adam, being away from home, asks a Newsbearer of the Skies, as he is called, "How is my Father, the Father of Light? How is my Mother, the mother of the living whom I left, and her brethren also? Rejoice with me, ye holy ones, for I have returned to my original glory again." And again, in leaving the earth, he says, "My hour has come. They summon me. I will go from your midst and return to my true home." Accordingly, "The Sent One comes to take the soul of Adam back to the great first house of his Father to the place where he formerly lived." And so his children were admonished, "Arise, old soul, return to your original home, to the place from which you were planted. Put on your garment of glory. Sit down upon your throne. Dwell in the dwellings among the *Uthras*, thy brethren." And again, "Now arise and return to the place of thy true family." "I came from the house of my Father," says the Psalm of Thomas, "in a far land, and I shall mount up until I return to that land of the pure." There is a moving scene at the end of the Pearl, the most moving of all the early Christian Syriac writings, where the hero finally returns to his home, his mission accomplished. He's met at the gate of greeting and honor by his entire family. He bows and worships his father and the Christ of the Father "who has sent me the garments and given me the orders while I was on the earth." All the princes of the house were gathered at the gate. They embraced him with tears of joy as the organ plays and they all walk back to the house together.

And Gregor of Nyssa, one of the three great Cappadocians, writing about this, says that in his time, the Fourth Century, the church was very confused about these teachings. They were being rapidly lost. He says, "Christians are all confused about the preexistence. Some say we lived in families there, and in tribes just as we do here, and that we lost our wings when we came down here and will get them back again upon earth." So they mix up tenable and untenable things; all sorts of strange ideas get in the picture. Regardless of what the true picture is, we know that the early Christians did believe very strongly in the preexistence. The mysterious word *propators*, which they used a lot, is now recognized as not meaning the Father who was before our Heavenly Father but our Heavenly Father as our forefather, our *propator*—"the father of our preexistent spirit," says a quotation from a newly found work. "When they ask you who you are," says the Apocryphon of James, "say 'I am a son and I come from the Father.' And when they ask you what sort of son and from what father, answer, 'From the preexistent Father and I am a son of the Preexistence.' " "The spirit existed before the flesh," says a psalm. Commenting on the teaching of this doctrine, the Clementine Recognitions, the editors of the

Patrologiae Graecae note that various fathers of the church represented every interpretation of the doctrine, from absolute acceptance to absolute denial. Most of the fathers temporized somewhere in between. Again, this is a good indication that we are dealing with an authentic teaching of the early church, since the early fathers are all for it. The later ones don't know; they are not so sure.

"The earth had already passed away," says one of these new writings, "and the Son had already had glory before this earth was ever created," reminding us that the fact that we do not know them does not mean that other times and worlds have not existed and do not now exist. From the Apocalypse of Abraham: "Before the worlds were I was a strong god who once created the light of the world." And he tells Abraham how "I explained my will to those who stood before me in this form that I am showing you in the spirit world before they came into existence." Abraham is shown the council of heaven in the spirit world in the preexistence. It is plain enough what is meant by "coming into existence."

Man's premortal existence was an illustrious one. There are descriptions of the glory we enjoyed before we came here. In these writings there is also a good deal about ordinances. We can't talk too much about them, or be too specific about them. These ordinances are vital. They are not mere forms or symbols, we are told. They are analogues.

Of extreme importance is Adam as Michael. And Adam is aroused by the three sent ones. Standing with the apostles in the prayer circle, the Lord tells them, "I will teach you all the ordinances necessary that you may be purged by degrees and progress in the next life. These things make it possible for you to achieve other exaltation, but they must be performed in this life. Unless one performs them here, one cannot become a Son of Light," since the Sons of Light are by very definition those who are perfect in the ordinances. Throughout these writings, no matter where they come from, whatever part of the Old World they come from, the code word is "Sons of Light." Nobody knew what it meant until now. It means "those who have received all the ordinances." Temple ordinances are what they are. And this is the way it is explained in Second Jeu also: The sons of light are by very definition those who are perfect in the ordinances. It is interesting that this same definition applies to the once mysterious title of Nazoraean, which means the same thing.

"Until Christ came," says the Pistis Sophia, "no soul had gone through the ordinances in their completeness. It was He who opened the gate and the way of life. Those who receive these ordinances are the dispensations of the Sons of Light. And they receive whatever they desire. They are those who are upon the right hand, for it is by their faithfulness in these very things that they show that they are worthy to return and inherit the kingdom. Without the ordinances, therefore, there is no foothold or foundation or anything in this life." In First Jeu 86: "If you want to go to the Father, you must pass through the Veil."

Recently I collected all the references I could find—I have twice as many now—of the forty-day mission of Christ. Whenever you find a very early Christian text, it almost always has a title referring to "the secret teachings of the Lord to the Apostles during the forty days." The fifty texts available to me then had four things in common.

The first was secrets, what the Lord taught the apostles after the forty days. When he came after the resurrection, he visited them and taught them. This was the really important thing, we're told. They didn't understand anything until then, yet in the Bible we are told hardly a word of what he taught them. Why not? It was secret.

The second point is that they all asked the Lord, "What's going to happen to us? What's going to happen to the Church?" And he tells them that it is going to be on earth for two generations; these things are not going to be

handed down; they are to be buried; they are to be kept secret. They are not to be passed on to the world. That's why
we didn't get them. We are just finding them now.

Third, he taught the strange doctrines the Christian
world did not like at all, the things we have been talking
about: other worlds, things like that. That was out of bounds
to the Christian doctors, because it wasn't Aristotle.

The fourth was the main thing he came to do. He took
them through the temple, he taught them temple ordinances. Only the apostles and the general authorities, the
seventies, were instructed in these—things to be handed
down, not divulged to the public. Though they were very
carefully kept from the public, we have these ordinances
now as they are described here, and this I have talked
about in the temple on occasion. I just mention here these
generalities, the importance of these documents, what
they meant to those people. The person who receives these
becomes a son. He both gives and receives (that is what a
son does—becomes a father) the signs and the tokens of
the God of Truth while demonstrating the same to the
Church, all in the hopes that these ordinances may some
day become realities.

Remember, they are only forms, only types, yet they
must be performed here. It is the same as going to school.
If you take a good course in math, you say you are just
working with symbols, dealing with things in the calculus
that are very abstract, or you are dealing with unreal or irrational numbers and things like that, even though they
aren't the real thing. Some day you will know what's behind
it all, in the hope that these things may some day become
reality.

"They may be mere symbols," says the Pistis Sophia,
"but they are an indispensable step to the attainment of real
power. Without the mysteries, one loses one's power."
Without the ordinances, one has no way of controlling
matter. For such control begins with control of oneself. The
ordinances provide the means and the discipline by which

light operates on material things. They are meant for instruction, they are meant for practice, and they are meant
as a test of obedience. Your level in the next world will depend on the ordinances you have received in this world,
and whoever receives the highest ordinances here will understand the whys and wherefores of the great plan. You
cannot hope to understand it all here. It is through the ordinances that one makes progress in knowledge. For those
who receive all the available ordinances and teachings here
shall pass by all intermediate places and not have to give
answers, signs, and stand certain tests hereafter. "John the
Baptist," another writing says, "who performed the ordinances with which he was entrusted, foretold in a special
language that Christ would bring the ordinances of a
higher priesthood as he had brought the ordinances of the
lower." And indeed it was the Lord who, during the forty
days, revealed these ordinances to the apostles.

There is much more to that effect. In most of our sources,
after explaining them to the apostles, the Lord gives a complete summary of all the rites and their meanings as they
stand in the prayer circle. (For a full discussion of this material, see "The Early Christian Prayer Circle," *BYU Studies*
19 (Fall 1978): 41-78.) This is mentioned in many writings,
and it much perplexed the early fathers of the church. The
topic finally was brought up in the Council of Ephesus, at
the Second Council of Nicea, which finally got rid of it, because the fathers couldn't understand what it was all
about. But the Syriac Church kept the rite down until the
Seventh Century. We have one writing, a very valuable
one, edited by Rahmani some years ago, long considered
the most valuable of all writings from the early Syriac
Church, called the Testament of Jesus Christ. We mention it
here because the author talks about the prayer circle and
how the saints in the Syriac Church used to perform it. In
the Pistis Sophia, at the end of the teachings and performing
of the ordinances, the Lord orders the apostles and their
wives to form a circle (which is one of the reasons these

texts were rejected with horror because they specifically
mention their wives being present, and they had to be in
this particular circle). He stands at an altar on one side,
while they recapitulate all the ordinances. The Savior
opens with a prayer, which is given in code. The words in
this code aren't always the same. In this one he says, "I ai
oh ah oh i oh i ah"—a special code in Coptic. There are lots
of codes in Coptic, and they are not as confusing as you
might think. They are to make sure that all is kept secret
from the world. This particular code is explained as meaning, "Hear me, Father." In First Jeu, the Lord calls on the
Father with different words, also cryptic: "Ie, ie, ie." We
are told that in every world, in every level (every *taxis*),
there are twelve who officiate under the direction of three,
and they always form a circle, without a lower and a higher,
because there is no head of the table in a circle. There is no
sense of rank whatever. They are instructed in all things.

It was to such a circle, First Jeu tells us, that God said in
the beginning, "These I will make my rulers," at the creation
of the world. Abraham was standing in that circle: "These
I will make my rulers. Abraham, thou art one of them."
(Abraham 2:23.) But it says specifically here they were
standing in a circle of twelve, and the Lord addressed them
that way, saying they were the ones who would be his rulers
on earth. The apostles, in other words, were appointed in
the preexistence.

Before forming the circle, the twelve sing a hymn. When
the circle is formed, the ordinances are pronounced, the
Lord recites, and then they recite after him. In most of the
cases they say "amen" after every sentence; in some they
simply repeat his words. In Second Jeu, the apostles and
their wives all form a circle standing around the Lord, who
says that he will lead them through all the ordinances of
eternal progression. Clothed in their holy garments they
form a circle, foot to foot, arm resting on arm. Jesus, as
Adam, takes the lead, and all the others say "amen" to each
phrase of the prayer. In the recently found Kasr al-Wizz

Manuscript (this one interests me particularly, because I got the first photographs of it): " 'And you shall recite after me,' and so we made a circle and surrounded Him and he said, 'I am in your midst in the manner of a little child,' and then He says, 'After everything I say you shall say Amen after me.' Gather to me, O Holy members of my body, when I recite the hymn do ye say 'Amen'?" There it breaks off, unfortunately.

This tradition is recalled a number of times in the earliest Christian literature. The Acts of John says, "Now, before he was taken by the lawless Jews [and at the same time he gave them the sacrament in the upper chambers he had them do this], He gathered us all together and said, 'Before I am delivered up to them, let us sing a hymn unto the Father,' so He commanded us to make as it were a ring, holding each others' hands, himself standing in the middle. And He said, 'Respond Amen to me,' and then He began to sing a hymn, 'Glory to Thee, Father,' and we, standing about in a ring said 'Amen.' " The phrases to which the apostles then pronounced "Amen" were: "We praise Thee, O Father." "We give thanks to Thee." "I would be saved and I would save." Then, "Amen." "I would be loosed and I would loose." "Amen." "I would be a Savior." "I would be pierced and I would pierce." Then he gave them the sign. "I would be born and I would bear," and so forth.

One is reminded of a statement in the Gospel of Philip: "Before one can give, one must receive." Another text adds, "I would wash myself and I would wash others." "I have no temple, and I have temples." Then the Lord commands, "Now see thyself in me who speaks, and when thou hast seen what I do, keep silence about my mysteries. You must see me as I suffer and what I suffer. Who am I? Thou shalt know when I go away." "Know thou suffering, and thou shalt have no power to suffer," He tells them. "That which thou knowest, I myself will teach thee." The prayer ring is mentioned not only in the Acts of Peter, but also in Irenaeus, in St. Augustine, in Photius, in First and Second Jeu, in the Testament of our Lord and Savior, in the Second Coptic Gnostic work, in the Pistis Sophia, and at various councils of the church.

St. Augustine, in reporting the episode of the prayer circle, says the whole thing was always kept most secret by the early Christians. Epiphanius says the Second Council of Nicea reported on it and included it among the lists of blessings handed down in the early Church. But they finally gave it up in the Eighth Century because they couldn't understand what it was all about, and it was never used again.

Following this pattern, in the early Syriac Church, the bishop takes his place at the altar. He first addresses the people in the circle and says, "If anyone has any ill feelings against his neighbor, let him be reconciled. If any feels himself unworthy, let him withdraw, for God is witness of these ordinances, and the Son, and the Angels." God, and the visiting or witnessing angels, are witnessing these things, so withdraw.

In the Bartholomew, there is some very interesting and personal stuff, some having to do with Mary. It is not the miraculous Mary literature in which the chariots of fire and that sort of thing happen. This is very homey, very natural. The apostles are having a prayer circle one day, and Mary asks if she might speak a few words. When she goes over to the altar, some of the apostles don't like it. They say she doesn't have authority, because she's a woman. Should they allow her to speak? But she says, "I have something I want to tell you, something that happened in the temple, because this is the proper occasion for it." Having finished the prayer, Bartholomew says, "She began by calling upon God with upraised hands, speaking three times in an unknown language" (the usual code introducing the prayer). Then, "having finished the prayer, she asked them all to sit on the ground." She asks Peter to support on her right hand and Andrew to support on her left hand. Then she tells that just before the birth of Christ, the veil was rent in the temple. On that occasion she saw an angel in the temple at the veil. He took her by the right hand, after she had been washed and anointed, wiped off, and clothed with the garment. She was hailed by him as a blessed vessel. "And he took me by the right hand and there was bread on the altar in the Temple and he took some and ate it and gave some to me. And we drank wine together. And I saw that the bread and wine had not diminished." (The same thing happened in 3 Nephi 20 at the administering of the sacrament.) All this happened in the temple. At this point, the Lord himself appeared and forbade Mary to tell any more, since all the creation, he said, had been completed that day.

The Apocalypse of Abraham says the same thing. "Abraham went with the Lord and fasted for forty days and God took him to Mt. Horeb and there was an altar but no offering." But God provided it miraculously, as he does elsewhere. He had a sacramental meal with his followers, and then the followers were ordered to stand in a ring and be instructed by Abraham in the proper manner of sacrifice under the old covenant. So under very much the same circumstances, he has them stand in a ring, and he instructs them.

A much vaster thing than we had ever imagined before is the doctrine of identity. This is the most interesting thing, the whole subject of identity. The expression occurs a great deal. You comprehend what you are like, don't you? In other words, you identify. We are told time and again that when Jesus came down to earth he took flesh so that we could comprehend him. He became like us. "Among the angels he was an angel. Among men he was a man." He descends to the level of the people whom he must teach, because he must do it in order to teach them. Because of this principle you comprehend what you are like, and comprehension means a lot. You comprehend others only to the degree that you are like them. One way to put it is, "Here, while we are on this earth, we are in ourselves and the world lies around us outside." We don't understand it all; it's a great mystery, not only psychologically, but scientifically and in every other way. We don't know how it is that we comprehend what's outside, how it's brought to us, how it's transmitted, or how it gets inside our heads. It's in there, you see. Whatever it is, we are comprehending because we are seeing both what is in here and out there. By comprehending something, you embrace it, literally; it is part of you; you identify with it completely. This means that life will look very different hereafter, when we can identify with, for example, animals. It wouldn't be unfair to lower creatures to compare them with ourselves—they would lose nothing by it. Can they not have joy in the sphere in which they were created without having our particular type of glory? They aren't missing anything at all, because we're sharing a common existence. The man comprehends a great deal more in the love of his dog, and the other way around. If there is a good feeling between the man and his dog, neither feels cheated; neither feels that he is being left out of anything, because they are actually sharing in each other's worlds. You can say that a man has a very intelligent dog of which he is very fond and that the dog is very fond of the man. They actually share a very real experience, so that neither has to envy the other at all.

You can heighten this greatly with our Heavenly Father and ourselves. We are not missing anything. We don't feel cheated by being so far below Him. We haven't missed a thing. It's just lovely to be near him, because he's trying to pull us up to him. He wants us to be like Him, to identify with him. We can't desire anything greater than that, so there is none of this dominance or submission business. God is not putting himself in charge. We are drawn toward him, and he wants us to be drawn.

SOURCES MENTIONED
Compiled by the Editors
(listed topically and alphabetically)

Modern Thinkers (including representative works)

H. A. Brongers
  Bibliotheca Orientalis 1948:38
  De Scheppingstradities bij de Profeten (Amsterdam: H.J. Paris,
    1945)

R. H. Charles
  Apocrypha and Pseudepigrapha of the Old Testament (Oxford: 1913)
  The Book of Enoch (Oxford: 1912)

Jean Danielou
  Biblica 28 (1947)
  Origen (N.Y.: Sheed and Ward, 1955)
  The Dead Sea Scrolls and Primitive Christianity (Baltimore: Helicon
    Press, 1958)

E. S. Drower
  The Canonical Prayerbook of the Mandaeans (Leiden: Brill, 1959)
  The Mandaeans of Iraq and Iran (Oxford: 1937)
  A Pair of Nasoraean Commentaries (Leiden: Brill, 1963)

Erwin Goodenough
  Jewish Symbols in the Greco-Roman Period, 13 vols. (N.Y.:
    Pantheon Books, 1953)

Fred Hoyle
  "The Universe: Past and Present Reflections," *Engineering and
    Science* (November 1981)

Isaac Newton
  The Mathematical Principles of Natural Philosophy, translated by
    Andrew Motte, 2 vols. (London: Dawson, 1968)

Johannes Pederson
  Israel: Its Life and Culture (London: Oxford University Press,
    1947)

Karl Popper
   "Science: Problems, Aims, Responsibilities," *Federation of*
      American Societies for Experimental Biology 22 (1963)

G. Santillana
   Hamlet's Mill (Boston: Gambit, 1969)

Carl Schmidt
   Epistola Apostolorum (Leipzig: Hinrichs, 1919)
   Gespräche Jesu mit seinen Jüngern nach der Auferstehung (Leipzig:
      Hinrichs, 1919)
   "Gnostische Schriften in Koptischer Sprache aus dem Codex
      Brucianus," *Texte und Untersuchungen* 8 (1892)
   Koptisch-Gnostische Schriften (Berlin: Akademie-Verlag, 1954)
   Manichäische Handschriften der Staatlichen Museen Berlin
      (Stuttgart: W. Kohlhammer, 1940)
   Pistis Sophia (Leiden: Brill, 1978)

Levi Strauss
   La Pensée Sauvage (Paris: Plon, 1962)

W. Richter
   "Urgeschichte und Hoftheologie," *Biblische Zeitschrift* NF 10
      (1966)

W. C. Van Unnik
   Evangelien aus dem Nilsand (Frankfurt am Main: H. Sheffler, 1960)
   "Newly Discovered Gnostic Writings; a Preliminary Survey of
      the Nag Hammadi Find," *Studies in Biblical Theology* 30 (1960)

George Widengren
   The Ascension of the Apostle and The Heavenly Book (Uppsala:
      Lundequistska Bokhandeln, 1950)
   The Gnostic Attitude (Santa Barbara: Inst. of Religious Studies, U.
      of Cal., 1973)
   "Der Iranische Hintergrund der Gnosis," *Zeitschrift für Religion
      und Geistesgeschichte* 4 (1952)
   Journal of Semitic Studies 2 (1957)

Ancient and Classical Texts

1 Enoch
1 Jeu

2 Jeu
Acts of John
Acts of Petrian Simon
Apocalypse of Adam
Apocalypse of Abraham
Apocryphon of James
Apocryphon of John
Askew Manuscripts
Berlin Manichaean Coptic Manuscript
Bodmer Papyri
Cathara Wiss Manuscript
Chester Beatty Papyri
Codex Brucianus
Epistle of the Apostles
Ginza
Gospel of Bartholomew
Gospel of Peter
Gospel of Philip
Gospel of Thomas
Gospel of Truth
Mandaean Prayerbook
Manichaean Psalm-Book
Odes of Pindar
Odes of Solomon
Oxyrhynchus Papyri
The Pearl
Pistis Sophia
Psalms of Thomas
The Second Coptic Gnostic Work
Sefer Yetzirah
Serekh Scroll
Sophia Christi
Testament of Jesu Christi
Testament of Our Lord and Savior
Zohar

Church Fathers

See generally *The Ante-Nicene Christian Library*, 23 vols., A.
    Robertson and J. Donaldson, eds. (Grand Rapids, Mich.:
    Eerdman's, 1951).

Aristides, Aelius

Aquinas, Thomas
Augustine, Bishop of Hippo
Clement, of Rome, *Clementine Recognitions, 1 Clement*
Epiphanius, Bishop of Salamis
Eusebius Pamphili, Bishop of Caesarea
Gregor, of Nyssa
Ignatius, Bishop of Antioch
Irenaeus
Jerome
Justin Martyr
Melito, Bishop of Sardis
Methodius
Origen
Papias, Bishop of Hieropolis
Photius, Patriarch of Constantinople
Synesius Sardicus
Timothy, Archbishop of Alexandria

7

Treasures in the Heavens

As Christianity has been deeschatologized and de-
mythologized in our own day, so in the Fourth Century it
was thoroughly dematerialized, and ever since then anything smacking of "cosmism," that is, tending to associate
religion with the physical universe in any way, has been instantly condemned by Christian and Jewish clergy alike as
paganism and blasphemy. Joseph Smith was taken to task
for the crude literalism of his religion—not only talking
with angels like regular people, but giving God the aspect
attributed to him by the primitive prophets of Israel, and,
strangest of all, unhesitatingly bringing other worlds and
universes into the picture. Well, some of the early Christian and Jewish writers did the same thing; this weakness
in them has been explained away as a Gnostic aberration,
and yet today there is a marked tendency in all the churches
to support the usual bloodless abstractions and stereotyped
moral sermons with a touch of apocalyptic realism, which
indeed now supplies the main appeal of some of the most
sensationally successful evangelists.

Over a century ago, J. P. Migne argued that the medi-
eval legends of the Saints were far less prone to mislead the
faithful than those scientifically oriented apocrypha of the
Early Church, since the former were the transparent inven-
tions of popular fantasy that could never lead thinking
people astray, while the latter by their air of factual reporting and claims to scientific plausibility led the early Christians into all manner of extravagant speculation, drawing

"Treasures in the Heavens: Some Early Christian Insights into the
Organizing of Worlds" was published in *Dialogue: A Journal of Mormon
Thought* 8 (Autumn/Winter 1973): 76-98.

the faithful astray in many directions. To appreciate the strength of their own position, Latter-day Saints should not be without some knowledge of both these traditions. Since the "cosmist" doctrines have been almost completely neglected, here we offer a look at some of them.

The canonical writings and the Apocrypha have a good deal to say about "treasures in the heavens." If we compare the "treasures" passages in a wide sampling of these writings, including those of Qumran, Nag Hammadi and the Mandaeans, it becomes apparent that "treasures in the heavens" is a part of a much larger picture, a "cosmist" view of the plan of salvation that was rejected by the official Christianity and Judaism that emerged triumphant in the Fourth Century but seems to have been prevalent throughout the Near East in an earlier period. There is no better approach to the study of this strange and intriguing doctrine than an examination of the Treasures in Heaven. We begin with the surprising fact that the Treasures in the Heavens were not allegorical but real.

That the life-giving treasures of the earth, particularly the golden grain that was anciently kept in a sacred bin, really comes from the sky is apparent to everyone.[1] The miracle of the bounties of heaven literally pouring from "the treasure-houses of the snow, . . . the terrible storehouses" is an awesome sight and a joyous one.[2] But without a benign intelligence to administer them, the same elements that bestow life on man can wreak frightful destruction; hence it is plain that a measure of knowledge, skill, and benevolence is necessary to convert the raw elements into useful gifts.[3] Thus when one speaks of treasures in the heavens, one means not only the vast secret chambers of the rain, snow, and hail, but also the deep hidden wisdom and the power necessary to control them; God's treasury is a source not only of the elements that sustain life but also of the light and knowledge that endow them with that power.[4]

The life-giving fusion of divine wisdom with primal element is often described in religious texts as a fountain, as "the overflowing waters which shine" coming from the "treasure-chest of radiance" along with all the other shining treasures.[5] "Thou hast established every fountain of light beside Thee," says Baruch, "and the treasures of wisdom beneath Thy throne hast Thou prepared."[6] The concept is more than a figure of speech; "the heavenly waters . . . important for life on earth," to be effectively used, must be "gathered in and assigned . . . to particular treasurehouses."[7] We are introduced to that physical part of the heavenly treasure in a grandiose scene in which we behold a great council in heaven being held at the creation of the world; there God, enthroned in the midst of his heavenly hosts, explains the plan of creation to them[8] and then opens his treasure chest before them to show them the wondrous store of stuff that is to be used in making a world;[9] but the new world is still in a preliminary state, "like unripe fruit that does not know what it is to become."[10] It is not until we get to the doctors of the Church, wholly committed to the prevailing teachings of the schools, that we hear of creation ⟨ *ex nihilo*.[11] Before then, creation is depicted as a process of imposing form and order on chaotic matter: the world is created for the specific purpose of carrying out a specific plan, and the plan, like the creation itself, requires strict organization—all creatures have their work assigned them in the coming world, to be carried out at predetermined times and places.[12] When the plan was announced to the assembled hosts, and the full scope and magnanimity of it dawned upon them, they burst into spontaneous shouts of joy and joined in a hymn of praise and thanksgiving, the Morning-song of Creation, which remains to this day the archetype of hymns, the great *acclamatio*, the primordial nucleus of all liturgy.[13]

The Creation drama, which is reflected in the great year-rites all over the ancient world, does not take place in a vacuum but "in the presence of God," seated in the midst of "His holy ones" with whom he takes counsel, they being his mind and mouth on the occasion as he is theirs.[14] Though the plan from first to last is entirely God's own, he discusses it with others, "consulting the souls of the righteous before deciding to create the world," not because he needs their advice, but because the plan concerns them and requires their maximum participation in it. The discussion was a lively one—apart from those rebellious angels who rejected it entirely, there was a general protest that the plan would be too painful for some parties and too risky for all; it was the generous voluntary offering of the Son of God that settled the question.[15] Those who embrace the plan wholeheartedly on this earth are the Elect, "the people of the Plan," chosen "from the foundation of the world";[16] they form on earth a community dedicated to "the faithful working out of God's plan" in close cooperation with the heavenly hosts;[17] they alone have access to the heavenly hidden treasure, because they alone covet and seek it.[18]

What most thrills the psalmist of Qumran as he sings of the bounteous fountain of God's hidden treasures is the thought that he is not only a beneficiary of God's plan, but was actually taken into his confidence in the making of it— he was there![19] When Clement of Alexandria recalls that "God knew us before the foundation of the world, and chose us for our faithfulness," he is attesting a well-known teaching of the early Church.[20] The recurring phrase "Blessed is he who is before he came into being" is not a paradox but refers to two states of being:[21] if (following Baruch) "we have by no means been from the beginning what we are now," it does not follow that we did not exist, for it is equally true that "what we now are we shall not afterwards remain."[22] We are dealing here not with existence and nonexistence but with a passing from one state to another, sometimes explained as a passing from one type of visibility to another.[23] It is common to speak of the Creation as a renewing,[24] even as a reorganizing of old matter, nay as the

building of a world from materials taken from the dismantling of older worlds.[25] Preexistent man had been around a
long time before it was decided to create this earth: the
whole thing was produced, when the time came, for his
benefit; and though he was created last of all to take it over,
in his real nature he is older than any of it.[26] He is the child
of an earlier, spiritual birth or creation.[27]

Nothing could be more gratifying to the ego or consol-
ing to the afflicted spirit of mortals than the secret intima-
tion of a glorious past and an exalted parentage.[28] The exciting foster-parent illusion was exploited by the Gnostics for
all it was worth;[29] but the idea was no invention of theirs: it
was the thought of his preexistent glory that was Job's real
comfort—"Where wast thou when I laid the foundations of
the earth . . . when the morning stars sang together and
all the sons of God shouted for joy?" is not a rhetorical
question. For it was the recollection of that same Creation-
hymn of joy and their part in it that sustained the Sons of
Light in the midst of terrible reverses.[30] "If you could see
your real image which came into being before you," says a
logion of Jesus, "then you would be willing to endure anything!"[31] The author of the Thanksgiving Hymn is simply
drunk with the idea of his own preexistent glory.[32] Such
glory, according to the Johannine writings, belongs not
only to the Lord but to all who follow him.[33]

But why leave one's heavenly home for a dismal earthly
one? To that question, constantly reiterated in the Mandaean writings, the Gnostic answer was that we were forced
to make the move as a punishment; but the "Treasure" doctrine was the very opposite—we are here as a reward, enjoying an opportunity to achieve yet greater things by being
tried and tested, "that each one might be promoted, according to his intelligence and the perfections of his way, or
be retarded according to his wrong-doings."[34] This is the
well-known doctrine of the Two Ways: For this reason the
world has existed through the ages, says the Clementine
Recognitions, so that the spirits destined to come here

might fulfill their number, and here make their choice between the upper and the lower worlds, both of which are
represented here.[35] In what has been regarded as the oldest
ritual document in existence, the so-called Shabako Stone
from Memphis, we find the concept full-blown: "To him
who doeth good will be given Life and [of] Salvation [htp].
To him who doeth evil will be given the Death of the Condemned [criminal] . . . according to that decree, conceived
in the heart and brought forth by the tongue, which shall
be the measure of all things."[36]

The element of opposition necessary for such a test is
provided by the adversary, who in the beginning openly
mocked God's plan and set up his own plan in opposition
to it.[37] Being cast out of heaven with his followers by main
force, he continues upon this earth during the set time allowed him by God's plan (for the irony of his situation is
that he is Mephistopheles, unwillingly if not unwittingly
contributing to the operation of that plan), attempting to
wreck the whole enterprise by drawing off as many spirits
and as much material as possible into his own camp.[38] The
devil and his hosts claim the Treasure for their own and attempt to pirate the treasure ships that cruise between the
worlds, using the loot in the outfitting of their own dark
worlds.[39] A neglected leitmotif of the New Testament is the
continuation on earth of the personal feud between the
Lord and the adversary begun at the foundation of the
world: from the first each recognizes the other as his old
opponent and rival;[40] they are matched at every point—
each claims identical gifts, ordinances, signs, and wonders;
each has his doctrine and his glory and his plan for the future of the race.[41] Above all, each claims to possess the
Treasure, the Lord promising treasures in the heavens while
the adversary offers a clever, glittering earthly imitation: it
is the choice between these treasures (for no man can have
both) that is a man's real test here upon the earth, deter-
mining his place hereafter.[42] It is the "poor" who recognize
and seek the true treasures, since they who are "rich as

to the things of this world" have deliberately chosen the fraudulent imitation.[43]

In coming to earth each man leaves his particular treasure, or his share of *the* Treasure, behind him in heaven, safely kept in trust ("under God's throne") awaiting his return.[44] One has here below the opportunity of enhancing one's treasure in heaven by meritorious actions, and also the risk of losing it entirely by neglecting it in his search for earthly treasure.[45] Hence the passionate appeals to men to remember their tremendous stake on the other side and "not to defraud themselves of the glory that awaits them" by seeking the things of the world.[46] To make the "treasure" test a fair one, the two treasures are placed before us on an equal footing (the doctrine of the Two Ways), their two natures being mingled in exactly equal portions in every human being.[47] To neutralize what would otherwise be the overpowering appeal of the heavenly treasure, the memory of its former glories has been erased from the mind of man, which is thus in a state of equilibrium, enjoying by "the ancient law of liberty" complete freedom to choose whatever it will.[48] In this state, whatever choice is made represents the true heart and mind of the one who makes it. What conditions the Elect to make the right choice is no unfair advantage of instruction—for all men are aware of the issues involved—but a besetting nostalgia, a constant vague yearning for one's distant treasure and happy heavenly home. This theme, akin to the Platonic doctrine of anamnesis, runs through all the Apocrypha and scriptures; it is beautifully expressed in the Hymn of the Pearl from the Acts of Thomas.

In this classic tale, a king's son has come down to earth to find a pearl which he is to return to its heavenly depository; here below he becomes defiled with the things of the world until a letter from heaven, signed by all the Great and Mighty Ones, recalls to him his true heritage and his purpose in coming to earth, whereupon he casts off his earthly garments and with the pearl returns to the waiting arms of his loved ones in the royal courts on high and to his robe of glory that has been carefully kept for him in the Treasury.[49] Our various "treasure" texts consistently refer to going to heaven as a return, a joyful homecoming, in which one follows the steps of Adam "back to the Treasury of Life from which he came forth."[50] A great deal is said about a garment that one changes in passing from one stage to another, the final garment of glory being often equated to the Treasure itself.[51] This garment introduces us to the very important ritual aspect of the treasure story, for it is generally understood that one can return to one's heavenly treasure only by the careful observance of certain rites and ordinances, which provide the means both of receiving instruction and demonstrating obedience.[52] In the Mandaean economy the ordinances *are* the Treasure, the knowledge of the proper procedures being the very knowledge by which the elements are controlled and the spirit of man exalted.[53] The other sectaries are hardly less concerned with ordinances, however, the paradox of Qumran being that a society that fled from the rites of the temple at Jerusalem should become completely engrossed in yet more rites and ordinances once it was in the desert.[54] Moreover, the most elaborate of all discourses on the initiatory rites are those of the Coptic Christians.[55]

As teacher and administrator of the ordinances, the priest holds the key to the spiritual Treasure House in which "the merit accruing from *ceremonial* worship is accumulated."[56] These ordinances, imported directly from that Treasury of Light to which they alone offer the means of return, are types of what is done above; through them "souls are led to the Treasury of Light. . . . Between us and the Great King of the Treasury of Light are many steps and veils," and it is only by "giving the proper replies to the Guardians" that one is able to approach and finally enter the Treasury of Light.[57] The ordinances are most secret (they are usually called "mysteries"), and it is through their scrupulous observance that every man "puts his own treasure in order."[58]

The archetype whom all must follow in the ordinances as is Adam, whose true home is the "Treasury of Light," and who belongs with all his children "to the Father who existed from the beginning."[59] The preexistent Adam, "the Adam of Light," having descended to earth fell into a deep sleep, from which he awoke with his mind erased like that of a little child.[60] He was thus in a state to undergo impartial testing, but in his new helplessness he needed instruction. This was provided by a special emissary from the Treasury of Light, the "Sent One." The Sent One is often a commission of three, the "Three Great Men" who wakened Adam from his sleep and immediately set about teaching him what he should know and do in order to return to the House of Light from which he had come.[61] The Sent One may be Michael, Gabriel, or the Lord himself, but whoever holds that office always has the same calling, namely to assist the souls of men to return to the Treasury of Light: when the Lord, as the supreme example of the Sent One, descends below to deliver the spirits that sit in darkness, they hail him as "Son of Glory, Son of Lights and of the Treasures."[62] Always a stranger on earth, recognized only by the "Poor,"[63] the Sent One comes to bring a treasure, and indeed he is sometimes called the Treasure, for he alone brings the knowledge men must have to return to the Father of Lights.[64] Letters sent from above to help men in their need—the prototype of those "Letters from Heaven" that have haunted Christian and Moslem society through the centuries—being directives or passports for getting to the Treasure House, if not written deeds to the Treasure itself (the scriptures are rated as such), are themselves among the Treasures of Heaven.[65]

While a treasure is anything precious and hidden, the early Christian idea of what was precious differed noticeably from the abstract and allegorical "spiritual" treasures of the philosophizing churchmen of a later time. The Patristic writers, trained in the schools, are offended and annoyed by the way in which many Christians cling to the old literalism of the Early Church.[66] When primitive Christians thought of a treasure, it had to be something real and tangible; theirs was the tradition of the Jews before them, for whom the delights of the other world "though including spiritual and intellectual joys are most tangible delights of a completely pleasing physical and social environment."[67] Much has been written about early Christian and Jewish concepts of time, but where the other world is concerned, the ideas of space are at least equally important. With what care Luke tells us exactly where the angel stood in the temple and exactly where on the map he found Mary! What tireless comings and goings and what constant concern with being in one place or another fill the pages of the gospels! If we are not to think in terms of real time and place, why this persistent use of familiar words that suggest nothing else? Scholars have pointed out that it is impossible to take such formulaic expressions as "to visit the earth" and "he went and preached" (referring to the descensus) in any but the most literal sense.[68] The insistence of our sources on depicting the hereafter in terms of "places" (*topoi*, the *ma'man* of the Dead Sea Scrolls) is a constant reminder that "heaven is not only a state but a place."[69] True, it is so far away that our sun "and all the world of men" look like nothing but a tiny speck of dust, "because of the vast distance at which it is removed"; but for all that it is still the same universe, and all made of the same basic materials.[70]

This preoccupation with locus assumes a plurality of worlds, and indeed in our "treasure" texts we often find *worlds, earths,* and *kosmoses* in the plural.[71] It is only the fallen angels, in fact, led by the blind Samael, who insist: "We are alone, and there is none beside us"![72] To the Sons of Light, on the other hand, there is opened up the grandiose vision of the "worlds" united in the common knowledge of him who made them, exchanging joyful and affectionate messages as they "keep faith with one another" in the common plan and "talk to each other . . . and establish concord, each contributing something of its own" to the common interest.[73] The members of the vast complex are kept in perfect accord by the sustaining Word of God, which reaches all alike, since it possesses "through the power of the Treasure" the capacity for traveling for unlimited distances with inexpressible speed.[74] This Word is also the Son, who "has betaken himself to the numberless hidden worlds which have come to know him."[75] The messages may also be borne by special messengers and inspectors, angels with special assignments and marvelous powers of getting around, who constantly go forth on their missions and return with their reports.[76]

With all its perfect unity and harmony, the system presents a scene not of monotonous uniformity but rather of endless and delightful variety: "They are all different one from the other, but He hath not made any one of them superfluous, the one exchangeth what is good, [in it] with the other."[77] At a new creation there is a reshuffling of elements, like the rearranging of notes in the musical scale to make a new composition;[78] it is even suggested, as we have noted, that old worlds may be dismantled to supply stuff for the making of newer and better ones.[79]

Beginning with the very old Egyptian idea, recently examined by E. A. E. Reymond, that the creation of the world was really a re-creation by "transforming substances" that had already been used in the creation of other worlds,[80] the Jewish and Christian apocryphal writers envisage a process by which the stuff of worlds is alternately organized into new stars and planets, and when these have served their time, scrapped, decontaminated, and reused in yet more new worlds. This "Urstoff" that is being constantly recycled is the *Tohuwabohu* of some Jewish teachers, according to Weiss, who saw the ultimate forms of matter in fire and ice.[81] Likewise, according to the same authority, the world-holocaust of the Stoics was merely a necessary preparation for the making of new worlds from old materials.[82] The whole thrust of Weiss's book is that until the early Christian apologists, we find no trace anywhere of a doctrine of *creatio ex nihilo*,[83] the Creation being everywhere conceived of as the act of organizing "matter unorganized" (*amorphos hyle*), bringing order from disorder, the basic prerequisites for the work being space (*chora*) and unorganized matter.[84]

And so we have in the Pistis Sophia, continuing the Egyptian teachings, the picture of a constant remixing (*kerasomos*) going on in the universe in which old, worn-out, contaminated substances, the refuse (*sorm*) of worn-out worlds and kingdoms (247-250), is first thrown out on the scrap-heap and returned to chaos as "dead" matter (134, 41, 68), then melted down in a dissolving fire for many years (365f.), by which all the impurities are removed from it (249), and by which it is "improved" (41, 68), and is ready to be "poured from one kind of body into another" (251). This whole process by which souls as well as substances are "thrown back into the mixing" (14) is under the supervision of Melchizedek, the great reprocessor, purifier, and preparer of worlds (35f.). He takes over the refuse of defunct worlds or souls (36), and under his supervision five great Archons process (literally "knead"—*ouoshm*) it, separating out its different components, each one specializing in particular elements, which they thus recombine in unique and original combinations so that no new world or soul is exactly like any other (338).

In this full-blown pleniarism there is no waste and no shortage: "If any were superfluous or any lacking, the whole body would suffer, for the worlds counterpoise one another like the elements of a single organism."[85] The worlds go on forever: "They come and come and cease not, they ever increase and are multiplied, yet are not brought to an end nor do they decrease."[86]

It was essential to the plan that all physical things should pass away; this idea is depicted by the ancient

Egyptian symbol of the *Uroboros,* the serpent with his tail in his mouth, representing the frustration of material things or matter consuming itself by entropy.[87] Indeed, the Pistis Sophia describes the *Uroboros* (which means "feeding on its own tail") in terms of the heat-death, when it reports that fire and ice are the end of all things, since ultimate heat and ultimate cold both mean an end to substance.[88] Though matter is replaced through an endless cycle of creations and dissolution, only spirit retains conscious identity, so that strictly speaking "only progeny is immortal," each "mounting up from world to world" acquiring ever more "treasure" while progressing toward His perfection, which awaits them all.[89] When the apostles formed a prayer circle, "all clothed in garments of white linen," Jesus, standing at the altar, began the prayer by facing the four directions and crying in an unknown tongue, "Iao, Iao, Iao!" The Pistis Sophia interprets the three letters of this word as signifying (1) *Iota,* because the universe took form at the Creation; (2) *Alpha,* because in the normal course of things it will revert to its original state, alpha representing a cycle; (3) *Omega,* because the story is not going to end there, since all things are tending towards a higher perfection, "the perfection of the perfection of everything is going to happen"—that is "syntropy." (Pistis Sophia, 358.)

The eternal process is thus not a static one but requires endless expansion of the universe *(p-sōr ebol mpterf)* (193ff., 219, 225, etc.), since each dispensation is outgoing, tending to separation and emanation, that is, fissure (220), so that "an endless process in the Uncontainable fills the Boundless" (219). This is the Egyptian paradox of expanding circles of life that go on to fill the physical universe and then go on without end.[90] Such a thing is possible because of a force that is primal and self-existent, having no dependence on other matter or its qualities. This is that "light-stream" that no power is able to hold down and no matter is able to control in any way. (Pistis Sophia, 227.) On the contrary, it is this light that imposes form and order on all else; it is the spark by which Melchizedek organizes new worlds (35); it is the light that purifies contaminated substances (388), and the light that enables dead matter to live (65; 134). Reduced to its simplest form, creation is the action of light upon matter *(hyle)* (64); matter of itself has no power, being burnt-out energy (65), but light reactivates it (134); matter is incapable of changing itself—it has no desire to, and so light forces it into the recycling process where it can again work upon it—for light is the organizing principle (50). If Melchizedek is in charge of organizing worlds, it is Michael and Gabriel who direct the outpouring of light to those parts of chaos where it is needed (130). As light emanates out into space in all directions it does not weaken but mysteriously increases more and more, not stopping as long as there is a space to fill. (129.) In each world is a gathering of light ("synergy"?), and as each is the product of a drive toward expansion, each becomes a source of new expansion, "having its part in the expansion of the universe." (193ff.)

The mere mechanics of the creation process as described in our "treasure" texts display truly remarkable scientific insight. For the making of the world the first requirements, we are told, are a segment of empty space, pure and unencumbered,[91] and a supply of primordial matter to work with.[92] Mere empty space and inert matter are, however, forbidding and profitless things in themselves, disturbing and even dangerous things for humans to be involved with—contemplating them, the mind is seized with vertigo until some foothold is found in the void.[93] The order and stability of a foundation are achieved through the operation of a "Spark." The Spark is sometimes defined as "a small idea" that comes forth from God and makes all the difference between what lives and what does not: "Compared with it all the worlds are but as a shadow, since it is the Spark whose light moves all [material] things."[94] It is the ultimate particle, the *"ennas* which came from the Father of those who are without beginning," emanating from the Treasure House of Light from which all life and power is ultimately derived.[95] Thanks to the vivifying and organizing power of the Spark, we find throughout the cosmos an infinity of dwelling-places *(topoi),* either occupied or awaiting tenants.[96] These are colonized by migrants from previously established *toposes* or worlds, all going back ultimately to a single original center.[97] The colonizing process is called "planting," and those spirits that bring their treasures to a new world are called "Plants," more rarely "seeds," of their father or "Planter" in another world.[98] Every planting goes out from a Treasure House, either as the essential material elements or as the colonizers themselves, who come from a sort of mustering-area called the "Treasure-house of Souls."[99]

With its "planting" completed, a new world is in business, a new Treasury has been established from which new Sparks may go forth in all directions to start the process anew in ever new spaces;[100] God wants every man to "plant a planting," nay, "he has promised that those who keep his Law may also become creators of worlds."[101] But keeping the law requires following the divine pattern in every point; in taking the Treasure to a new world, the Sent One (who follows hard on the heels of the colonists) seeks nothing so much as complete identity with the One who sent him; hence, from first to last one mind alone dominates the whole boundless complex. Because each planting is completely dependent on its Treasure House or home base, the system never breaks up into independent systems; in this patriarchal order all remains forever identified with the Father from whom all ultimately come forth.[102]

We on earth are not aware of all this because we comprehend only what *we* are like.[103] Not only is God rendered invisible by the impenetrable veil of light that surrounds him,[104] but he has purposely "placed veils between the worlds," that all treasures may be hid from those who do not seek them in the proper way.[105] On the other side of the veil of the temple lay "the secrets of heaven," the celestial spaces that know no bounds, and all that they contain.[106] The *wilon* (veil) quarantines this polluted world mercifully

from the rest.[107] "Beyond the veil are the heavens,"[108] and
that goes for other worlds as well as this one, for each is
shut off by its veil, for there are aeons and veils and firmaments: "He made a veil for their worlds, surrounding them
like a wall."[109] Behind the ultimate veil sits Jeu, "the Father
of the Treasury of Light," who is separated from all others
by the veils (katapetasmata),[110] a veil being that which sepa-
rates that which is above from that which is below.[111] When
a cycle has been completed in the existence of things, "the
Great Sabaoth the Good looks out" from behind the veil,
and all that has gone before is dissolved and passes into ob-
livion.[112] Only the qualified can pass by one of these veils,
of course; when Pistis Sophia presumed to look behind the
veil before she was ready, she promptly fell from her
former glory.[113] Only Jesus has passed through all the veils
and all the degrees of glory and authority.[114] As one grows
in faith, more and more is revealed, until finally "the
Watchers move the veils aside and you enter into the Presence of the Father, who gives you His name and His
seal."[115]

These veils seem to serve as protecting as well as confining fences around the worlds: The light of the sun in its
true nature (morphe) is not seen in this place, we are told,
because it passes through "many veils and regions (topoi)"
before reaching us;[116] its protective function is represented
by a wonderful super-bird, called "the guardian of the inhabited earth," because "by spreading out his wings he ab-
sorbs (dechetai) the fire-like (pyrimorphos) rays" of the sun;
"if he did not receive [absorb] them, the human race could
not survive, nor any other form of life." On a wing of the
bird is an inscription declaring, "Neither earth nor heaven
begot me, but the wings of fire." Baruch was informed by
an angel that this bird is the phoenix, the sun-bird, which
feeds on the manna of heaven and the dews of earth.[117] It
blocks the sun with its wings outspread, suggesting solar
prominences or zodiacal light. At any rate, it is an interest-

ing example of how the ancients explained things that most men cannot see or comprehend in terms of things they can.

The plan calls for universal participation in the accumulation of treasure in a course of eternal progression.[118] The "Treasures in the Heavens" is heady stuff; E. L. Cherbonnier has observed that the discovery that man really belongs to the same family as God, "to share in the same kind of existence which God himself enjoys," is "like learning that one has won the sweepstakes."[119] The Evangelium is good news—the only *good* news, in fact, since all else ends in nothing. But it is also *news*, the sort of thing, as C. S. Lewis points out, that no human being could possibly have invented. Granted that the Treasures in the Heavens are something totally alien to human experience, something that "eye hath not seen, nor ear heard, neither hath entered into the heart of man," they must be nonetheless real.[120] "For the plan of Salvation," as E. Soggin has recently put it, "only exists when we are dealing with reality, not with artificial contrivances; . . . as Hesse notes, 'We are only interested in what really took place, all the rest being of little or no concern whatever.'"[121] Likewise the religion of Egypt "n'est pas une mystique, mais une physique," as we are now discovering.[122] This attitude, diametrically opposite to that of Christian and Jewish scholars (for example, C. Schmidt) in the past, is gaining ground today. The old literalism has been dismissed as Gnostic, and indeed much of the appeal of Gnosticism lay in its exploitation of certain "cosmist" aspects of early Christian teaching; but the basic teachings of Gnosticism and Neoplatonism were spiritualized concepts that followed the prevailing line of the schools and ran directly counter to the old literalism of the Treasures of Heaven.[123]

While our sources contain "extremely confused and contradictory records of creation," all seem to betray "a single organic foundation."[124] And while the relationship between them all still remains to be established, it becomes

clearer every day that there was a relationship.[125] The "cosmist" idea is not the monopoly of any group, Gnostic or
otherwise. Indeed, cosmism was essentially anti-Gnostic.[126]
The doctors of the Christians and the Jews who adopted
the Neoplatonic and Gnostic ideas of the schools opposed
the old literalism with all their might, so that to this day
cosmism has remained the very essence of heresy.[127] Still,
the very fathers who opposed the old teaching admitted
that it was the original faith of the Saints, and they could
not rid themselves of it without a real struggle.[128]

In view of its age, its universality, its consistency, and
its scientific and aesthetic appeal, the doctrine of the Treasures in the Heavens should be studied more closely than it
has been. What we have presented in intensely concentrated
form is enough to show that references to treasures in religious writings may well conceal far more than a mere figure
of speech.

NOTES

1. We have treated this theme in "Sparsiones," *Classical Journal*
40 (1945): 515-43.

2. Secrets of Enoch 5:1; cf. 6:1; Jer. 51:16; Ps. 135:7; Job 38:22; 1
Enoch 18:1; Slavonic Enoch (in J.A.T. Robinson, *Apocrypha Anecdota*
[Cambridge: 1897], II, p. 58); Pseudo-Philo 32:7 (in M. R. James,
Antiquities of Philo [SPCK, 1917], 176). "Clouds of radiance drip
moisture and life," Psalms of Thomas 1:11 (A. Adam, in *Zeitschrift
für die Neutestamentliche Wissenschaft* [hereinafter, ZNTW], Beih.
No. 24 [1959], 2); text in *A Manichaean Psalm-Book* (Stuttgart: 1938),
pp. 203-28. On the heavens as a general storehouse and treasure
house, K. Ahrens, in *Zeitschrift der Deutschen Morgenländischen Gesellschaft* (hereinafter, "ZDMG") 84 (1930): 163, discussing Koran 15:21;
cf. Ben Sirach 43:14ff. In the Enuma Elish, Tab. 7:8, God's "treasure
is the abundance which is poured out over all." On the relevance of
this source, see W. Bousset, *Hauptprobleme der Gnosis* (Göttingen:
1907), p. 246.

3. They are "for a blessing or a curse as the Lord of Spirits
willeth." (1 Enoch 59:1ff.; 60:22.) They must undergo a transforma-
tion to be useful to man. (Deut. 28:12; 1 Enoch 18:2; 60:15, 21-22; 3
Baruch 10:9-10.) They may serve "against the day of battle and war"

(Job 38:22-23), for unless benignly restrained they are dark and destructive. (J. A. T. Robinson, *Apocrypha Anecdota;* cf. Odes Sol. 16:15-17; Pseudo-Philo 15:5).

4. "I am the Treasure of Life who descended upon the King of Glory, so that he was radiant in his understanding," M. Lidzbarski. *(Das Johannesbuch der Mandäer* [hereinafter, *"Johannesbuch der Mand."*] [Giessen: 1905], p. 203, no. 57.) God holds the keys to control and administer the treasure (K. Ahrens, in *ZDMG* 84 [1930]: 163); he restrains the elements as by a dam. (1 Enoch 60:1ff.), keeping them "sealed up" (Pseudo-Philo 13:6-10) in places of peace and order. (1 Baruch 3:12-15). His treasury is a shrine of wisdom. (Jer. 51:15-16.) For the Mandaeans, *treasure* means "capability, ability, worthiness." (E. S. Drower, *The Thousand and Twelve Questions* [hereinafter, *"1012 Questions"*] [Berlin: Akad-Verlag, 1960], p. 117, n. 8.) An impressive treatment of the theme is in the Thanksgiving Hymns (hereinafter, "IQH"), especially 1, 3, 10-11, and 14.

5. Quotation is from E. S. Drower, *A Pair of Nasoraean Commentaries* (hereinafter, *"Nasoraean Commentaries"*) (Leiden: Brill, 1963), p. 69, n. 1; cf. 2 Baruch 54:13; Odes Sol. 4:10. The treasure is a fountain. (Cf. Prov. 8:24.) He has "a multitude of waters in the heavens." (Jer. 51:16.) The source of all earthly treasure is a pool in heaven. (3 Baruch 10:1-10.) The "treasures of glory" are the clouds and earthly fountains, says the Battle Scroll (hereinafter, "IQM") 10:12, the latter being fed by the former. (Pseudo-Philo 19:10; cf. N. Sed, "Une Cosmologie juive du haut moyen-age," in *Revue des Etudes Juives* 124 [1965], 64-65.) In the treasuries of the heavens are "the living waters" (1 Enoch 17:5); blessings pour from "the holy dwelling and the eternal fountain that never deceives" (IQSb [Isaiah Scroll—Hebrew University] 1:3); this is also temple imagery (1 Enoch 39:5). God's creative intelligence is "a strong fountain" (IQH 12:11); Pindar, *Olympian Odes* 1:1ff.; 3:65ff.; and Aeschylus, *Persians*, ll. 234-47, 405; 1207-18, equate the life-giving gold and silver of the divine treasure-house of oracular wisdom with golden grain and silver fountains. The light of the treasure is also a stream. (Pistis Sophia 65 [132-33]). The creative process is an ever-flowing Jordan of Light. (M. Lidzbarski, *Ginza* [Göttingen: 1925], pp. 61-63, 67.)

6. 2 Baruch 54:13.

7. K. Koch, "Wort und Einheit des Schöpfergottes im Memphis und Jerusalem," *Zeitschrift für Theologie und Kirche* (hereinafter, *"ZThK"*) 62 (1965): 276. This is one of many recent studies pointing out the relevance and importance of early Egyptian texts for the study of Jewish and Christian concepts. So L. V. Zabkar, *Journal of Near Eastern Studies* (hereinafter, *"JNES"*) 13 (1954):87; R. Anthes, *JNES* 18 (1959): 169-212; L. Speleers, *Les Textes des Cercueils* (Brussels:

1946), p. 28. The five *stoicheia* "gush forth" from the five treasure-houses. *(Manichäische Handschriften der Staatl. Museen Berlin* [hereinafter, *"Berlin Manich. Hs."*] [Stuttgart: 1940] 1:30.)

8. Such a scene is depicted in the archaic text of the so-called Shabako stone (K. Sethe, *Das 'Denkmal Memphitischer Theologie,' der Schabakostein des Britischen Museums* [Leipzig: 1928], pp. 23-32, 60-70); in the *Pyramid Texts* (Louis Speleers, Brussels: 1923-24), e.g., No. 468 (895); and *Coffin Texts* (A. de Buck, ed., Univ. of Chicago: 1938), e.g. no. 39 (166-67); in Enuma Elish, Tab. 3:132-38; 4:6. On the general Near Eastern background of the Council in Heaven, see F. M. Cross, *JNES* 12 (1953): 274-77; H. W. Robinson, *Journal of Theological Studies* (hereinafter, *"JTS"*) 45 (1944): 151-57. On the presentation of the plan, see J. Fichtner, *Zeitschrift für die Alttestamentliche Wissenschaft* (hereinafter, *"ZATW"*) 63 (1951): 16-33. The scene is presented in the Serekh Scroll (or Manual of Discipline; hereinafter, "IQS") 10:1ff.; Ben Sirach 17:11-12; *1012 Questions*, p. 112.

9. Thus in the Shabako stone (see above, note 8) as rendered by J. Breasted, *The Development of Religion and Thought in Ancient Egypt* (London: 1912), p. 46: "Then he assembled all the gods and their *kas* [saying to them]: 'Come ye and take possession of the Meb-towe, the divine store-house . . . whence is furnished the Life of the Two Lands.'" Cf. Pindar, *Pythian Odes* 11:5: "Come to the hidden Melian treasury of the golden tripods, . . . the storehouse of true counsels, where the host of heroes assembles." Cf. Jer. 10:12-13; 4 Ezra 8:20-21; Ben Sirach 39:12-17; IQH 1:10; 13:1; IQS 10:1-2; Odes Sol. 15 and 16; 19:1ff.; Acts of Thomas, ch. 136 (A. F. J. Klijn, *The Acts of Thomas* [Leiden: Brill, 1962], p. 137); Psalms of Thomas 1:7-14; the Second Gnostic Work, 39a (C. Schmidt, *Texte u. Untersuchungen* [hereinafter *"TU"*], 8 [1892]: 254, 301). At the great council in heaven the Son said to the father: "If it please Thee . . . speak, open Thy treasury, and take therefrom a boon," the boon being the plan of salvation. (Prayerbook of the Mandaeans, No. 250, in E. S. Drower, *The Canonical Prayerbook of the Mandaeans* [hereinafter *"CPM"*] [Leiden: Brill, 1959], p. 207); the scene is also described on pages 225 (No. 318), 227 (No. 321), 228 (No. 323), 252 (No. 358, cf. 365-68), 269 (No. 375), 271ff. (No. 376). There is a dramatic description of the opening of the chest in the Alma Rishaia Zuta 3:199ff. (in E. Drower, *Nasoraean Commentaries*, p. 69). So *Ginza*, p. 493. There are five treasuries of the senses; when the mind *(enthymesis)* wants to create, it opens the appropriate treasure chest to get the things it needs *(Berlin Manich. Hs.* 1:138-40), the things being the elements in an unformed state (ibid., p. 54). Though they were later corrupted by mixture with a lower state of matter or ground-substance, the physical elements are

in themselves pure and holy (ibid., p. 239); in their corrupt earthly form they are gold, silver, copper, lead, and tin (ibid., p. 33). God also opens a treasure chest to bring forth healing elements for man. (*Manichaean Psalm-Book*, II, 46.)

10. Gospel of Truth (M. Malinine et al., *Evangelium Veritatis* [Zürich: 1956], fol. XIVv, 5-7.) Smoke, fire, wind, and water were the chaotic contents of the divine storehouse. (*Manichaean Psalm-Book*, II, 9.) In *Ginza*, p. 259, there is a leavening substance, a "Sauerteig der Welt," kept in the divine treasure house, and from this the world and the planets are created, as higher worlds are created of a like substance (p. 261). God furnishes "the whole creation" from "the treasuries of all the winds" (1 Enoch 18:1), which are in the midst of "secret things" amidst mountains of precious stones and minerals (ibid. 52:5). On wind as the "Urstoff," see *Coffin Texts*, Spell 162, II, 401; on water, see W. Lambert, *JTS* 16 (1965): 293.

11. For a thorough treatment, see H. F. Weiss, *Untersuchungen zur Kosmologie des hellenistischen und Palästinischen Judentums* (Berlin: Akad.-Verlag, 1966), pp. 59-74, and notes 81-84, below; see also W. Richter, "Urgeschichte und Hoftheologie," *Biblische Zeitschrift* (hereinafter "*BZ*"), NF 10 (1966): 97; H. A. Brongers, *De Scheppingstradities bij de Profeten* (Amsterdam: 1945), pp. 3-18.

12. The idea is carried over into the widespread ritual dramatizations of the Creation, whose essence is the strict regulation of persons, times, and places. (S. Mowinckel, *Religion und Kultus* [Göttingen: 1953], pp. 53-59; see esp. Pistis Sophia 128-135 [pp. 325-57]).

13. This is an unfailing part of the picture: the Hallelujah chorus with its refrain of "Forever and ever!" is the closing section of almost any ritual text. See W. F. Otto, *Die Musen und der göttlichen Ursprung des Singens und Sagens* (Düsseldorf-Köln: E. Diederich, 1956); H. Nibley, "The Expanding Gospel," *BYU Studies* 7 (1965): 3-27.

14. K. Koch, in *ZThK* 62 (1965): 271, 281-82, shows that the "creative word of God" originally refers to a conversation, a discussion with others. The Egyptian concept is discussed by H. Junker, *Die Götterlehre von Memphis* (Berlin: Akad. d. Wiss., 1940), pp. 36-37, 42, 55; the holy ones are "as it were extensions of the Great God." (H. Grapow, *Das 17. Kapitel des aeg. Totenbuches* [Berlin: 1912], p. 40.) See above, notes 8 and 9. May not the *logos* of John 1 also be a "council" discussion?

15. Quotation from D. Winston, in *History of Religions* 5 (1966): 212, citing Jewish and Persian sources. It was a real discussion, in which many divergent views were expressed, as described in Timothy Archbishop of Alexandria, *Discourse on Abbaton* (hereinafter "Abp. Timothy on Abbaton") fol. 10a-12a (in E. A. W. Budge, *Coptic*

Martyrdoms [Br. Mus.: 1914], pp. 232-34); *Ginza*, pp. 331-33; Mandaean Prayerbook, No. 361 (*CPM*, 255); Alma Rishaia Zuta 3:215ff. (in E. Drower, *Nasoraean Commentaries*, pp. 67, 70); Alma Rishaia Rba 4:150ff. (in E. Drower, *Nasoraean Commentaries*, p. 7).

16. IQM 12:2-3; IQSa (Isaiah Scroll—St. Marks) 1:1ff. The world was created on their behalf. (Ascension of Moses 1:12; 4 Ezra 9:13-14.) All the elect were known and the kingdom with "the riches of his glory" (i.e., the treasure) appointed to them "from the foundation of the world." (Matt. 25:34, 41; Rom. 9:23; Odes Sol. 23:1-3; Psalms of Solomon 7:30; Didache 10:3; *Test. Dom. nostri J. Christi* [J. E. Rahmani, ed.; Mainz: 1899], p. 25.) They are the pearls in the treasure house of Life. (*Ginza*, pp. 590-91.) They alone share the secrets of the treasure. (Ibid., p. 296; cf. IQH 17:9.)

17. IQM 13:2; 7:6; 15:13; IQSa (Isaiah Scroll—St. Marks) 2:8-9, 14-15, 20; IQH 3:20-21. Every major event in the New Testament is marked by the presence on the scene of heavenly beings participating with the Saints in the activities.

18. IQM 5:10; Clementine Recognitions 3:53-54, 58; 5:5-7; Oxyrhynchus Frg., No. 654:5ff.; Gospel of Thomas 80:14-18; 94:14ff.; 19:1ff.; Gospel of Truth, fol. IXr, 2-4; Lactantius, *Div. Inst.* 4:2. "The Chosen people alone understand what the others have rejected." (K. Koch, *ZThK* 62 [1965]: 292.)

19. IQH 1:21; 2:7, 13, 17; 3:19ff.; 4:27; 5:25; 6:10-11; 7:26-30; 10:4, 14ff., 22ff., 29; 11:4-8, 10; 27-28; 12:11-12; 13:18-19; 15:21-22; cf. IQS 11:6-7; 9:16-18; Isa. 45:3; Matt. 11:25ff.; Rom. 11:33, 12; Eph. 3:8-9; Col. 1:26-27; 2:2-3, 26-27; Phil. 4:19; *Ep. Barnab.* 6; Odes Sol. 11:4-5; Gospel of Truth, fol. XVIr, 17; *Test. Dom. nostri J. Christi* 43 (Rahmani, 103); Ben Sirach 17:11-13; *Manichaean Psalm-Book*, II, 120, 126. "In a certain way, election is pre-existence," writes J. Zandee in *Numen* 11 (1964): 46, citing Logion No. 49 of the Gospel of Thomas. Not only the Son of Man but Isaac, Jacob, Jeremiah, the Twelve Apostles, Peter, etc., are specifically said to have been chosen and set apart in the preexistence.

20. Clement of Alexandria, *Paedagog.*, I, 7 (in Migne, *Patrologiae Gracae* [hereinafter "*PG*"] 8:321), citing Jer. 1:7, 5; cf. Eph. 1:4; 1 Pet. 1:20. The awards and assignments handed out at the Creation must have been earned in a preexistent life. (Origen, *De princip.*, I, 8:4; II, 9:6-8; cf. Zadokite Document 2:7; IQS 1:7; 3:15; 4:22.)

21. The expression occurs in Gospel of Thomas 84:17; Gospel of Philip 112:10; cf. Secrets of Enoch 23:4-6; IQH 1:19; 13:8; Odes Sol. 7:11.

22. 2 Baruch 21:16; cf. Gospel of Philip 112:10: "For he who is both was and shall be." "By not yet existing, I do not mean that they do

not exist at all." (Gospel of Truth, fol. XIVv, 22-23.) The formula "out of the eternities and into the eternities" is found in IQS 2:1 and indicates an endless past as well as an endless future for man, "for Thou didst establish them before eternity." (IQH 13:8.) "When he prepared the heavens I was there. . . . Then I was by him, as one brought up with him; and I was daily his delight." (Prov. 8:27, 30; see H. Donner, *Aegypt. Zeitschr.* 81 [1956]: 8-18, for Egyptian parallels.)

23. With a new creation, things become visible on a new level. (Secrets of Enoch 24:5–25:1; 24:2; 30:10-11; 65; 2 Baruch 51:8.) This is consistent with the doctrine that one sees or comprehends only what one is like. (See below, note 103.) In the Genesis creation hymn, "everything is as it were created twice, in two different ways." (J. B. Bauer, *Theol. Zeitschr.* 20 [1964]: 7.) Albright has shown that "in the beginning" does not refer to an absolute beginning but to the start of a new phase in a going concern. (Ibid., p. 1.) *Ex ouk onton* refers to such a phase rather than to creation *ex nihilo*. (W. Richter, *BZ*, NF 10 (1966): 97, citing 2 Macc. 7:28 and *Homil. Clem.* 19:4, 9, 16, 18.)

24. The concept of Gen. 1 and Ps. 94 and 104 is the same as the old Egyptian idea that the Creation was the beginning of a new cycle of time following a different kind of age. (K. Koch, *ZThK* 62 [1965]: 257.) At the Creation, God showed his children "what they did not know before, creating new things and abolishing old agreements, to establish that which should be eternally." (IQH 13:10-12; Ben Sirach 36:6-8.) Passing from one life to another is a renewal (IQH 11:12ff.); one's existence does not begin with the womb, though a new life begins there (IQH 15:12-15; Apocalypse of Adam 78:1). When the "treasury of the heavenly King is opened" the Saints become heirs to a new kingdom by a renewal of the mind. (Acts of Thomas, ch. 136.) To become a Christian is to accept a new creation. *(Epist. to Diognetus 11.)*

25. See below, note 79. The Egyptians taught that a creation was the reuniting of existing things in new forms. (R. Anthes, *Aegypt. Zeitschr.* 82 [1957]: 3.) Untamed chaotic matter is represented as a raging beast, e.g., Pistis Sophia 54 (104); 55 (105); when the beast is subdued, an orderly world is composed of its substance. (Ibid., 70 [154].) Can this be the origin of the common tradition of creation from the body of some slain monster?

26. *Clementine Recognitions* 1:28. So *Ginza*, pp. 506, 508-10, 438. The spirits are equal in age but not in power and glory, in which they compare as fathers to sons, without any rivalry or jealousy. (Sophia Christi 97:2ff.)

27. Every man has a *dmuta*—"likeness, counterpart, image"— which is the "spiritual or ideal counterpart or double. *(1012 Ques-*

tions, p. 11); it is "the pre-existent pneumatic part of man" (Ibid., pp. 122, n. 5; 161; 173, n. 3). Thus Paul (in the Apocalypsis Pauli 18:22ff.) and Tobit (in an Aramaic text of Tobit from Qumran) both see their spiritual doubles. In the remarkable Vision of Kenaz, in the Pseudo-Philo 28:8, that early prophet sees the spirits of men walking about in another spirit world while waiting for this world to be created. This is the Mandaean "Ether-Earth." (Mandaean Prayerbook [*CPM*, p. 290, n. 4].) Before the creation of the world, "the souls still sat in the Kanna, without pain and without defect." (*Johannesbuch der Mand.*, 55, No. 13.) All creatures are double. (Pastor Hermae, II [Mand., 8], 1), and all souls existed before the formation of the world (Secrets of Enoch 23:5). The related Platonic doctrine "became a prevailing dogma in later Judaism," according to R. H. Charles. (*Apocrypha and Pseudepigrapha of the Old Testament* [Oxford: 1913], II, 444, n. 5.)

28. "God has shed upon man the splendor of his glory at the creation of all things." (IQH 16:9; 7:24ff.; Secrets of Enoch 24:1-5; 22:8B; Odes Sol. 28:14-15; 41; 24:5; 36:3-5; Gospel of Thomas 90:2; Gospel of Philip 112:12, 14-15; The Nature of the Archons 144:20 [in *Theologische Literaturzeitung*, 83 (1958), 668]; Pastor Hermae, Simil. 1:1; Mandaean texts cited by R. Bultmann, "Die neuerschlossenen mandäischen Quellen . . . ," *ZNTW* 24 [1925]: 108-9.) One is awed by the thought that this thing of wet dust once "praised amongst the praising ones . . . [was] great . . . amongst the mighty ones." (Odes Sol. 36:4; IQS 11:20-22; IQSb [Isaiah Scroll—Hebrew University] 3:28.) To know one's true identity is the great treasure. (Gospel of Thomas 80:26; 81:3-4; 87:1-2.) "I am a Son and come out of the Father . . . descended from the pre-existing Father," etc. (Apocryphon of James 1:333, 15-16.)

29. Thus a fragment from Turfan, cited by Bultmann, p. 126: "I come from the light as one of the gods, and here I have become a stranger." With characteristic vanity, the Gnostics reserved such glory for themselves alone. (Irenaeus, *adv. Haeres.*, I, 6; cf. Odes Sol. 41:8; The Pearl 11, 31-44, 56.)

30. Job 38:3-7, 21. This last is not stated as a question in the Masoretic Text, but as a flat declaration (IQM 17:20-27); " . . . peace was prepared for you before ever your war was," and God will not take back the promises made at the Creation. (Odes Sol. 4:12-14.)

31. Gospel of Thomas, Log. 84. When Adam complained of his hard lot on earth, a heavenly messenger shamed him by reminding him of the throne awaiting him in heaven. (*Johannesbuch der Mand.*, 57, No. 13.) "Endure much; then you will soon see your treasure!" (*Ginza*, p. 493; cf. Apocryphon of John 20:19-22; 17.)

32. E.g., IQH 3:22; 7:32; 10:1ff., and above, note 19; cf. Acts 1:23, 26.

33. Those who will go to heaven are they who came from there in the first place. (John 3:13.) They recognize the Lord on earth even as they once acclaimed him above. (John 17:8, 10-12.)

34. Justin Martyr, *Apol.*, 1:10, 59; 2:4-5, 7. So Zadokite Frg. 2:3-6. "When you lay your hand on the treasure the soul enters the scales that will test her." (Alma Rishaia Rba [in E. Drower, *Nasoraean Commentaries*, pp. 44-46].) Only when you have overcome here "is your name called out from the Book of Those Who Were Valiant, and you become the heir to our Kingdom." (The Pearl 46-48.) For the reward aspect, see Origen, *De princ.*, I, 8:4; II, 9:6-8; cf. *Manichaean Psalm-Book*, II, 4, 58, on this "world of testing."

35. *Clementine Recognitions* 1:24.

36. K. Sethe, *Das 'Denkmal Memphitischer Theologie' der Schabakostein des Britischen Museums* (Leipzig: 1928), I, 64-65.

37. A specific counterplan is mentioned in *Clementine Recognitions* 3:61; cf. IQH 13:4; IQS 2:4ff.; 4QFlor. 1:8; Gospel of Philip 123:2ff.; 103:14ff.; Apocryphon of John 74:1ff.; 36:16ff.; 72:10ff.; Sophia Christi 122:1ff. There are those in the Church who preach the doctrine of the Serpent, according to the Pseudo-Epistle of Paul to the Corinthians in Bodmer Papyrus 10:54:15, describing his ambitious opposition to God's plan in the beginning. (Ibid. 10:53:11-15.)

38. "Now the Prince, not being righteous and wanting to be God . . . enchains all the flesh of men." (Bodmer Papyrus, 10:53.) So Irenaeus, *adv. Haer.*, 5:25; Creation Apocryphon 151:11ff. (in A. Böhlig u. P. Labib, *Die Koptisch-Gnostische Schrift ohne Titel aus Cod. II von Nag Hammadi* [Berlin: Akad.-Verlag, 1962], pp. 48-49); 155:25ff.; 150:27, 35; 151:3, 7, 15, 18, 24; 154:19ff., 14-15; 156:1; Psalms of Thomas 2:1-2; 1:30-37, 22-25, 43-47; 7:1-3; *Test. Dom. nostri J. Christi* 23:43, Acts of Thomas (A. J. Klijn) 204:22-25; Book of John the Evangelist (ed. M. R. James), pp. 187-89; Vita Adae et Evae 15:3; 16:1, 4 (in R. H. Charles, *Apocrypha and Pseudepigrapha of the Old Testament*, p. 137); hypostasis of the Archons 134:9 (after Isa. 46:9); 140:26; 141:1; Abp. Timothy on Abbaton, fol. XIIIa; Pseudo-Philo 34:2-3; Sibylline Oracles 3:105ff. (in Charles, 381); Ascension of Isaiah 2:1-9; 7:3-5, 9-10, 15; Secrets of Enoch 10:1-6; 31A:3-5; *Johannesbuch der Mand.*, 3 (14-15, 17ff.), No. 2; Alma Rishaia Zuta 3:215ff. (in E. Drower, *Nasoraean Commentaries*, p. 70); *Ginza*, pp. 18, 263.

39. When God sent forth a ship of light "laden with the riches of the Living," Satan and his pirate crew coming "I know not from where" seized "the treasure of the Mighty One" and "distributed it

among their worlds," until they were forced to give it up. (Psalms of Thomas 3:1-15, 29-32, 35; *Manichaean Psalm-Book*, II, 53, 163, 178; cf. the image of the three ships, Berlin Manich. Hs. 1:50; Psalms of Thomas 12:1-13.) The Second Coptic Work 14a (ed. C. Schmidt, in *TU* 8:236, 286) has Christ coming out of the *monas* of Setheus "like a ship laden with all manner of precious things," so also the *Manichaean Psalm-Book*, II, 151-152, 168, 171, 174; in the *Johannesbuch der Mand.* 206, No. 58, a ship moves between the worlds bearing the glory of the Treasure of Life from one to the other. In the Egyptian Victory Over Seth 1:19-22, the god passes through dangerous straits in his ship while Seth and his robber band try to waylay him. (In the Book of the Dead, the battle of the gods takes place on board a ship [H. Grapow, *Das 17. Kapitel des Totenbuches*, p. 37].) When Adam returns to "the Treasure of Life," he is asked by the guardians "what wares he is bringing in his ship." (J. Leipoldt, *Religionsgeschichte des Orients* [Leiden: Brill, 1961], pp. 86-87). In numerous Acts of Thomas, the Captain of the ship or the rich merchant is Christ in disguise, e.g., A. Klijn, Acts of Thomas 2-3. The same commercial imagery of the ship appears in the *Johannesbuch der Mand.*, 84-86, No. 20-21; cf. *Ginza*, p. 324. The seven planets are described as floating ships (Mandaean Prayerbook, No. 286 [*CPM*, p. 288]); these seven try to rob man of his treasure (Psalms of Thomas 5:4 [in *ZNTW*, Beih. 24 (1959): 123]); *1012 Questions*, pp. 251, 258. The Ark itself was not a ship but a luminous cloud in space, according to the Apocryphon of John 73:5-12.

40. Mark 5:5ff.; Luke 4:34-35. The recognition is mutual. (Luke 4:41; 8:27-28; 10:17-18.) The contest is continued in the desert (Matt. 4:1), with Satan still claiming the rule and challenging the Lord's title (Matt. 4:10, 3). The war we wage here (Eph. 6:12) is a continuation of the conflict in the beginning. (Hypostasis of the Archons 134:20). Those who follow either leader here, followed the same there. (John 8:44, 7; Odes Sol. 24:5-9.)

41. Apocryphon of James 53:12ff. (the gifts); Apocryphon of Adam 85:1-2 (ordinances); *1012 Questions*, II, 3b, 86 (226-27) (signs); 2 Thes. 2:9 (wonders); Bodmer Papyrus 10:54 (doctrine); Apocalypse of Elias 1:8ff. (glory); they are even rival fishermen (Logion, No. 174, in M. Osin et Palacias, "Logia et agrapha D. Jesu," *Patrologia Orientalis* [hereinafter "*PO*"] 19:574).

42. Matt. 6:19-21; 13:10ff.; 19:21, 29; Mark 10:21; 12:41ff.; Luke 18:21-22; 12:21, 32; Rom. 2:5; 1 Tim. 6:17-19; Jer. 48:7; Ben Sirach 5:2. Many Logia deal with the theme. (M. A. Palacias, "Logia et agrapha," Nos. 13-14, 34, 42, 44, 50, 53-55, 77 [in Graffin, *PO* 13:357ff.].)

So the Gospel of Thomas, 37, 137, 147; Apocalypse of Elias 8:12-13; Psalms of Thomas 1:17-19; Apocryphon of James 2:53; Acts of Thomas 37, 137, 147; Gospel of Thomas 85:6ff.; 86:24-29; 92; 94:14-22; 95:15; 98:31–99:4; Slavonic Adam and Eve 33:1ff. It is important not to confuse the treasure or to falsify. (*Ginza*, pp. 19, 40, 123-24, 334, 394, 433; cf. Pistis Sophia 100 [249-51]; *Berlin Manich. Hs.* 1:223, 228-29; *Manichaean Psalm-Book*, II, 75, 79, 82.)

43. Hence the paradox that the "poor" are the rich. (*Epist. to Diognetus* 5; *Manichaean Psalm-Book*, II, 157.) See below, note 45.

44. Treasures now "prepared" and awaiting the righteous on the other side (Mark 10:40; Gospel of Truth, fol. XXIv, 11-17) can be claimed only by meeting certain stipulations (Gospel of Philip 108:1ff.). All treasures are held in trust, "dedicated" (1 Chron. 26:20; Pseudo-Philo 21:3), and will be handed over when the time comes (1 Enoch 51:1). The righteous "without fear leave this world," because they have with God "a store of works preserved in treasuries." (2 Baruch 14:12; 24:1.) Whatever part of the Treasure we enjoy on earth is not ours but has only been entrusted to our keeping. (*1012 Questions*, I, i; 111-12; 122-23.) On the "treasury of good works" as an old Oriental doctrine, see K. Ahrens, *ZDMG* 84 (1930): 163. One's good works will lead to future rewards and recompense, says Ignatius, *Epist. ad Polycarp* 6. The Christian (Manichaean) and Chinese versions are compared by A. Adam, in J. Leipoldt, *Religionsgeschichte des Orients*, p. 109; for the Iranian version, see D. Winston, in *History of Religions* 5 (1966): 194-95, who also mentions concealing the treasure under God's throne (p. 212), to which parallels are supplied by 2 Baruch 54:13; *Ginza*, p. 281; the Shabako Stone, line 61; and the Ark of the Covenant "under the feet of the statue of God," W. H. Irwin, *Revue Biblique* 72 (1965): 164. This is the theme of The Pearl.

45. Matt. 25:14-29. The rich man is welcome to his treasures on earth but cannot claim treasures in heaven. (Matt. 19:21, 24; 6:19-20; Mark 10:25; Luke 18:22; 12:33-34; 2 Baruch 44:13-15; Secrets of Enoch 1:5; Gospel of Thomas 88:34-35; 89:1ff.; Acts of Thomas 146; *1012 Questions*, II, iv, 159 [245].) It is a Jewish, Christian, and Mandaean tradition that earthly prayers are laid up in God's treasure-house. (*Johannesbuch der Mand.*, 10, n. 2; Mandaean Prayerbook, No. 379 [*CPM*, 293].) If a righteous one strays, "his treasure will be taken from him." (Alma Rishaia Zuta, 1 [in E. Drower, *Nasoraean Commentaries*, p. 55]; *Berlin Manich. Hs.* 1:73.)

46. Apocalypsis Pauli, 19 (text in *Orientalia* 2 [1933]: 22); cf. 2 Baruch 52:7; *1012 Questions*, vib, 379 (279).

47. IQS 4:16-18. This is an "Abbild" of the cosmic struggle. (J. Schreiner, in *BZ*, NF 9 (1965): 180; J. M. Allegro, in *Jnl. of Semit. Stud.* 9 (1964): 291-94.

48. For the erasing of the memory, see below, note 60. The "Law of Liberty" (*Khoq kherut*) of IQS 10:6, 11, is "the Ancient Law of Liberty" of *Clementine Recognitions* 2:23-25; 3:26, 59; 4:24, 34: 10:2; cf. Minucius Felix, *Octav.* 27; Cyril of Jerusalem, *Catehesis* 4:19-20 (in Migne, *PG* 33:481). Having such freedom, the wicked have deliberately rejected God's plan. (IQS 4:25-26.) Though the evil spirits are fiercely opposed to this liberty (*Clementine Recognitions* 1:42), the "testing of election for every single individual" goes on without coercion in "truth, righteousness, humility, judgment," etc., while the self-willed are free "to go the way of their own heart . . . according to the plan of his own devising" (IQS 5:3-5), the spirit being "immortal, rational and independent" (*Const. Apostol.* 6:11; Tatian, *Adv. Graecos* 7). The present test was appointed from the beginning. (IQM 13:14ff.) "This is the condition of the contest which every man who is born on the earth must wage; if he be overcome, he shall suffer; . . . if he be victorious, he shall receive what I said." (4 Ezra 7:127-29; cf. IQH 14:23.) It is "a testing-time in the common light." (Sibylline Oracles, frg. 18.) See further J. B. Bauer, *Theolog. Zeitschr.* 20 (1964): 2-3.

49. A. Adam, "Die Psalmen des Thomas u. das Perlenlied," *ZNTW*, Beih. 24 (1959): 49-54. The Syriac text is given by G. Hoffman in *ZNTW* 4 (1903): 273-83, bearing the title "Song of Judas Thomas the Apostle in the Land of India." Thomas's situation in India resembles that of the hero in the Land of Egypt. The pearl itself comes from the other world and is that part of the heavenly knowledge that is to be found here (*Mandaean Prayerbook.* No. 252 [*CPM*, 208-9]); when it is taken away the world collapses (*Ginza*, p. 517); it is the pure pearl that was transported from the treasuries of Life (*Mandaean Prayerbook*, No. 69). The robe of glory, left behind with the Treasure, is to be regained with it. (Bartholomew, "Book of the Resurrection of Christ," Fol. 18b [in E.A.W. Budge, *Coptic Apocrypha*, p. 208]; Pistis Sophia 6 [9-10].)

50. J. Leipoldt, *Religionsgeschichte des Orients*, p. 86; Abp. Timothy on Abbaton, fol. 20b. The joyful homecoming is a conspicuous Egyptian theme from the beginning: there is rejoicing among the great ones, for one of their own has returned. (*Pyramid Texts*, No. 606 [1696], 217 [160]; 222 [201]; 212, 213, etc.; *Coffin Texts* [de Buck], II, Spells 31, 132.) The theme is discussed by H. Brunner, in *Aegypt. Zeitschr.* 80 (1955): 6-7. The righteous are homesick. (1 Enoch 14:4; 42:1ff.; *Manichaean Psalm-Book*, II, 197-200, 87.) Going to heaven is a

return. (4 Ezra 7:78; John 17:5-6; 3:7-13; Rev. 5:12.) The Saints desire "to be received back again" into "the first Church [that] . . . existed from the beginning," before the Creation. (2 Clem. Epist. 14; Clementine Recognitions 3:26; Test. Dom. nostri J. Christi, 28 [61]; Abp. Timothy on Abbaton, fol. 20b; 12a; Gospel of Phillip 115:13.) The Saints find the Kingdom because they came from there. (Gospel of Thomas 89:27; Pastor Hermae, III [Simil. 1, the Pearl motif]; Apocalypsis Pauli 43:9; 44:6ff.; Apocryphon of James 1:27:5ff., 12; 31:13-25; 2:58:2ff.) "The Living Ones will return again to the Treasure which is theirs." (Psalms of Thomas 1:49; cf. 18:1ff.; 17:20ff.) In the end everything returns to its "root." (Creation Apocryphon 175:4; cf. J. Zandee, Numen 11 [1964]: 66.) Those above are equally impatient for the reuniting. (Pistis Sophia, 10 [16-19]; Manichaean Psalm-Book, II, 201, 72, 136.)

51. In reclaiming its treasure, the spirit "becomes what it was before removing its garment." (Apocryphon of James 2:56:11ff.; cf. Gospel of Philip 105:19; Psalms of Thomas 2:70-72, 74, 77; Acts of Thomas 6-7 (lines 35-55 of The Pearl); Second Gnostic Work i-a; Ginza pp. 487, 26-27; Odes Sol. 11:10.) The garment is the treasure for both men and angels (Ginza, p. 13); the garment of Adam and Eve "was like the Treasure of Life" (ibid., p. 243); it is a protection for the righteous that the evil ones try to seize and possess (ibid., pp. 247, 259, 132).

52. The garment represents ritual in general. (C. Schmidt, in TU 8 [1892]: 347.)

53. 1012 Questions, pp. 212, 241; the ordinances are "the treasures that transcend the world." (Ibid., p. 245.) "Ginza" means "a treasure, mystery, sacrament, . . . what is hidden and precious." (Ibid., p. 12.) As guardian of these secrets and mysteries, the Eldest Son is called "the Treasurer." (Ginza, p. 150.) The eldest are they who observe the ordinances secretly in this world (ibid., pp. 153-54), and their highest duty is to transmit and explain these rites to their children (Mandaean Prayerbook, No. 373 [CPM, 266]). See S. A. Pallis, Mandaean Studies, p. 192.

54. Discussed by B. Gärtner, The Temple and Community in Qumran and the New Testament (Cambridge Univ.: 1965), pp. 16ff. The temple with its rites is the earthly counterpart of the heavenly treasury. (1 Baruch 4:3-5.) Since the Creation, the ordinances have been essential to God's plan. (Jubilees 6:18.) It is in the cultus that the cosmic plan is unfolded. (N. A. Dahl, in W. D. Davies and D. Daube, eds., Background of the New Testament, pp. 430-31.) And the return of the temple is the return of the heavenly order. (4QFlor. 1; 6.)

55. That is, 1 and 2 Jeu and the Second Gnostic Work. Without

the "mysteries," one has no power and no light (Pistis Sophia 55 [107]); this is a "Hauptthema" of the Gospel of Phillip 124. The old temple rite of the shewbread is an initiation to the Treasury of Light (Pistis Sophia 4:142). One's station (*taxis*) hereinafter depends entirely on the mysteries one has "received" on earth. (Ibid., 90 [202]; 86 [195]; 32 [52]; 125 [317]; 129 [329].) Without the performance of certain ordinances, no one, no matter how righteous, can enter into the Light. (Pistis Sophia 103 [263].) Hence the rites are all-important. (Ibid., 107, 11 [279], 100 [249-250].) One becomes "an heir of the Treasure of Light by becoming perfect in all the mysteries." (2 Jeu 76; 1 Jeu 5; Apocryphon of John 53:11ff.)

56. K. Ahrens, in *ZDMG* 84 (1930): 163; quotation is from D. Winston, *History of Religions* 5 (1966): 195, giving Jewish and Avestan sources; cf. 1QS 10:4, 2:3, Secrets of Enoch 40:9-10. At the fall of the temple "the heavens shut up the treasure of the rain" and the priests "[took] the Keys of the sanctuary, and cast them into the height of heaven." (2 Baruch 10:18.) The key to the Mandaean *kushta* (initiation rights) is held by the Master of the Treasurehouse. (*Ginza*, pp. 429-30.) So also in the Pistis Sophia 133 (351), the ordinances are "the keys to the Kingdom of Heaven." The keys that Christ gave to Peter were those to "the Heavenly Treasure." (Epistola XII Apostolorum, Frg. 2, in Migne, *PO* 2:147.)

57. 2 Jeu 73 (in C. Schmidt, *TU* 8:211-12); the same image is in Pistis Sophia 14 (23); cf. IQH 17:21: "God has chosen his elect . . . instructed him in the understanding of his mysteries so that he could not go astray . . . fortified by his secrets." Through definite ordinances one progresses in the community and helps others to progress (IQH 14:17-18), teaching of "the Creation and of the Treasures of Glory" (IQM 10:12-13), and testing the knowledge of the members (IQM 17:8; IQSb [Isaiah Scroll—Hebrew University] 3:22-26). In the Coptic works, all the rites "serve a single *oekonomia*, i.e., the gathering in of the spirits who have received the mysteries, so that they can be sealed . . . and proceed to the *kleronomia* (heritage) of Light . . . called in the literal sense of the word of the Treasure of Light." (C. Schmidt, in *TU* 8 [1892]: 365.) In Pastor Hermae, I, Vision 3:5, the Saints are raised up by degrees, being tested at each step, to be incorporated into the precious tower.

58. *1012 Questions*, pp. 212, 241. See Morton Smith, *The Secret Gospel* (N.Y.: Harpers, 1972), pp. 96, 115, 83.

59. J. Zandee, in *Numen* 11 (1964): 44. Adam is the type of the initiate (*Ep. Barnab.* 6:11-16) from whom the mysteries have been handed down (Apocryphon of Adam 85:19ff.). He was privy to the whole plan of creation (2 Baruch 4:2ff.; Secrets of Enoch 30:13ff.),

being in the "Creation Hymn" (Gen. 1:26ff.) as "God's counterpart as a speaking, active, personal being" (J. B. Bauer, in *Theol. Zeitschr.* 20:8), a historical, *not* a mythological, character (ibid., p. 7). He "came forth out of the light of the invisible place" (Pseudo-Philo 28:9) and received the first anointing (Creation Apocryphon 159:5; *Clementine Recognitions* 1:47). It is "the light of Adam" that leads men back to the Light (Psalms of Thomas 4:9ff.); and the faithful are promised "all the glory of Adam" (IQS 4:23). He is called "the son of the Treasuries of Radiance" in the *Mandaean Prayerbook*, No. 379 (*CPM*, 290).

60. On the sleep of forgetting, see The Pearl 34; Psalms of Thomas 15:5-10; Apocryphon of Adam 65:14-21; Abp. Timothy on Abbaton, fol. 15b; Sophia Christi 106:1-10; Creation Apocryphon 158:25; Apocryphon of James 1:28:14, 22-23; Hypostasis of the Archons 137:1-5. It is the "Sem-sleep" of the Egyptian initiation rites. It is also expressed in terms suggesting Plato's Cup of Lethe (*Manichaean Psalm-Book*, II, 7, 57, 117), and as the dropping of a veil (Sophia Christi 120 [in *TU*, 60:280]; Pistis Sophia 131 [336-38]; *Ginza*, p. 34); the Cup of Lethe plays an important role in the Greek mysteries; to a lesser extent the Cup of Memory is discussed by C. Schmidt in *TU* 8 (1892): 405-6.

61. Called "Three Great Men" in Apocryphon of Adam 66:12ff., they are three archangels. (Creation Apocryphon 152:23; Sophia Christi 96:3ff.; Second Gnostic Work 19a.) They are sent down to instruct and accompany Adam. (*Ginza*, pp. 15, 33-35.) They are the Three Uthras, "sent into the world to fetch the Elect . . . back to the House of Light." (R. Bultmann, in *ZNTW* 24 [1925]: 132.) Thus Enoch is fetched by three men in white (1 Enoch 90:31), who also visit Abraham (Gen. 18:1-2; Genesis Apocryphon 21:21). For the Jewish version of the Three Men in White, see R. Goodenough, *Jewish Symbols in the Greco-Roman Period* (New York: Pantheon, 1958) 9:102-4, 84-89; 10:91-96. Cf. J. Barbel, "Zur Engel-trinitätslehre im Urchristentum," in *Theological Review* 54 (1954): 48-58, 103-12; K. Rudolph, *Die Mandäer*, I, 162, noting that these three were the arch-types of the Sent Ones in general.

62. Cf. Odes Sol. 29:1ff.; 22:1; Psalms of Thomas 5:28; Gospel of Truth, fol. XIv, 22; 1 Jeu 3; *Berlin Manich. Hs.* 1:56; not only Adam but every patriarch after him is instructed by a Sent One. (*Johannesbuch der Mand.*, 57ff., No. 13, 14; 60, n. 6.) Indeed, the Sent Ones are to help every mortal back "to the place from which he came." (*Ginza*, p. 244; cf. IQS 11:1; Luke 1:76-79 [John the Baptist as a Sent One].) The adversary also has his sent ones. (Pistis Sophia 66 [136].)

63. Being rejected like the poor, the Sent Ones may be identified

with them. (R. Bultmann, in *ZNTW* 24 [1925]: 124.) The evil spirits accuse the Sent Ones of being aliens and meddlers in the earth (*Ginza*, pp. 263-64) and accuse Adam and his descendants of the same thing. The poor are the true heirs. (4QPs 37:3-10; Odes Sol. 8:6-13); see K. Romaniuk, in *Aegyptus* 44 (1964): 85, 88, citing Old Testament and New Testament parallels to Egyptian teachings. Their "angels" have unbroken contact with the Father. (Matt. 18:10.)

64. The Sent One is the treasure. (C. Schmidt, in *TU* 8 [1892]: 349.) The Saints receive the law "by angels" (literally, "sent ones") (Acts 7:53), there being six angels (cf. six dispensations) (Pastor Hermae, I, Vision 3:4). "For there has come from the plains of heaven a blessed man . . . and [he] has restored to all the good the wealth [treasure] which the former men took away," namely, the ordinances of the temple. (Sibylline Oracles 5:414-33.) "Thou didst appoint from the beginning a Prince of Light to assist us." (IQM 13:10.) Enos, Enoch, Moses, and Joshua were such Sent Ones (*Const. Apostol.* 7:38), as was John the Baptist, restoring lost ordinances and preparing the people for things to come (John 1:6; Luke 1:16-17; Heb. 1:14; cf. IQS 9:11). Those who accept the plan had a pure begetting through the First Sent One. (Sophia Christi 82:12.) Like Adam, everyone is awakened from the sleep of forgetfulness by a Sent One. (Ibid., 94:5ff.) Angels and prophets are sent to bring men "what is theirs" (Gospel of Thomas 96:7), instructing them in the mysteries (Mysteries of Heaven and Earth 4:1, in Graffin, *PO*, 4:428; Bodmer Papyrus, 10:53). Adam himself became a Sent One to help his children. (Psalms of Thomas 5:26-28; 4:1-10, 12-17.) The instructions to the Sent One and his two counselors were to teach Adam and his posterity what they must know and do to return to the Light. (*Ginza*, pp. 16, 17, 18, 41, 57ff., 113 [on the teaching of ordinances], 119); for the Sent One is in special charge of the Treasure of Life in this world and the other (ibid., p. 96).

65. It was by "a letter of command from the Father" that "the Son of Truth inherited and took possession of everything." (Odes Sol. 23:15-17; The Pearl.) The "King's Letter" is one's passport to heaven. (*1012 Questions*, p. 198.) As a knowledge of the ordinances, the Treasure is an actual scroll, written by the hand of the Lord of Greatness. (Alma Rishaia Zuta 72.) Writing is one of the Ten Treasures of the Creation. (Pesachim, fol. 54a.) The heavenly books are "Beweisdokumente" (L. Koep, *Das himmlische Buch* . . . [Bonn: Hanstein, 1952], pp. 54-61); for example, The Book of Deeds is a written contract between Christ and Adam (ibid., p. 64). "Thou hast engraved them on the Tablets of Life for kingship." (IQM 12:3, discussed by F. Notscher in *Revue de Qumran* 1 [1959]: 405-12.) For the Mandaeans the holy books *are* heavenly treasures. (*1012 Questions*, p. 158-59, 170,

252.) The holy books were often literally treasures, being inscribed on precious metals and buried in the earth like other treasures. (H. Nibley, "Qumran and the Companions of the Cave," *Revue de Qumran* 5 [1965]: 191-92.) The idea of books as treasures is a natural one. "The treasures of the wise men of old are the books they have left us." (Xenophon, *Memorab.*, I, 4:14.)

66. We have given some examples in "Christian Envy of the Temple," *Jewish Quarterly Review* (hereinafter cited as *"JQR"*) 50 (1959): 97ff., 229ff.; reprinted in *When the Lights Went Out* (Salt Lake City: Deseret Book Co., 1970), pp. 54ff.

67. J. B. Frey, in *Biblica* 13 (1932): 164.

68. For the first formula, see M. R. James, *Biblical Antiquities of Philo*, pp. 44, 56. Luther called the second *"locus vexatissimus,"* and indeed it "makes impossible a spiritual interpretation" of the *kerygma*. (M. H. Scharlemann, in *Concordia Theological Monthly* 27 [1956]: 86, 89-90.)

69. Quotation from J. Frankowski, in *Verbum Domini* 43 (1965): 149. See also below, notes 91, 96, 97.

70. Pistis Sophia 84 (185-86), 85 (189); on the basic materials, ibid., pp. 247-48.

71. In the Genesis Apocryphon 2:4, Lamech swears by "the King of all the Ages [*'olamim*]" (cf. the common Moslem expressions); God made the "worlds" (Odes Sol. 16:19; 12:4, 8); all the worlds worship the Sent One as "Illuminator of their worlds" (ibid., 11:12; so Psalms of Thomas 8:13, 6ff.; *1012 Questions*, p. 112); "other worlds" have been going on forever (Gospel of Philip 106:18-19). The created world is plural in Apocryphon of John 21:22; the worlds assemble before him (Psalms of Thomas 8:6). The angel who came to Isaiah was of another firmament and another world. (Ascension of Isaiah 6:13.) The adversary opposed the plan of God "to create another world" and to put Adam in charge. (Secrets of Enoch 31:3.) A logion depicts the Saints hereafter moving freely through space among the spheres. ("Logia et agrapha," No. 127, in Graffin, *PO* 19:547; cf. 2 Baruch 48:9.) The Father is in the worlds *(kosmois)*, and the Son is first and highest among those worlds *(en toisde tois kosmois)*, according to an early Liturgy, in Graffin, *PO* 18:445-46, 448. Each heaven is completely equipped with thrones, dwellings, temples, etc., and there are many such heavens. (Creation Apocryphon 150:18ff., 23-25.) The Archon Jaldaboth created beautiful heavens for his sons (ibid., 150:9-10; Hypostasis of the Archons 144:5-10), furnished with stolen materials (see above, note 39).

72. Ascension of Isaiah 10:13; Creation Apocryphon 148:29-30; *Ginza*, p. 80; they say, "There is only one world—ours!"

73. Odes Sol. 12:3; 16:14-16; Gospel of Truth, fol. XIVr, 11-16; Apoc-

ryphon of John 26:2-3; 21:1ff.; 1 Enoch 2:1; 43:1; 2 Baruch 43:9; *Epist. 1 Clement* 20. When God created this world, all the other worlds rejoiced together. (Second Gnostic Work 47a.) The worlds borrow light from each other and exchange all they know (*Ginza*, pp. 10-11); they form a single lively community (*Mandaean Prayerbook*, No. 379, 303, 298-99), all the mysteries being "shared out amongst the worlds of light" (*1012 Questions*, pp. 112, 164). In a pinch, the "Treasures" help each other out. (Psalms of Thomas 23:25.)

74. Quotation is from the *Johannesbuch der Mand.*, 207, No. 59. See also Odes Sol. 12:4-9; *1012 Questions*, p. 213; *Mandaean Prayerbook*, No. 379 (*CPM*, p. 296). This seems to be an Eastern tradition, the others being more concerned with emissaries and messengers; see the following notes.

75. Second Gnostic Work 45a; cf. *Manichaean Psalm-Book*, II, 23, 66. On his visits each world implores him to stay "and be our King and bring peace to our city!" (*Ginza*, p. 258.) In other words, it is a true Parousia. (Psalms of Thomas 8:1-14; cf. John 10:16.)

76. Two hundred angels act as interplanetary messengers. (Secrets of Enoch 4:1.) The business of the angels is to coordinate the working of the central plan among the worlds. (F. Dieterici, *Thier und Mensch vor dem König der Genien* [Leipzig: 1881], pp. 78-79.) The heavenly bodies receive commands from a single center (M. R. James, *Biblical Antiquities of Philo*, p. 43), the highest heaven being the "indispensable exchange-center between the spheres" (K. Koch, in *ZThK* 62 [1965]: 275); the affairs of "the incomprehensible expanse of the structure of heaven" are directed from a command-post in the center (Creation Apocryphon 146:15-20). The rulers dispatch "letters from world to world and reveal the truth to each other, and there are some souls that travel like an arrow and cleave through all the worlds." (*1012 Questions*, p. 192, cf. p. 164.) Adakas "is a 'go-between' between the worlds" (*Mandaean Prayerbook*, p. 293), and Manda d-Haiai, called "the Capable" by his brother úthras, is called "to regulate and to station the úthras in their places" among the worlds (ibid., p. 294). In the beginning of the Apocalypse of Paul 1:1-2, Paul is ordered "to go down and speak to the planet earth" (*lé alma de arga*). Visitors to celestial regions in the various Testaments (Abraham, Isaac, Isaiah, the 12 Patriarchs, Adam, etc.) report a traffic of chariots in the spaces. (See, for example, 1 Enoch 75:8.) By whatever means, they circulate ceaselessly among the worlds with marvelous ease. (*Ginza*, pp. 13, 42.) The Mandaean faithful are urged to "be informed about all worlds" as far as possible. (*1012 Questions*, p. 289.) The worlds of darkness also communicate, but on another level. (*Berlin Manich. Hs.* 1:32.)

77. Ben Sirach 42:24-25; Odes Sol. 12:9; "each is more wonderful than the other!" (*Ginza*, pp. 11-13); so also *Johannesbuch der Mand.*, No. 59, 207, explaining that it is "the power of the Treasure" that makes such rich variety possible. Among ten thousand times ten thousand worlds "every world is different from the others." (*Ginza*, p. 152.) Even the worlds of darkness are all different. (*Berlin Manich. Hs.* 1:68.) One cannot describe how another world differs entirely from every other (Pistis Sophia 88:199); no other world can be described in terms of this one, so different are they all (ibid., p. 84 [183]).

78. Wisdom of Solomon 19:18. On the letters of the alphabet as elements of creation, see "Sefer Yeshira," texts by P. Mordell, in *JQR*, N.S. 3 (1913): 536-44.

79. The Creation is compared to the smashing of inferior vessels to use their substance for better ones (Gospel of Truth, fol. XIIIv, 25ff.), or the melting down of scrap metal for reuse (*Manichaean Psalm-Book*, II, 11), or the breaking of an egg that a more perfect form might emerge (*Clementine Recognitions* 3:27-29; cf. *1012 Questions*, p. 183; *Ginza*, pp. 83-84). God spares some worlds from dismantling until they have fulfilled their purpose. (Psalms of Thomas 2:30-31.) While treasure ships carry matter through space (see above, note 38), the Seven Planets "intercept all the goods bestowed by the constellations and divert them to the use of the demons" in furbishing their worlds. (D. Winston, *History of Religions* 5 [1966]: 193.) The fullest treatment is in *Berlin Manich. Hs.* 1:109, 111-14, 177, where it is even necessary to decontaminate older materials before reusing! (Ibid., pp. 113-14, 130.)

80. E. A. E. Reymond, *The Mystical Origin of the Egyptian Temple* (Manchester Univ. Press: 1969), p. 187.

81. H. F. Weiss, *Hellenist. Judentum*, pp. 92-99.

82. Ibid., pp. 22ff.

83. Ibid., p. 146.

84. Ibid., pp. 29-36, citing many sources. It is the business of the Demiurge to *organize* rather than to produce out of nothing. (Ibid., pp. 44ff.)

85. *1012 Questions*, p. 164. "There is abundant room in thy Paradise, and nothing is useless therein." (Odes Sol. 11:20.) There is a remarkable picture of the struggle for survival, however, when life began in the waters: "They attacked one another and slew one another, saying to one another: 'Move off out of my way. . . . Move on that I may come!'" (*1012 Questions*, p. 184.)

86. *1012 Questions*, p. 111; Gospel of Philip 104:18-19; the *physis* itself is "imperishable, complete, and boundless" (Creation Apocryphon 146:11).

87. It represents "die Begrenzung und Begrenztheit der Welt." (E. Hornung, *Aegypt. Zeitschr.* 97 [1971]: 78.)

88. Pistis Sophia 127 (323-24); L. Kakosy, in *Aegypt. Zeitschr.* 97 (1971): 104-5.

89. Worlds come and go; only progeny (sonship) is eternal (Gospel of Philip 123:6-13); "The man of heaven, many are his Sons, more than the man of earth. If the sons of Adam are many but die, how many more the sons of the perfect man, they who do not die but are begotten at all times" (ibid., 106:17). "Mounting up from world to world" is from *1012 Questions*, p. 192, and his "perfection" from the Gospel of Truth, fol. XXV, 4-14. The ultimate objective is to receive the same glory that the Son received from the Father in the beginning (John 17:22); the *Epistle to Diognetus* 10 tells us not to marvel at this—man must become the heir of divinity in the fullest sense (C. Schmidt, in *TU* 8 [1892]: 319-20; Gospel of Philip 100:1ff., 11; 101:1ff.; Psalms of Solomon 1:3-4). It is important not to get stuck "in the middle" and so delay progress (C. Schmidt, *op. cit.,* p. 335), this world being merely a bridge,according to the famous logion(Graffin, *PO*, 13, No. 75). The fundamental nature of Godhood is to beget and create. (Sophia Christi 87:1-88:1.)

90. G. Thausing, *Mitt. dt. Inst. Kairo* 8 (1939): 63-64.

91. This is the *ametretos bathos* in which a sector is staked out for a new creation. (Second Gnostic Work 9a.) Ptahil-Uthra is ordered: "Go down to a place where there are no *Shkinas* (dwellings) and no other worlds, and make thee a world as the Sons of Salvation do." (*Ginza*, p. 98.) God plans for the occupancy of all the "spaces" ahead of time. (Gospel of Truth, fol. XIVr, 11-16.) One seeks release by moving "from the more confined to the more spacious places." (Pistis Sophia 47 [83].) The role of space in creation is vividly depicted in Egyptian temple-founding rites, in which the king, representing God creating the world, takes sightings on the stars in a pure and empty place. (A. Moret, *Du caractere religieux de la royaute pharaonique* [Paris: 1902], pp. 130-42; R. T. R. Clark, *Myth and Symbol in Ancient Egypt* [London: Thames, 1959], p. 80.) Preparing for the creation of the world, "Marduk went into the heavens, inspecting the places, and there he established a new one, an exact replica . . . of the dwelling place of Ea." (Enuma Elish 4:142.) "Space and time are the plan of the world-system." (G. S. Fullerton, *Philosophical Review* 10 [1910]: 595.)

92. The work begins with *hyle*. (C. Schmidt, *TU* 8 [1892]: 365, 372.) Although "we do not know whether Hyle was already present in the Treasury of Light or not," there was a "*kerasmos* in which Light and Matter are mixed in various proportions." (Ibid., p. 383.) "Kenaz" in the *Visio Kenaz* (M. R. James, *Apocr. Anecdota*, II, No. 3 [Cambridge:

1893], pp. 178-79) sees "flames that do not consume and fountains stirring into life" amid a vague substance taking form at the Creation. Those who were with God "before his works of old" are later "to inherit substance, and fill their treasures" (Prov. 8:19-22), referring perhaps to a new, material phase of creation; see above, notes 80-84.

93. It is well for men not to contemplate the *bathos* too intently. (Gospel of Truth, fol. XIXr, 8-9; 1 Enoch, frgs. in R. H. Charles, *The Book of Enoch* [Oxford: 1912], p. 297; Evang. Barthol., frg. 3, in *Revue Biblique* 10 [1913]: 326.) "Matter having no fixity or stability" is repellent. (Gospel of Truth, fol. XIIIv, 15ff.; Pistis Sophia 39 [63]; Apoc. of Abraham 16-17.) Sophia's first advice to her son was, "Get a foothold, O youth, in these places!" (Creation Apocryphon 148:12; 149:6.) The foothold idea may have inspired the ubiquitous image of the "Rock," e.g., in IQS 11:5; R. Eisler, *Iesous Basileus* (Heidelberg: 1930), II, 286-87. Preparing for the Creation, Marduk, having found his space, established the stations (fixed points of reference) beside the star *Nibiru*, firmly bolted on the left and on the right. (Enuma Elish 5:8-10.)

94. Second Gnostic Work 2a-3s; 18a. The *fundamentum* of a world begins to take form when touched by a *scintilla*, but "the spark ceases and the fountain is stopped" when the inhabitants transgress. (*Visio Kenaz.*) Matter without Light is inert and helpless (Pistis Sophia 55 [107]; *Berlin Manich. Hs.* 1:130); it is the "first light" which reproduces "the pattern of the heavenly model" wherever it touches. (Creation Apocryphon 146:20.) For "rays from the worlds of light stream down to the earthly world" for the awakening of mortals (*1012 Questions*, pp. 199-200); sometimes a column of light joins earth to heaven ("Synax. Arab.," in Graffin *PO* 11:754), even as the divine plan is communicated to distant worlds by a spark (Second Gnostic Work 29a-30a); it is the *"dynamis* of Light" that animates one world from another (C. Schmidt, *TU* 8 [1892]: 331). God's assistants, "the faithful servants of Melchizedek," rescue and preserve the light particles lest any be lost in space. (C. Schmidt, *TU* 8 [1892]: 404; cf. Second Gnostic Work.) The spark is also called a "drop" (Sophia Christi 104:7ff.); it is "the divine drop of light that he [man] brought with him from above" (ibid., 119:1ff.). The Spark can reactivate bodies that have become inert by the loss of former light. (Pistis Sophia 65 [134].) It is like a tiny bit of God himself, "die kleine Idee." (C. Schmidt, *TU* 8 [1892]: 396; H. Zandee, *Numen* 11 [1964]: 67.)

95. C. Schmidt, *TU* 8 (1892): 333. Knowledge of the divine plan is communicated to the worlds by a spark (Second Gnostic Work 29a-30a); the Father "let an idea come out of His Treasury" (1 Jeu 7), even as "the Son of Radiance" is sent forth to enlighten the worlds" (Psalms of Thomas 8:12); such an ambassador is himself a "treasure-

chamber of Life" (ibid., 3:18). All the mysteries are "shared out" among 380 Worlds of Light "as they emanate from the Supreme Celestial World." (*1012 Questions*, p. 112.) God is "pure radiance, a precious Treasure of Light, the Intelligence which correcteth the hearts of all our kings!" (Ibid., p. 123.) The "Emanation" (*probole*) is a sharing of treasures, so that "der Lichtschatz ist also der Gipfelpunkt des Universums." (C. Schmidt, *TU* 8 [1892]: 325, 266.) "The sparks from the Crown scatter to every Place" (*Ginza*, p. 7); the Power of Light, radiating into surrounding chaos, produces a higher type of *topos* wherever it goes (Pistis Sophia, 58 [112]), the creation process being the adding of Light and its power to dark chaotic matter (ibid., 47 [84], 48 [85-86], 50 [90]). Every *phoster* goes back to the same Root. (*Manichaean Psalm-Book*, II, 26, 138.)

96. An important part of God's plan is the providing of a proper *topos* for the Saints. (Pastor Hermae, III, Simil. 5:6.) Each *topos* awaiting occupants is the result of the diffusion of the Treasure. (1 Jeu 11.) For "there has previously been prepared a place [*topos*] for every soul of man" (Secrets of Enoch 49:2; 58:4ff.), "mansions . . . without number" (6:12). The work of Jesus was to collect the treasures of the Father into one blessed *topos* of meeting. (Acts of Thomas 48.) While the elect have their mansions (1 Enoch 41:1-9), there are special places set apart for spirits in transition (ibid., 22:3, 9). For each specific group yet to be born, a place has been prepared. (2 Baruch 23:4.) The earthly and heavenly hosts alike have their assigned places. (IQM 12:1-2.) There is an assigned place of glory for each hereafter (*Epist. 1 Clem.* 5, 6; Polycarp, *Epist. ad Phil.* 9; Apocryphon of Adam 69:19ff.); everyone should know to what *topos* he has been called and live accordingly (*Epist. 2 Clem.* 1, 5; Ignatius, *ad Magnes.* 5; Polycarp, 11; Oxyrhynchus Frg., No. 654:22). No one gets a *topos* without earning it. (Ignatius, *ad Smyrn.* 6; Pastor Hermae, III, Simil. 8:3, 5, 8; Apocalypse of Elias 6:6ff.) The *topothesias* of the angels greatly interested the early Saints. (Ignatius, *ad Trall.* 5.)

97. The central *topos* is the Treasury of the true God (C. Schmidt, *TU* 8 [1892]: 367); it is "the topos from which all aeons and all cosmoses take their pattern and their origin" (Sophia Christi 116 [in *TU* 60:266ff.]). It is "the self-produced and self-begotten topos" from which all others are derived (Second Gnostic Work 1a); it is called "the God-bearing" *topos*, or "land of the begetting of gods" (ibid., 21a). Early views of the Creation can be related to the establishment of God's reign over a particular land. (W. Richter, *BZ*, NF 10 [1966]: 96-105.) The colonization of worlds is always a family affair: "All of them He raised Him up" to "fill the face of the earth with their seed." (Zadokite Doc. 2:10.) The inhabitants are the progeny or seed of

those who sent them (1 Enoch 39:1; *1012 Questions*. pp. 118, 170-71; Sophia Christi 88:7ff.; 98:1-99:5ff.; Apocryphon of James 1:43:5ff.), called "chosen seed, or seed of promise" (J. Zandee, in *Numen* 11 [1964]: 45-46). When "elect and holy children . . . descend from heaven, . . . their seed will become one with the children of men." (1 Enoch 39:1.) Simat-Hiia, the primordial Eve, is "mother of all kings, from whom all worlds proceeded." (Alma Rishaia Rba 6:388ff. [in E. Drower, *Nasoraean Commentaries*, p. 29].) A colonizing activity is described in Pistis Sophia 16 (26-27), 25 (36-37), 24 (34-35). Lactantius mentions polemically the idea of real seeds floating around in space. (*Div. Inst.* 3:17.)

98. "Planting" can here mean create, beget, establish, or assist; that is, it is the proper work of the "Sent One," according to M. Lidzbarski, *Johannesbuch der Mand.*, p. 60, n. 6, and *Berlin Manich. Hs.* 1:53-54. Eden was God's planting on earth. (W. Richter, *BZ*, NF, 10 [1966]: 101-2.) "I said that the world should be, . . . [saying] I will plant a great vineyard, and out of it I will choose a plant," that is, the Chosen People (Pseudo-Philo 28:4); the Qumran Community calls itself a planting (IQS 8:5; 11:15), as does the early Church (Irenaeus, *adv. Haeres.*, V, 36:1). God's "planting in the world of men" includes providing necessary physical substances (Psalms of Thomas 3:29-35) and the "planting" of light in a place of darkness (ibid. 7:17). God, before the world existed, planted the earth and then planted the Garden in it (4 Esdras 3:4, 6); He is the "Greatest of Gardeners," "the Planter" par excellence (H. F. Weiss, *Hell. Judent.*, p. 50). Those who share in God's plan are his "plants" (*1012 Questions*, pp. 127, 140, 150), who in turn have their disciples or plants (ibid., pp. 130, 216-17). The human race is Adam's "planting" (*Mandaean Prayerbook*, No. 378 [*CPM*, 283, 286]; No. 386 [*CPM*, 290]). The elect are "the plants that God has planted," and they must plant their own plants through marriage. (*Ginza*, pp. 61-62.) The "planting" of the earth is described as a colonizing enterprise in *Ginza*, pp. 335, 337; they move from place to place in winged wagons, looking for places to settle (ibid., pp. 337-40); the Planter is expected to provide the necessary helpers for new settlers (ibid., p. 404). Ritually, the planting is a *sparsio*, a sowing or begetting of the race. (H. Nibley, "Sparsiones," *Classical Journal* 40 [1945]: 515ff.)

99. On the "Treasure-house of Souls," see R. H. Charles, note on 4 Ezra 4:35 (*Apocrypha and Pseudepigrapha of the Old Testament*. II, 567); 2 Baruch 30:2; Pseudo-Philo 32:13; C. Schmidt, in *TU* 8 (1892): 368. The souls of the righteous, like the Treasure itself, are beneath the throne of God. (Sabbath, fol. 152b.; cf. Rev. 7:9.) The "planting" of a world is always from the "House of Light, the shining Home," in

other words, the Treasure-house. (*Johannesbuch der Mand.*, p. 218, No. 63.) It is "through the power of the Treasure" that "earths of radiance" are created, "thrones of glory are established and Chiefs of worlds appointed" (ibid., p. 207, No. 59), the Treasure being the source of everything within as well as between the worlds (ibid., No. 57, 203-5). Every world comes into existence by a sort of fission from the Treasure of the Secret Mysteries. (Oxford Mand. Scroll 55-56.) What Adam plants then grows and so increases his Treasure. (*Mandaean Prayerbook*, p. 285.) The bestowing of the "Treasure of the Mighty One" on men to test them is called a "planting of plants" in Psalms of Thomas 13:5-14; 3:24-27; Acts of Thomas 10.

100. On the hierarchy of emanations, see C. Schmidt, *TU* 8 (1892): 367. In the system of 1 Jeu 5-7, one put in charge of a new *topos* as "Chief" is a Jeu, who then becomes the Father of "other emanations to fill other toposes," each of which in turn becomes a "Father of Treasures"; in the end "myriads of myriads will go forth from them." (Ibid., 6.) Every Son begets sons, and these in turn consult in the making of "other worlds" (*Ginza* p. 240); just so "a Jordan produces Jordans without number and without end—living waters" (ibid., pp. 65-67). Through the power of the Treasure, earths are created, places made inhabitable, "chiefs of worlds are appointed," so that the Treasures may be handed down from the older worlds to newer ones. (*Johannesbuch der Mand.*, p. 207, No. 59.) It is perhaps from this Manichaean experience that St. Augustine derives the image of sparks springing from a central fire, each becoming a focal center for more sparks, an idea conveyed in the *Berlin Manich. Hs.* 1:35-36.

101. Quotation from the Second Gnostic Work 49a. He who is begotten is expected to beget. (Gen. 1:29; 9:1.) In the Egyptian rites, the First-born is commanded "to create men, to give birth to the gods, to create all that should exist" (R. Reymond, in *Chronique d' Egypte* 40 (1965): 61); the work of the Creation is repeated indefinitely and daily in ritual (H. Kees, in *Aegypt. Zeitschr.* 78 [1942]: 48). One becomes a Son in order to become a Father; one receives in order to give. (Gospel of Philip 123:10-14.) The Son is commanded, "Go, confirm kings, create new Jordans, and help Chosen Ones [to] arise with thee to the Father." (*1012 Questions*, p. 123.) The Sent Ones say to the Father, "O our Lord, Lord of all worlds, Thou didst command that we should create worlds and propagate species!" and God informs them that that is the secret treasure, bestowed only on "one who is our son (plant)." (Ibid., p. 137.) All who behold the creative process have a normal desire to become creators themselves (*Ginza*, pp. 67-68), creation being the essence of godhood (see above, notes 8, 9, 14).

102. The patriarchal line is never broken: "Let us, Father, create

other worlds in order to raise to *Thee* a planting." (*Ginza*, p. 241.) One does not create without the express permission of the "Creator of the Treasures." (Ibid., pp. 67-68.) He who is "planted from above" does his own "pure planting" under the auspices of *his* Planter. (*Johannesbuch der Mand.*, p. 207, No. 59.) Hence "all gloried in the knowledge that their Father had transplanted them from the House of life" (Alma Rishaia Rba 1 [in E. Drower, *Nasoraean Commentaries*]); in the end, all come "into existence for his sake" (*Johannesbuch der Mand.*, pp. iv, 30-35, 70). Even to the greatest Sent Ones he is the "lofty King by Whom our Treasure ascends!" (Alma Rishaia Zuta 64-65.) At the council in heaven the Son was hailed as "the Father of those who believe" (Second Gnostic Work 29a-30a); this identity of Father and Son to and with believers is a basic teaching of the Fourth Gospel (R. Bultmann, *ZNTW* 24 [1925]: 122).

103. "The dwellers upon earth can understand only what is upon the earth" (4 Ezra 4:21), and the same applies to other worlds. Beings comprehend only what they are like, so that the Lord must take the form of those to whom he appears (C. Schmidt, *Kopt-Gnost. Schrift*, I, 342; Gospel of Philip 101:27-36; 105-106:10; Ascension of Isaiah 7:25; Pistis Sophia 7 [12]; cf. U. Bianchi, in *Numen* 12 [1965]: 165; *Manichaean Psalm-Book*, II, 42.)

104. Gospel of Thomas 95:20-23; cf. Gospel of Truth, fol. Xv, 20-23; Ex. 3:6; Matt. 17:5-6; Mark 9:5-7; E. L. Cherbonnier, *Harvard Theological Review* 55 (1962): 198-99. "He . . . is within the Veil, within his own *shkinta*" (dwelling tabernacle). *Mandaean Prayerbook*, No. 374 (*CPM*, 267); his *topos* is completely out of our cosmos, being the ultimate Treasure, "the Treasure of the Outer Ones" (1 Jeu 5; 59; Second Gnostic Work 2a), surrounded by veils and guarded gates (C. Schmidt, *TU* 8 [1892]: 402); hence it is "beyond the veil, a place of shadowless light" (ibid., p. 366; Sophia Christi 116:9ff.), "the great secret Dwelling of Light" (*1012 Questions*, p. 163). By night all the other worlds strain to see the Father . . . because of the invisibility that surrounds him" (Second Gnostic Work 5a), even as the angels yearn to see the ultimate place of the Saints (L. Guerrier,in Graffin, *PO* 9:153; cf. 1 Pet. 1:12).

105. Sophia Christi 118; Second Gnostic Work 47a; *Berlin Manich. Hs.* 1:118; "the veil at first concealed how God controlled the creation" (Gospel of Philip 132:23); there is a veil between us and the heavens (N. Sed, *Revue des Etudes Juives* 124 [1965]: 39). All treasures are hidden treasures until God reveals them. (Zadokite Doc. 5:1; 2 Baruch 51:7-8; Evang. Barthol. 3:2-7; Gospel of Thomas 86:4-5, 24.) "If you want to go to the Father you must pass through the veil." (2 Jeu 42.) God isolates hostile worlds from each other lest they unite

against him. (*Ginza*, p. 177.) "As the doctrine of the body is hidden in its treasure-house, so God the Father is hidden in his Kingdom, invisible to the wastelands without." (*Berlin Manich. Hs.* 1:151.)

106. A. Pelletier, *Syria* 35 (1958): 225-26.

107. M. J. bin Gorion, *Sagen der Juden* (1913), I, 59.

108. N. Sed, *Revue des Etudes Juives* 124 (1965): 39.

109. Second Gnostic Work 47a; Pistis Sophia 125 (317); Sophia Christi 118.

110. C. Schmidt, in *TU* 8 (1892): 368.

111. Hypostasis of the Archons 143:20.

112. Pistis Sophia 139 (366).

113. Ibid., 28 (42-44).

114. Ibid., 14 (23).

115. 1 Jeu 39; Pistis Sophia 125 (317-18).

116. Pistis Sophia 84 (184).

117. 3 Baruch 6:3ff.

118. The progress of the soul in the afterworld, with three main degrees of glory, is found in the Egyptian funerary literature, that is, the Book of Breathings, lines 2-3, in *Biblioth. Egyptol.* 17:113. So Pindar, *Olymp.* 2:75. For Jewish and Christian concepts, see H. P. Owen, *New Testament Studies* 3 (1957): 243-44, 247-49; K. Prumm, *Biblica* 10 (1929): 74; K. Kohler, *JQR* 7 (1894/5): 595-602; C. Schmidt, in *TU* 8 (1892): 478, n. 1; 489-91, 496-97, 519-21, 524-25. Eternal progression is indicated in IQH 7:15, and in the formula "out of the eternities and into the eternities" (IQS 2:1); "press on from glory to glory," says "Hymn of Serverus" (in Graffin, *PO* 5:683; Second Gnostic Work 5a; Gospel of Thomas 90:4ff.) ("a forward motion, and then a resting-time."). You master the places in this world so that you can master them in the next. (Gospel of Philip 124:33-34.) He who receives all the ordinances "cannot be held back in the way." (*Ginza*, p. 19.)

119. E. L. Cherbonnier, *Harvard Theological Review* 55 (1962): 206.

120. This idea is forcibly expressed in the Pistis Sophia 88-89 (199), 84 (183); *Ginza*, pp. 14, 493-94.

121. J. Soggin, *Theologische Literaturzeitung* 89 (1966): 729. Those who receive the mysteries of the gospel will also come to know the mysteries of the physical Cosmos. (Pistis Sophia 96 [232].)

122. A. Piankoff, in *Inst. Français Archeol. Orient.*, Bibl. Et., 19, 1.

123. The Schoolmen have always avoided "cosmism" and still do. (See H. F. Weir, *Hell. Judaism.*, 79ff.; K. Koch, *Ratlos vor der Apokalyptik* [Gütersloher Verlag, 1970], esp. 55ff.)

124. The contradictions are emphasized by S. A. Pallis, *Mandaean Studies*, pp. 1, 2, 4, 8, 188, and by A. Brandt, *Mandäische Religion*, 48ff., while the "einheitliche und organische Grundlage" is noted by

K. Rudolph, *Mandäer*, I, 141, following H. Jonas. The Mandaeans frequently refer to other sects, Jewish and Christian, as bitter rivals, not because of the differences but because of the many resemblances and common claims between them. (See, for example, *Ginza*, pp. 28-30, 48-52, 135, n. 4, 223-32; *Mandaean Prayerbook*, No. 357, 251; *Berlin Manich. Hs.* 1:21.) While A. Loisy, *Le Mandeisme et les Origines Chretiennes* (Paris: Nourry, 1934), p. 142, maintains that "le Mandeisme n'est intelligible qu'en regard du chrétianisme," M. Lidzbarski, *Ginza*, p. 9, insists that it is older than the captivity of 587 B.C. Such disagreements are typical.

125. See K. Rudolph, *Mandäer*, I, 19-22, 36-41, 59ff., 112ff., 173-75, 251-54, seeing the common source in the early Taufsekten. Since the rites are "sinnlos und unerklärbar" without the peculiar doctrines (ibid., I, 254), the common rites indicate a common doctrinal tradition (E. Drower, *Nasoraean Commentaries*, p. 7).

126. In their main points, the two doctrines are in striking contrast, for example: (1) The idea that all matter is evil heads the list of "orthodox" charges against the Gnostics. (Bodmer Papyrus 10:51:10; Const. Apostol. 6:10; C. Schmidt *TU*, 8 [1892]: 402-3; cf. *Clementine Recognitions* 4:23: "absolute dicimus in substantia nihil esse mali.") Cf. the Gnostic denial of a physical resurrection with the attitude of the Gospel of Philip 105:9-19. (2) The Gnostic idea that Adam was "predisposed to evil" and that souls come to the earth to be punished is the opposite of that of man's preexistent glory. (J. Zandee, *Numen* 11 [1964]: 31; Creation Apocryphon 171:10ff.; Cyril of Jerusalem, Migne, *PG* 33:481. (3) Gnostic dualism—between physical and non-physical states of being—is *anti*-cosmist. (U. Bianchi, *Numen* 12 [1965]: 165-66, 174, 177; S. Giverson, *Studia Theologica* 17 [1963]: 69-70. (4) The Gnostics put God utterly beyond man's comprehension, not in the same family as the "Treasure" concept does (Bodmer Papyrus 10:51:10; Const. Apostol. 6:1); *Israel* means "man who is God," according to the Creation Apocryphon 153:25. (5) Whereas the true Gnostic achieves complete spirituality on earth and goes directly to heaven (or the sun) at death (C. Schmidt, *TU* 8 [1892]: 521ff.; Puech, "Epist. to Rheginos," in *Vigiliae Christianae* 8 [1956]: 44-46), the idea of a long and gradual progress of the soul is older than the Gnostics (K. Kohler, *JQR* 7:598; cf. IQS 2:23ff.; IQH 10:28). (6) Whereas pessimism is the hallmark of all Gnostic systems (*Numen* 11 [1964]: 17; 12 [1965]: 165), the "Treasure" doctrine is completely optimistic and joyful. (7) The Gnostics show the influence of the schools (Bianchi, *Numen* 12 [1965]: 162), while the other teaching is characteristic neither of the schools nor of religions in general (K. Koch, *ZThK* 62 [1965]: 263). (8) Following the schools, Gnosticism

shuns literalism and turns everything into abstraction and allegory: it is not a real system but poetic fantasy (C. Schmidt, *TU* 8 [1892]: 397, 413, 421-22); but "of mystical rapture there is no hint" in the other tradition (H. P. Owen, *New Testament Studies* 3 [1957]: 251; K. Koch, *ZThK* 62 [1965]: 263).

127. C. Schmidt, *TU* 8 (1892): 345-46; there was nothing the Patristic Fathers combatted more vigorously than "the cosmist heresy." Having chosen the way of the Gnostics and Neoplatonics, they condemned all literalism. (Ibid., p. 421, and C. Schmidt, *TU* 43:524-25.)

128. Tertullian and Irenaeus wavered between the two views. (C. Schmidt *TU* 43:520-21.) The fundamental "Treasure" doctrine of the descensus disappears after the 3rd century. (F. Kattenbach, *Das Apostolische Symbol* [Leipzig: 1894], I, 104; II, 913-14.) The *Epist. to Diognetus*, 6, compromises, but for Athanasius, Basil, John Chrysostom, and so on, heaven has become a state of mind, pure and simple.

8

Great Are the Words of Isaiah

I have reached the stage where I have nothing more to say. As far as I am concerned, the scriptures say it all. "Behold, I say unto you, that ye ought to search these things. Yea, a commandment I give unto you that ye search these things diligently; for great are the words of Isaiah. For surely he spake as touching all things concerning my people which are of the house of Israel; therefore it must needs be that he must speak also to the Gentiles. And all things that he spake have been and shall be, even according to the words which he spake." (3 Nephi 23:1-3.) That quotation alone spares us the trouble of an apology for Isaiah. The book of Isaiah is a tract for our own times; our very aversion to it testifies to its relevance. It is necessary to remind us of its importance, however, because Isaiah's message has not been popular, and he tells us why. The wicked do not like to be told about their faults. Every society, no matter how corrupt, has some good things about it—otherwise it would not survive from year to year. Isn't it much pleasanter to talk about the good things than the bad things? The people of Zarahemla, said Samuel the Lamanite, wanted prophets that would tell them what was right with Zarahemla, not what was wrong. There is a great danger in that: the many things that are right with any society can hardly damage it, but one serious flaw can destroy it. One goes to the physician not to be told what parts are functioning well, but what is making him ill or threatening him with the worst.

But, says Isaiah, the people of Israel want to hear

"Great are the Words of Isaiah" is an address given at BYU's sixth annual Sidney B. Sperry Symposium on January 28, 1978.

smooth things: "Prophesy not unto us right things, speak unto us smooth things." (Isaiah 30:10.) And ever since, the process of interpreting Isaiah has been one of smoothing him out. Consider some conspicuous examples of this.

1. The idea that Isaiah is moralizing, not talking about doctrine. Yet he starts out (1:2) calling Israel God's children; he insists on this all along—God is their Father. It is the first Article of Faith. But they won't see it (1:3), they want nothing of the doctrine (1:4). They don't see anything that they don't want to see, says Isaiah. They are functionally blind. They have deliberately cut the wires, and then they complain that they get no message. Isaiah is full of obvious things that nobody sees, especially for Latter-day Saints. The rabbis have always made fun of the suggestion that he is actually referring to Christ. But we go further than that. We see in the Book of Mormon even the particular calling of the Prophet Joseph. And who is to say that we are wrong?

2. The idea that the God of Isaiah is the savage, vengeful Old Testament God of wrath, the tribal God. This means we do not have to take him too seriously. It lets us off the hook. But Isaiah's God is kindness itself. "Come now, and let us reason together," he says; "though your sins be as scarlet, they shall be as white as snow." (Isaiah 1:18.) There is nothing authoritarian about him; he is constantly willing to discuss and explain. His most threatening statements are instantly followed by what seems a reversal of mood and judgment. He is always willing, ready, waiting, urging, patiently pleading; it is Israel that will not hear, it is they who break off the discussion and walk away, turning their back upon him and asking him to please be quiet.

3. The idea that Isaiah is addressing special groups. Indeed he talks about good people and bad people—but they are the same! Woe to Israel! Good tidings to Israel! One and the same Israel. And not just to Israel but to all mankind; he addresses the nations and their leaders by name. And not

only to his generation does he speak, but to all. Nephi applied the words of Isaiah to his own people in the desert "that it might be for our profit and learning." (1 Nephi 19:23.) Six hundred years later Jesus Christ called upon the Nephites to do the same thing, and the angel Moroni handed the same message over to our generation. Isaiah has just one audience because he has but one message. He is addressing whatever mortals upon the face of the earth happen to be in need of repentance. This takes us to our next point.

4. The idea that there is more than one Isaiah and that they all tell different things. Since there is only one message and one audience, this is a mere quibble. The message is a happy one: "Repent—and all will be well—better than you can ever imagine!" Only to those who do not intend to repent is the message grim. Isaiah does not distinguish between the good and the bad but only between those who repent and those who do not. He does not ask where we are—he knows that—but only the direction in which we are moving. Of course, only those can repent who need to, and that means everybody—equally. Does not one person need repentance more than another? Ezra and Baruch protested to God that while Israel had sinned, the Gentiles had acted much worse, and asked why they should be let off so much more easily. But God was not "buying" that argument. You can always find somebody who is worse than you are to make you feel virtuous. It's a cheap shot: those awful terrorists, perverts, communists—*they* are the ones who need to repent! Yes, indeed they do, and for them repentance will be a full-time job, exactly as it is for all the rest of us.

5. The Doctors, Jewish and Christian alike, love to labor the idea that for Isaiah the supreme and unforgivable sin was the worship of idols. Well, he says that's foolish and irrational but never that it is the unforgivable sin. The darling illusion of the schoolmen is that as modern, enlightened, rational thinkers they have made a wonderful

discovery: that wood or metal dolls or images cannot really see or hear, and so on. They labor the point to death. But the ancients knew that as well as we do. That is exactly *why* they patronized the idols. There is the famous story of the Eloquent Peasant from the Middle Kingdom in Egypt that tells how the rascally manager of an estate, when he saw a peasant passing by on his way to the market with a load of goods, cried out, "Would that I had some idol that would permit me to rob this man's goods." A dumb image would offer no opposition to any course he chose to take. That was the beauty of idols: They are as impersonal and unmoral as money in the bank—the present-day as well as the ancient equivalent of a useful idol.

6. This is matched by the idea that the greatest of moral and intellectual virtues was the acknowledgment of the One and Only God. Again, that was another ancient commonplace. Isaiah does not denounce polytheism as the greatest of sins. Indeed, a number of researchers have shown that polytheism as such is nowhere condemned in the Bible. But Isaiah does lay heavy emphasis on oneness. There is to be no compromise. There is only *one* way for a person to go, *one* God for Israel or the *one* human race to serve. To defuse this uncomfortable teaching, the doctors have converted it into a theological exercise for the schools.

7. The idea that Isaiah is denouncing pagan practices before all else. But it is the rites and ordinances that God gave to Moses and that the people were faithfully observing that Isaiah describes as an exercise in desperate futility.

The quickest way to get an overview of the immense book of Isaiah is simply to read the first chapter. Scholars have long held that this is not part of the original book but a summary by a disciple. If so, that makes it nonetheless valuable, and indeed it is remarkable that this, the most famous chapter of Isaiah, is never quoted in the Book of Mormon. Let's take it verse by verse.

1:2. The people of Israel are God's children—he is their

Father. This is the doctrine they have forgotten, and they will be in no condition to receive it again until they have undergone the moral regeneration that is the burden of Isaiah's preaching.

1:3. That doctrine they have rejected: they refuse to hear it.

1:4. Because they can't live with it in their sinful state, they have run away from it. This is inexcusable; God does not look upon it with forbearance. He knows that they are quite capable of understanding and living by the gospel. Accordingly, he is more than displeased; he is angry.

1:5. Yet it is not he who has been giving them a hard time. They decided to go their own way, openly revolting against him. And their system is simply not working. They are not able to cope with the situation mentally nor do they have the spirit to carry it through. Men on their own are a pitiful object.

1:6. The whole thing is sick, sick, sick. Every attempt to correct the situation fails miserably. Nothing works.

1:7. The result is internal depression and international disaster.

1:8. God's chosen people are holed up, trusting in their miserable defense, trapped by their own walls.

1:9. The reason they survive at all so far is that there are still a few righteous, a small remnant of honest people among them.

1:10. So it is time they were considering the alternative, which Isaiah herewith offers them.

1:11. You are not going to appease God by trying to buy him off, by going through the pious motions of religious observances, your meetings and temple sessions.

1:12. It is not for you to decide what to do to please God—it is for him to decide, and he has not required all this display of piety from you.

1:13. Your most dedicated observances, even following my ancient prescriptions, if done in the wrong spirit are actually iniquity—not to your credit but to your loss.

1:14. God is not impressed but disgusted by it.

1:15. Even when you pray I will not hear you. Why not? Answer: Because there is blood on your upraised hands.

1:16. The blood and sins of this generation are on you in the temple. What blood and sins? Your evil ways.

1:17. What evil ways? What should we be doing? Answer: Dealing justly, relieving those oppressed by debt instead of collecting from them, giving a fair deal to the orphans and assistance to the widow, in other words, showing some thought for people without money.

1:18. God is not being capricious or arbitrary. He is eminently reasonable. Is his way the only way? Let him tell you why, and then see if you do not agree: "Come now, and let us reason together, saith the Lord." Then a surprising statement: "Though your sins be as scarlet, they shall be as white as snow." Plainly God does not take pleasure in these rebukes, he does not gloat as men would (for example, Thomas Aquinas) over the punishment in store for the wicked; he loves them all and holds forth the most wonderful promises for them. There is a way out, and that is why Isaiah is speaking, not because he is a puritanical scold.

1:19. Have they had enough? They need only to listen and to follow advice and all will be well.

1:20. But you cannot go on as you have been. You will be wiped out by war if you do. "For the mouth of the Lord hath spoken it." The "consumption decreed" (D&C 87) is another quotation from Isaiah.

1:21. You can do it—because you once did. And then you lost it all—went over to unbridled sex and murder.

1:22. And for what? Property and pleasure, for silver that is now as worthless as garbage and wine that is flat.

1:23. The leaders set the worst example. They work with crooks, everybody is on the take: "Every one loveth gifts, and followeth after rewards," while the poor don't get a break in court and a widow can't even get a hearing.

1:24. God wants nothing to do with such rascals; he is going to get rid of them. They have made themselves his enemies.

1:25. This calls for a thorough housecleaning. All that dross must be purged away.

1:26. To bring back the old order, "restore thy judges as at the first" (as quoted in the well-known hymn). It is still possible, and God is going to bring it about. There will yet be "The city of righteousness, the faithful city."

1:27. There is going to be a Zion redeemed with many of these same sinful people living in it, along with a lot of converts from the outside.

1:28. All the rest will have to go, but not because God chooses to throw them out. They will walk away from safety right into destruction; with eyes wide open they will forsake the Lord and be consumed.

1:29-31. These verses are the only references to paganism—popular cults that will wither and be burned up—not be destroyed, however, because they follow pagan manners or forms, as the doctors, ministers, and commentators love to tell us, but because they were part of the cover-up for avaricious, hard, and immoral practices.

For the rest of the time I want to talk about those human qualities Isaiah describes as pleasing to God and those he despises. They both come as a surprise. As to the first, the traits and the behavior Isaiah denounces as the worst of vices are without exception those of *successful* people. The wickedness and folly of Israel do not consist of indolence, sloppy dressing, long hair, nonconformity (even the reading of books), radical and liberal unrealistic ideas and programs, irreverence toward custom and property, contempt for established idols, and so on. The wickedest people in the Book of Mormon are the Zoramites, a proud, independent, courageous, industrious, enterprising, patriotic, prosperous people who attended strictly to their weekly religious duties with the proper observance of dress standards. Thanking God for all he had given them, they bore testimony to his goodness. They were sustained in all their doings by a perfectly beautiful self-image. Well, what is wrong with any of that? There is just one thing that spoils it all, and that is the very thing that puts Israel in bad with the Lord, according to Isaiah. The Jews observed with strictest regularity all the rules that Moses gave them—"and yet . . . they cry unto thee . . . *and yet*" they are really thinking of something else. "Behold, O my God, their costly apparel, . . . all their precious things . . . ; their hearts are set upon them, *and yet* they cry unto thee and say—We thank thee, O God, for we are a chosen people unto thee, while others shall perish." (Alma 31:27, 28; italics added.)

God sums up the cause of anger against Israel in one word: "For the iniquity of his covetousness was I wroth, and smote him: I hid me, and was wroth." With what affect? It didn't faze the guilty, but "he went on frowardly in the way of his heart." (Isaiah 57:17.) Like the Zoramites, covetous Israel was quite pleased with itself, just as in these last days. Modern Israel was put under "a very sore and grievous curse" because of "covetousness, and . . . feigned words," that is, greed and hypocrisy. (D&C 104:4.) By far the commonest charge Isaiah brings against the wicked is "oppression," *ashaq*. The word means to choke, to grab by the neck and squeeze, grasp, or press, to take the fullest advantage of someone in your power, in short, to maximize profits. It is all centralized in "Babylon, . . . the golden city,"—"the oppressor." (Isaiah 14:4.) Which gives us instant insight into the social and economic structure of Isaiah's world. It is a competitive and predatory society, "Yea, they are greedy dogs which can never have enough, and they are shepherds that cannot understand [they do not know what is going on, because everyone is looking out for himself]: they all look to their own way, every one for his gain, from his quarter." (Isaiah 56:11.)

The charge applies to our own day, when "every man

walketh in his own way, and after the image of his own god, whose image is in the likeness of the world, and whose substance is that of an idol, which waxeth old and shall perish in Babylon, even Babylon the great, which shall fall." (D&C 1:16.) Babylon had flourished long before Isaiah's day, and it was to flourish long after. At that particular time it was on the way up again, but the word is used throughout the scriptures as the type and model of a world that lived by "the economy." Its philosophy is nowhere better expressed than in the words of Korihor: "Every man fared in this life according to the management of the creature; therefore every man prospered according to his genius, and . . . every man conquered according to his strength, and whatsoever a man did was no crime." (Alma 30:17.)

In Isaiah, the successful people are living it up. It is as if they said, "Come ye, . . . I will fetch wine, and we will fill ourselves with strong drink." (Isaiah 56:12.) We'll have drinks and a party at my place. And tomorrow more of the same, but even better, even richer. The economy looks bright, all is well.

Isaiah has a good deal to say about the beautiful people in words that come uncomfortably close to home:

28:1. "Woe to the crown of pride, to the drunkards of Ephraim, whose glorious beauty is a fading flower, which are on the head of the fat valleys of them that are overcome with wine!"

28:2. "Behold, the Lord hath a mighty and strong [wind], which . . . shall cast down to the earth with the hand."

28:3. "The crown of pride, the drunkards of Ephraim, shall be trodden under feet."

28:7. "But they also have erred through wine . . . ; they stumble in judgment."

He describes the party-people, the fast set: "Woe unto them that rise up early in the morning, that they may fol-

low strong drink; that continue until night, till wine in-
flame them!" (Isaiah 5:11.) They are stupefied by the endless beat of the Oriental music that has become part of our
scene: "And the harp, and the viol, the tabret, and pipe,
and wine, are in their feasts: but they regard not the work
of the Lord, neither consider the operation of his hands."
(Isaiah 5:12.) And of course there is the total subservience
to fashion: "Because the daughters of Zion are haughty,
and walk with stretched forth necks and wanton eyes,
walking and mincing as they go" (Isaiah 3:16)—in the immemorial manner of fashion models. An instructive list of
words from the boutiques that only the fashion-wise will
know tells us that "The Lord will take away . . . their cauls,
and their round tires like the moon, the chains, and the
bracelets, and the mufflers, the bonnets, and the orna-
ments of the legs, and the headbands, and the tablets, and
the earrings, the rings, and nose jewels" (Isaiah 3:18-21),
and of course clothes, "the changeable suits of apparel, and
the mantles, and the wimples, and the crisping pins."
(Isaiah 3:22.) Their beauty aids will defeat their purpose as
their hair falls out and their perfumes are overpowered.
(Isaiah 3:24.)

Naturally there is the more lurid side of sex, the more
reprehensible: "Hear the word of the Lord, ye rulers of
Sodom; . . . ye people of Gomorrah. . . . How is the faithful city become an harlot!" (Isaiah 1:10, 21.) Just as Nephi
"did liken all scriptures unto us, that it might be for our
profit and learning" (1 Nephi 19:23), so right at the outset
Isaiah here not only likens Jerusalem to the long vanished
cities of Sodom and Gomorrah but addresses them directly
by name as actually *being* Sodom and Gomorrah—showing
us that we may not pass these charges off as not applying
to us because we live in another time and culture. Is the
scene so different?

The costly fashions reflect a world in which people are
out to impress and impose themselves on others. Everyone

is after a career, everyone is aspiring to be a VIP: "The mighty man, and the man of war, the judge, and the prophet, and the prudent, and the ancient. The captain . . . , and the honourable man, and the counsellor, and the cunning artificer, and the eloquent orator." (Isaiah 3:2-3.) What about them? "I will give children to be their princes, and babes shall rule over them." (Isaiah 3:4.) So much for their authority—and why? Because everyone is out for himself in this game of one-upmanship: "And the people shall be oppressed, every one by another, and every one by his neighbour [there's competition for you!]: the child shall behave himself proudly against the ancient [what else can you expect?], and the base against the honourable." (Isaiah 3:5.) Everything will get out of control. A man will take hold of his brother saying, "You have clothes, so you be our ruler; you be responsible for this mess!" But he will refuse the great honor, saying, "Don't try to make me a ruler—I'm flat broke!" (See Isaiah 3:6-7.) Because everybody will be broke, Isaiah continues: "For Jerusalem is ruined" (Isaiah 3:8)—all because they stubbornly think they can go it alone: "Woe to the rebellious children, saith the Lord, that take counsel, but not of me: and that cover with a covering, but not of my spirit, that they may add sin to sin" by justifying themselves at every step. (Isaiah 30:1.) The rebellious people, the lying children will not hear the law of the Lord. The law of God have they rejected; they reject the law of sacrifice. Oh yes, they sacrifice, but they do not do it the way the Lord wants them to—"Have I required this thing at your hands?" (See Isaiah 1:12.) They have violated the law of chastity, for Israel is a harlot. They have violated the law of consecration, for they are idolators— coveting for themselves is now their consecration. They have rejected the law of God, for they will not do things his way, as they covenanted. (See Isaiah 30.)

The one who sets the supreme example for the people is that most inspiring and amibitious of all spirits. "How art thou fallen from heaven, O Lucifer, son of the morning! how art thou cut down to the ground, which didst weaken the nations! For thou hast said in thine heart, . . . I will exalt my throne . . . : I will sit also upon the mount of the congregation." Isaiah 14:12, 13.) He is out to rule the world, which he does, with disastrous effect; the result is depression and ruin; "Behold, the Lord maketh the earth empty, and maketh it waste, and turneth it upside down, and scattereth abroad the inhabitants thereof. And it shall be, as with the people, so with the priest; as with the servant, so with his master; . . . as with the buyer, so with the seller; as with the lender, so with the borrower; as with the taker of usury, so with the giver of usury to him. The land shall be utterly emptied, and utterly spoiled: for the Lord hath spoken this word." (Isaiah 24:1-3.)

Isaiah knows how to describe a world in total collapse, and we have a rich and very ancient lamentation literature, both of the Egyptians and the Babylonians, appearing periodically over a span of thousands of years, along with abundant business documents, letters, and ritual texts to confirm that such conditions actually did prevail in the world from time to time exactly as Isaiah tells them, always with the same combination of social, economic, and political hysteria. Notice the strong emphasis on economy and finance in the passage just cited. "Ye do always remember your riches," says Samuel the Lamanite, and for that very reason you will lose them. (See Helaman 13:22, 31.) They are cursed and will "become slippery" is the way he puts it, and Isaiah has a comparable expression: "The land shall be utterly . . . spoiled. . . . [it] fadeth away. . . . because they [the people] have transgressed the laws, changed the ordinance, broken the everlasting covenant," to suit themselves. (Isaiah 24:3-5.) "Therefore hath the curse devoured the earth" (Isaiah 24:6); few men are left, everything is desolate; there are no crops, it doesn't rain; therefore, many people are gone into captivity because they have no knowledge, and their honorable men are famished, the multitude is dried up with thirst. "For it is a people of no understanding. Therefore he that made them will not have mercy. He will show them no favor."

Plainly, men are held responsible by God to show some sense. Self-deception costs dearly: He "frustrateth the tokens of the liars, and maketh diviners mad; . . . turneth wise men backward, and maketh their knowledge foolish." (Isaiah 44:25.) They have despised his word and trust oppression and perverseness, and persist in it. These are tough-minded people. They hold out to the end, like the breaking of "a high wall." They will hold out in their ways with great tenacity. Nothing will move them. Like a high dam when it breaks, it breaks all at once. (This is the principle of "the 29th day.") First the wall begins to bulge, then everything goes: The "breaking cometh suddenly at an instant." (Isaiah 30:12-13.) He will not spare even a shard.) The smashup is quick and complete.

All this because everything is out of line. No one can trust anyone else in this freely competitive society. "None calleth for justice, nor any pleadeth for truth: they trust in vanity, and speak lies." (Isaiah 59:4.) "The act of violence is in their hands. They shed innocent blood. Their thoughts are the thoughts of iniquity." This reads like a prospectus of TV fare. Such a course can only leave a trail of distrust: "The way of peace they know not; . . . they have made them crooked paths" (Isaiah 59:8); "speaking oppression and revolt, conceiving and uttering from the heart words of falsehood. . . . Yea, truth faileth; and he that departeth from evil maketh himself a prey." (Isaiah 59:13, 15.) It is profitable to break the rules only as long as there are people simple and gullible enough to keep them. And if you don't play the game, you can expect to become a victim. Isaiah does not applaud such realism: "Woe to thee that spoilest, and thou wast not spoiled; and dealest treacherously, and they dealt not treacherously with thee!" (Isaiah 33:1.) The

Lord goes even further in our dispensation, telling us that we have no right to cheat even those clever people who are trying to cheat us: "Wo be unto him that lieth to deceive because he supposeth that another lieth to deceive." (D&C 10:28.)

Naturally Isaiah takes us into the law courts: "Woe unto them that call evil good, and good evil" (Isaiah 5:20)—that being the rhetorical art, the art, as Plato tells us "of making good seem bad and bad seem good by the use of words," which in the ancient world came to its own in the law courts. "Woe unto them that are wise in their own eyes, and prudent in their own sight! . . . which justify the wicked for reward, and take away the righteousness of the righteous from him!" (Isaiah 5:21, 23.) This recalls how the Gadianton robbers, when they finally got control of the government and the law courts, when "they did obtain the sole management of the government," at once turned "their backs upon the poor and the meek" (Helaman 6:39), "filling the judgment-seats" with their own people (Helaman 7:4), "letting the guilty and the wicked go unpunished because of their money." (Helaman 7:5.) They "justify the wicked for reward," says Isaiah (5:23), and he warns them in their own legal language that God will bring charges against the elders of Israel and "the princes thereof: for ye have eaten up the vineyard; the spoil of the poor is in *your* houses!" (Isaiah 3:14; italics added.) The stuff that is in your houses really belongs to them. "What mean ye that ye beat my people to pieces, and grind the faces of the poor?" (Isaiah 3:15.) "Woe unto them that decree unrighteous decrees [in their untouchable authority], and that write grievousness which they have prescribed" (Isaiah 10:1)— serving their own interests by the laws and regulations they make, "to turn aside the needy from judgment, and to take away the right from the poor of my people, that widows may be their prey, and that they may rob the fatherless!" (Isaiah 10:2.)

Everything is rigged; everybody is on the take; the harlot city is full of murderers; the princes are rebellious, companions of thieves; "every one loveth gifts, and followeth after rewards: they judge not the fatherless, neither doth the cause of the widow come unto them." (Isaiah 1:23.) Even when right is plainly on his side, the poor man doesn't stand a chance, for "the churl . . . deviseth wicked devices to destroy the poor with lying words, even when the needy speaketh right." (Isaiah 32:7.) "For the vile person will . . . practise hypocrisy, and . . . utter error . . . to make empty the soul of the hungry, and he will cause the drink of the thirsty to fail." (Isaiah 32:6.) Real estate is a special province for such people, and the ancient record is full of the slick and tricky deals by which they acquired their great estates, from the earliest of Greek preachers, Hesiod and Solon, to the last of the Roman satirists, including the terribly modern Petronius. "Woe unto them that join house to house, that lay field to field, till there be no place, that they may be placed alone in the midst of the earth!" (Isaiah 5:8.)

Isaiah has a lot to say about trade and commerce, "The burden of Tyre," the crowning city, "whose merchants are princes, whose traffickers are the honourable of the earth." The Lord intends "to stain the pride of all glory, and to bring into contempt all the honourable of the earth." (Isaiah 23:1, 8, 9.) They are a restless lot, these enterprising people: "Peace, peace to him that is far off, and to him that is near, saith the Lord. . . . But the wicked are like the troubled sea, when it cannot rest, whose waters cast up mire and dirt" (remember Lehi's "filthy waters"). (Isaiah 57:19-20.) "There is no peace, saith the Lord, unto the wicked." (Isaiah 48:22, 57:21.) Babylon is at once restless and busy, selfish and carefree; "None seeth me," she says, there is "none else beside me." (Isaiah 47:10.) She has all the technical and commercial know-how at her command. All the experts are working for her—the charmers, the as-

trologers, the expert analysts, the skillful accountants—
and all will be burned as stubble. In the thirteenth chapter
of Isaiah we see the burden of Babylon, the vast activity,
the noise, the bustle, the self-importance, the consuming
hunger for profits in this great world center that is also
another Sodom, a sink of moral depravity.

By a great miracle King Hezekiah of Judah was
snatched from death and given fifteen more years of life. In
an outburst of joy and gratitude he voiced his thanks and
his infinite relief at knowing that God was able to give
whatever one asked of him, even life itself; what is the security of all the world's wealth in comparison to that? And
then a significant thing happened. Ambassadors arrived
from Babylon, and Hezekiah simply could not resist showing them through his treasury, displaying his wealth and
power. "Then came Isaiah the prophet unto King Hezekiah,
and said unto him, What said these men? and from whence
came they unto thee? And Hezekiah said, They are come
from . . . Babylon. Then said he, What have they seen in
thine house? And Hezekiah answered, All that is in mine
house have they seen. Then said Isaiah to Hezekiah, Hear
the word of the Lord of hosts: Behold, the days come, that
all that is in thine house . . . shall be carried to Babylon."
(Isaiah 39:3-6.) The man couldn't resist showing off, and by
his vanity he only whetted their greed. They liked what
they saw and came back later to fetch it. He had played
right into their hands.

Isaiah is very much into the international picture in
which the fatal flaw is the assumption that things are in the
hands of the great men of the earth, while in fact there are
no great men but just ordinary guys with disastrous delusions of grandeur. *Haughty* is a favorite word with Isaiah.

> And I will punish the world for their evil, and the
> wicked for their iniquity; and I will cause the arrogancy
> of the proud to cease, and will lay low the haughtiness of
> the terrible. (Isaiah 13:11.)

I will make a man more precious than fine gold; even a man than the golden wedge of Ophir. (Isaiah 13:12.)

The lofty looks of man shall be humbled, and the haughtiness of men shall be bowed down, and the Lord alone shall be exalted in that day. (Isaiah 2:11.)

Behold, the Lord, the Lord of hosts, shall lop the bough with terror: and the high ones of stature shall be hewn down, and the haughty shall be humbled. (Isaiah 10:33.)

The earth mourneth and fadeth away, the world languisheth and fadeth away, the haughty people of the earth do languish. The earth also is defiled. . . . Therefore hath the curse devoured the earth, and they that dwell therein are desolate: therefore the inhabitants of the earth are burned, and few men left. (Isaiah 24:4-6.)

What makes a nation great? Power and gain is the answer we give today; the thing is to be number one in military and economic clout. They thought so in Isaiah's day too: Woe unto them that rely on horses and chariots because they are powerful, but "look not unto the Holy One of Israel." "The Egyptians are men, and not God; and their horses flesh, and not spirit." (Isaiah 31:1, 3.) No real security is to be gained by alliances, no sword either of the strong or of the weak power shall overcome Assyria; the Lord had his own plans for Assyria, and no one could have guessed what they were. Where does security lie? In digging the defenses of Jerusalem you are merely digging your graves! The only true defense is the calling of the priesthood in the temple. If you play the game of realistic power politics, you can't expect any but the usual reward.

The Assyrians guaranteed security. They were the top nation militarily. "Go along with us," they said to Jerusalem (and Isaiah has preserved their letters), "and you

will be safe. You are fools. How can God deliver you if you
have no army? You need us. God is on the side of the big
battalions." This is what is called *Realpolitik*, which has repeatedly destroyed its practitioners in modern times.
When Isaiah tells the people to trust God and not Egypt,
the people say that that is not realistic! So here come the
Assyrians, those super-realists, with their irresistible
might—and they were wiped out in their camp as they
were sleeping. The great nations? "Behold, the nations are
as a drop of a bucket, and are counted as the small dust of
the balance." (Isaiah 40:15.) All the nations before him are
as nothing, and they are counted to him as less than nothing and vanity because they pretend to be something.
(Isaiah 10:33.) "For Tophet is ordained of old" and is waiting for them right now—("a prison have I prepared for
them," the Lord tells Enoch). "Yea for the king it is prepared"—for *Assyria*. "He hath made it deep and large: the
pile thereof is fire and much wood; the breath of the Lord,
like a stream of brimstone, doth kindle it." (Isaiah 30:33.)
Don't be impressed by "the mighty man, and the man of
war, the judge, and the prophet, and the prudent, and the
ancient." (Isaiah 3:2.) There is only one in whom you can
put your trust. Assyria vanished overnight and was never
heard of again, while lesser nations as ancient as Assyria
who could not afford to gamble for supremacy on the winning of battles are still with us.

As surprising as the traits Isaiah despises are those he
prizes—not drive, initiative, industry, enterprise, hard
work, thrift, piety—none of the Zoramite virtues, though
they are truly virtues when they are not vitiated by selfish
motives or a morbid obsession with routine. And let me observe in passing that work is, after all, not a busy running
back and forth in established grooves, though that is the essence of our modern business and academic life, but the supreme energy and disciplined curiosity required to cut *new*
grooves. In Isaiah's book the qualities that God demands of

men are such as our society looks down on with mildly patronizing contempt. Isaiah promises the greatest blessings and glory to the meek, the lowly, the poor, the oppressed, the afflicted, and the needy. What! Is being poor and oppressed an achievement? Are we encouraged to join the ranks of the down-and-outers? What possible merit can there be in such a negative and submissive stance? Well, there *is* virtue in it, and it is the presence of Satan in the world that is the deciding factor. In Zion, we are promised there will be no poor. That is because Satan will not be present there with his clever arrangement of things. But he is the prince of this world, freely permitted for a time to try men and to tempt them. There he calls the tune.

And how does he try and tempt us? In the worldwide mythology of the human race the devil is the Lord of the underworld who sits on the treasure of the earth in his dark kingdom; he is Pluto, the god of wealth, who by his control of the earth's resources dictates the affairs of men. Aristophanes' last play, the *Plutus,* is one long, bitter commentary on the kind of people who succeed in this world. Indeed, "the spurns that patient merit of the unworthy takes" is a stock theme of the world's literature from the Egyptian story of the two brothers through Lazarus and Dives to the vicissitudes of the Joad family in the *Grapes of Wrath.* If we believe Isaiah, the Son of Man himself was "despised and rejected" (Isaiah 53:3), from which one concludes that to be highly successful in this life is hardly the ultimate stamp of virtue. For Satan's golden question, "Have you any money?" has a paralyzing and intriguing effect that enlists all but the noblest spirits in the great conspiracy: "And judgment is turned away backward," says Isaiah, "and justice standeth afar off: for truth is fallen in the street, and equity cannot enter. Yea, truth faileth; and he that departeth from evil maketh himself a prey." (Isaiah 59:14, 15.) Whoever refuses to put up with this sort of thing, in their words, must expect to take a beating. "The

Lord saw it," continues Isaiah, "and it displeased him that there was no judgment." (Isaiah 59:15.) Everybody is cheating, and God does not like it at all. "Behold the world lieth in sin at this time, and none doeth good, no not one, . . . and mine anger is kindling against the inhabitants of the earth to visit them according to this ungodliness." Such were the opening words of the Lord in this dispensation spoken to the Prophet Joseph in the grove.[1] The words "the world lieth in sin" call for a more particular statement in the manner of Isaiah, and we find the same expression explained in D&C 49:20: "It is not given that one man should possess that which is above another, *wherefore* the world lieth in sin." (Italics added.) Mammon is a jealous God; you cannot serve him and any other master. To escape the powerful appeal of the things of this world and the deadly threat that hangs over all who do not possess them takes a meek and humble soul indeed—and a courageous one.

What does Isaiah say that God demands of those who would be justified? First of all, they must be clean of all defilement: "Wash you, make you clean," he says in the first chapter. (Isaiah 1:16.) Don't make your prayers when your hands are covered with blood. And the person with clean hands, says the psalmist, "he that hath clean hands, and a pure heart," is one "who hath not lifted up his soul unto vanity, nor sworn deceitfully." (Psalms 24:4.) Isaiah agrees: it is "he that despiseth the gain of oppressions, that shaketh his hands from holding of bribes, that stoppeth his ears from hearing of blood, and shutteth his eyes from seeing evil." (Isaiah 33:15.) The people fasted as God had commanded and asked Isaiah in perplexity why God had not heard them. In reply he told them, "Is not this the fast that I have chosen? to loose the bands of wickedness . . . and that ye break every yoke? Is it not to deal thy bread to the hungry, . . . bring the poor that are cast out to thy house?" Cover the naked? (Isaiah 58:6-7.) This is a reminder that our own fasts require an offering for the poor. God is not impressed by the magnificent temples people build for him—he owns it all anyway, "but to *this* man will I look, even to him that is poor and of a contrite spirit, and trembleth at my word." (Isaiah 66:2; italics added.) If they go on justifying themselves—"Yea, they have chosen their own ways, and their soul delighteth in their abominations" (66:3)—God will not curtail their agency; he will give them all the rope they want: "I also will choose their delusions, . . . because when I called, none did answer; . . . they . . . chose that in which I delighted not." (Isaiah 66:4.)

After describing the way of Israel, the burden of Damascus, the burden of Egypt, the burden of Babylon and of Assyria, in short, the world as it is and as it should not be, Isaiah in glowing terms depicts the world as it should be—as it was meant to be and as it was created to be. "He created it not in vain, he formed it to be inhabited." (Isaiah 45:18.) Under his rule, he is the Lord and there is none else. Unto him every knee shall bow and every tongue confess. "In that day . . . the fruit of the earth shall be excellent." (Isaiah 4:2.) All that remain are Zion and Jerusalem. "The Lord shall have washed away the filth of the daughters of Zion, and shall have purged the blood of Jerusalem." (Isaiah 4:4.)

With Babylon gone from the scene, a huge sigh of relief goes up; at last the world is quiet and at rest. The golden city, the oppressor, is no more. (Isaiah 14:4.) The whole earth is at rest. "Good tidings unto the meek; he hath sent me to bind up the brokenhearted, to proclaim liberty to the captives, and the opening of the prison to them that are bound." (Isaiah 61:1.) "Violence shall no more be heard in thy land, wasting nor destruction within thy borders." (Isaiah 60:18.) On the contrary, "with righteousness shall he judge the poor, and reprove with equity for the meek of the earth." (Isaiah 11:4.) "Where is the fury of the oppressor?" (Isaiah 51:13.) "Ho, . . . he that hath no money; come ye, buy, and eat; yea, come, buy wine and milk without money and without price. Wherefore do ye spend money for that which is not bread? . . . Come unto me: hear, and your soul shall live." (Isaiah 55:1-3.) Wonder of wonders, in that day a man will be worth more than gold—a complete reversal of values. At the same time the forests return and the trees rejoice: "No feller is come up against us." (Isaiah 14:8.) Isaiah often equates the growing wickedness of the world with the brutal and wasteful exploitation of nature, which has reached an all-time climax in the present generation. We all know his most poetic lines: "The leopard shall lie down with the kid; and the calf and the young lion and the fatling together; and a little child shall lead them. And the cow and the bear shall feed; their young ones lie down together: and the lion shall eat straw like the ox." (Isaiah 11:6, 7.) In my school days this was the prize illustration of the unrealistic Isaiah, zoological nonsense. It was not the "nature red in tooth and claw" of our own neo-Darwinian world. Since then a lot has been learned about the true nature of certain savage beasts. "They shall not hurt nor destroy in all my holy mountain: for the earth shall be full of the knowledge of the Lord, as the waters cover the sea." (Isaiah 11:9.) "The wilderness and the solitary places shall be glad for them; and the desert shall rejoice, and blossom as the rose. It shall blossom abundantly, . . . In the wilderness shall waters break out, and streams in the desert. And the parched ground shall become a pool, and the thirsty land springs of water" (Isaiah 35:1, 2, 6, 7); "that they may see, and know, and consider, and understand together, that the hand of the Lord hath done this" (Isaiah 41:20).

And this happy world is for everybody, even as Isaiah's message of warning and promise of forgiving is for everyone. The sons of the stranger, taking hold of the covenant, "even them will I bring to my holy mountain." They will come to the temple, which will "be called an house of prayer for all people." (Isaiah 56:7.) The Lord God, who gathers the "outcasts of Israel" and all the "beasts of the field," says there won't be any watchdogs to frighten them off anymore; it will be a happy time of man and beast. (Isaiah 56:8-10.) "Great are the words of Isaiah!" We have been commanded to search them, study them, ponder them, take them to heart, and understand that the calamities and the blessings therein are meant for our own generation. May the words of this great prophet prepare us for these calamities and blessings.

NOTES

1. Jessee, Dean C., "The Early Accounts of Joseph Smith's First Vision," *BYU Studies 9 (Spring 1969): 280.*

9

More Voices from the Dust

Even if it were only fiction, the story of the finding of the Qumran Manuscripts (also called the Dead Sea Scrolls and the 'Ain Feshkha manuscripts) would be exciting reading. In a hundred journals the tale has now been repeated of how in June 1947 an Arab shepherd looking for a lost sheep came across the all-but-invisible entrance to a cave in which reposed "the first major biblical manuscripts of great antiquity" ever found—"older by more than a millennium than the Hebrew texts which are the basis of our biblical translations."[1]

In the same cave with the now famous Isaiah text were found fragments of Genesis, Judges, Deuteronomy, Leviticus, the apocryphal book of Jubilees, and the extensive writings dealing with the doctrines and practices of an ancient Jewish sect that had inhabited that part of the desert in the time of Christ. Small wonder that "the little world of biblical scholarship has been turned topsy-turvy by the discoveries," or that "the howling wilderness of Ta'amireh also has been turned upside down in consequence of the finds."[2] As a result of this feverish search, more than forty caves have now come to light, many of them containing ancient writings; for example, the first six caves opened around Qumran "have produced manuscript material representing an original collection of some four hundred to five hundred works that included all of the Old Testament books, numerous apocrypha, both known and unknown, and sectarian documents of all kinds."[3] From another group of caves nearby, two of which are described as noth-

---

"More Voices from the Dust" appeared in the *Instructor* (March 1956), pp. 71-72, 74.

ing less than "mighty caverns," even richer treasures came forth in 1952. The now famous Cave IV at Qumran has yielded three hundred fragments of writings, some of which are thought to go back to the fourth century B.C. As a result of these finds "we now have larger or smaller fragments of every book of the Old Testament except Esther, most of the known Apocrypha, and many new ones."[4]

Thanks to this material, the conventional ideals of Christian and Jewish religion are even now undergoing major revisions. We are told, for example, that "one conclusion is difficult to avoid: John, so far from being the creation of Hellenistic Christianity, has exceedingly close ties with sectarian Judaism, and may prove to be the most 'Jewish' of the Gospels."[5] At the same time we learn that the all-but-discredited Septuagint is really a very ancient and reliable text, "a literal and faithful translation of its Hebrew predecessor."[6] As to church history, "All the problems relative to primitive Christianity—problems examined for so many centuries—all these problems henceforth find themselves placed in a new light, which forces us to reconsider them completely."[7]

The texts are packed with matter of greatest interest to Latter-day Saints. The people who wrote and hid these records had our own conception of continued revelation, of this life as a probation, of the preexistence and resurrection, of the dispensations of the gospel with falling away and restoration; their covenants and ordinances closely resemble ours; and their book of doctrine and covenants (now called the Manual of Discipline) is surprisingly like our own, as are their ideas of priesthood, prophecy, heaven and earth, marriage and eternal progeny, and so on. To go through the scrolls illustrating these things point by point would require a whole book. Here one significant illustration must suffice.

Speaking of the Qumran manuscripts, *Time* magazine recently reported:

The most startling disclosure of the Essene documents so far published is that the sect possessed, years
before Christ, a terminology and practice that have always been considered uniquely Christian. The Essenes
practiced baptism and shared a liturgical repast of bread
and wine presided over by a priest. They believed in re-
demption and in the immortality of the soul. Their most
important leader was . . . a Messianic prophet-priest
blessed with divine revelation. . . . Many phrases, symbols, and precepts similar to those in Essene literature
are used in the New Testament, particularly in the Gospel of John and the Pauline Epistles.[8]

This was not only a "startling disclosure" but also a
very disturbing one. Many Jewish and Christian scholars
heaped scorn on the scrolls years after their discovery, or
even *refused* to consider them at all, calling them a hoax, a
"conglomeration of words . . . written by an uneducated
Jew in the Middle Ages," "a garbage collection," and what-
not,[9] for a Dupont-Sommer pointed out from the first, if the
scrolls are genuine, then the scholars have been wrong all
along in their conception of Christianity and Judaism.
Worst of all is the maddening habit these writings have of
"jumping the gun" on the New Testament. The Gospel of
John, for example, "employs the vocabulary characteristic
of the DSD," that is, the Manual of Discipline, written
years before the gospel.[10] Much of this literature is biblical,
and yet it is not biblical: thus "the hymns in the collection
are reminiscent of the latest biblical psalms, and more especially the psalm in the prologue of Luke. They draw heavily
on the Psalter and Prophetic poetry for inspiration, and
borrow direct phrases, cliches, and style. However, neither
in language, spirit, or theology are they biblical."[11] That is
to say, they are not "biblical" in the sense that *modern* critics
use the word, though they were obviously believed by
their authors to be completely biblical. Either those ancients did not understand the Bible, or else the moderns

don't. Yet Dr. Brownlee is willing to concede that *their* rendering of the scriptures "greatly enriches and improves upon the original form [sic]," and that "it will no doubt receive considerable use on the part of both ministers and rabbis who become familiar with it."[12]

Forced to accept the proofs that something like a New Testament church was in full bloom before New Testament times, Mr. G. L. Harding, who has been a most active figure in the discovery and preservation of the scrolls, can only conclude that John the Baptist and even Christ must have acquired much of what they taught in the bosom of the Qumran community itself: "John the Baptist . . . must have studied and worked in this building [the main assembly hall of the sect, near the Qumran caves]: he undoubtedly derived the idea of ritual immersion or baptism from them. Many authorities consider that Christ himself also studied with them for some time. . . . These, then, are the very walls He looked upon, the corridors and rooms through which He wandered and in which He sat, brought to light once again after nearly 1900 years."[13]

Now with the discovery and admission of the existence of typical New Testament expressions, doctrines, and ordinances well before the time of Christ, the one effective argument against the Book of Mormon collapses.[14] Within the past year a distinguished European scholar has written an ambitious study on the Book of Mormon, in which he praises it as the most significant work or historiography to appear in America, but at the same time denounces it as a fraud and forgery, stating as his proof that "the character of the forgery is made clear by the revamping of biblical accounts and expressions, especially in the founding of the Church, baptism, and sacrament as accompanying the appearance of Christ in America."[15] That is exactly what was held against the scrolls when they first appeared and almost up to the present moment: they were accused, like the Book of Mormon, of being nothing but a phony rehash of the Bible, with a new slant on particulars and a totally in-congruous setting. And had not the evidence continued to pour forth, year after year and cave after cave ("discoveries tread on the heels of discoveries," says Mr. Cross), the learned could never have been persuaded to admit that the documents were anything but clumsy forgeries.

Dr. Cross, eager to allay the misgivings that must in-evitably follow the overthrow of accepted ideas of Church history and doctrine, explains the resemblance between the Christian and pre-Christian churches as traceable to a common tradition: both "draw on common resources of language, common theological themes and concepts, and share common religious institutions."[16] But this common tradition was not that of conventional Judaism, let alone Hellenistic philosophy; it was the ancient tradition of the righteous few who flee to the desert with their wives and children to prepare for the coming of the Lord and escape persecution at the hands of the official religion. Qumran seems to have been the camping-place of such holy fugi-tives as early as the eighth and seventh centuries B.C., that is, as early as the days of Lehi.[17] The Book of Mormon clearly states that its people consider themselves to be in this particular and peculiar line of Israelite tradition.[18] The discoveries at and near Qumran now prove not only that such people existed, but also that they produced a peculiar type of literature, and it is to the Book of Mormon that one may turn for some of the most perfect examples of that lit-erature. And so the voices whispering out of the dust on the shores of the Dead Sea may yet provide some of the most powerful confirmation of the authenticity of the Book of Mormon.

NOTES

1. Cross, Frank Moore, "The Manuscripts of the Dead Sea Caves," *The Biblical Archeologist* 17, 1 (February 1954): 3. The fullest general description of the finding of the scrolls is still Harold Henry

Rowley, *The Zadokite Fragments and the Dead Sea Scrolls* (Oxford University Press, 1952).

2. Cross, p. 4.

3. Fritsch, Charles Theodore, "Herod the Great and the Qumran Community, *Journal of Biblical Literature* 74 (September 1955): 174.

4. Harding, G. Lankester, "Where Christ Himself May Have Studied: An Essene Monastery at Khirbet Qumran," *Illustrated London News* 227 (September 3, 1955): 379.

5. Cross, p. 3.

6. Cross, p. 18. It should be noted that the Inspired Version of the Bible as we have it from Joseph Smith greatly favors the Septuagint.

7. Dupont-Sommer, A., *The Dead Sea Scrolls: A Preliminary Report* (New York: Macmillan, 1952), p. 100. Time has vindicated this verdict, which Dupont-Sommer has repeated in his latest work. (See *Time*, "Dead Sea Jewels" [September 5, 1955], p. 34.)

8. Courtesy *Time;* copyright Time, Inc., 1955.

9. Nibley, Hugh W., "New Approaches to Book of Mormon Study," *Improvement Era* (March 1954), pp. 148ff.

10. Brownlee, William H., "A Comparison of the Covenanters of the Dead Sea Scrolls with Pre-Christian Jewish Sects," *The Biblical Archeologist* 14, 3 (September 1951): 58.

11. Cross, p. 3; compare Brownlee, "Biblical Interpretation among the Sectaries of the Dead Sea Scrolls," *The Biblical Archeologist* 14, 3 (September 1951):58.

12. Brownlee, ibid., p. 60.

13. Harding.

14. We pointed this out in 1954, (note 9 above), but the recent admissions of such authorities as Cross, Brownlee, and Harding now lend real force to the argument.

15. Meinhold, Peter, "Die Anfänge des Amerikanischen Geschichtsbewusstseins," *Saeculum* 5 (1954): 86.

16. Cross, "The Scrolls and the New Testament," *The Christian Century* 72 (August 1955): 971.

17. Kelso, James L., "The Archaeology of Qumran," *Journal of Biblical Literature* 74 (September 1955):145. "The roots of the Sect undoubtedly do go back to the pre-Maccabean Hasidim," according to Fritsch, ibid., p. 177.

18. Nibley, *Improvement Era* (May 1954), pp. 326-30.

10

The Dead Sea Scrolls:
Some Questions and Answers

What are the Dead Sea Scrolls?

Ancient religious writings found in caves and ruins in the Judaean desert.

When were they discovered?

The first in the summer of 1947. Other major discoveries were in 1952 and 1956. More than two hundred caves have been explored, and the search still goes on.

Where were they discovered?

The most important finds have come from eleven caves in the precipitous walls of the Wadi Qumran, a gorge on the western shores of the Dead Sea, about a mile from the water's edge near the north end, seven miles south of Jericho. Also important are the four huge caves in Wadi Murabba'at, twelve miles southwest of Qumran; and the ruins of Khirbet Mirdi, on a hilltop about five miles west-southwest of Qumran. Important finds have come from other hiding places known only to the Bedouins.

How were they discovered and by whom?

The first was accidentally discovered by a shepherd boy of the seminomadic Arabic tribe of the Ta'amireh. Most

"The Dead Sea Scrolls: Some Questions and Answers" was originally an address given to the Seminary and Institute faculty at BYU on July 5, 1962. It then appeared in the *Instructor* 98 (July 1963): 233–35.

subsequent discoveries have been made by members of that tribe, who have now become expert in the excavation and preservation of the documents. At first, clandestine digging (by dealers and monks as well as Arabs) destroyed much material.

In 1949 the experts withdrew, convinced that there was no more to be found; but the Arabs continued searching with such success that in 1951 formal expeditions were organized by the British Army and Jordanian government. The walls of the Wadi Qumran were systematically explored, leading to the discovery in 1952 of Cave IV—the richest find of all—and the disclosure by the Arabs of the great caves of the Wadi Murabba'at.

Accounts of the discovery and procurement of the various scrolls are complicated and conflicting.

How many scrolls are there?

In Cave IV alone thousands of fragments of more than 382 manuscripts were found. In all more than 500 manuscripts have come from Qumran in tens of thousands of leather fragments.

Who owns the scrolls and how were they acquired?

The first four scrolls were acquired by the Syrian Orthodox Metropolitan of Jerusalem (the story is very obscure), who took them to America and later sold them to the Hebrew University for a reputed quarter of a million dollars. Professor Sukenic, of the Hebrew University, picked up some fragments in a Jerusalem antique shop.

The Jordanian government has legal right to the finds and, being short of funds, has sold them at a fixed rate of one pound ($2.80) per square centimeter. Before the owners can claim them, the fragments must go to the Palestine Archaeological Museum to be cleaned, photographed, and edited for publication.

Dead Sea manuscripts have been acquired by McGill, Manchester, and Heidelberg Universities; by the McCormick Theological Seminary; and by the Vatican Library. New finds are acquired from the Arabs through the agency of intermediate dealers; the channels are devious and often shady.

What is the age of the scrolls?

It ranges from the seventh century B.C. (one fragment), to A.D. 68. Texts of Samuel, Jeremiah, and Exodus may date from about 200 B.C.; but most of the biblical scrolls come from the first century B.C.

What subjects are treated in the scrolls?

A quarter of all the manuscripts are biblical, every book of the Old Testament except Esther being represented. The most numerous manuscripts are of Deuteronomy, Isaiah and the Psalms. The first discovery was a Hebrew text of Isaiah, a thousand years older than any previously known. The Apocryphal works are richly represented, including two books in cryptographic writing, a book of Enoch, and a treatise on the book of Moses. The most famous nonbiblical scrolls are the Manual of Discipline, the Habakkuk Commentary, the Thanksgiving Psalms, the ancient ritual Order of Battle, the Genesis Apocryphon (a fuller story of Genesis, including a new account of Abraham in Egypt), a "Description of the New Jerusalem," and a lost Commentary on Job. The investigation and publication of such writings has just begun.

Who wrote the Dead Sea Scrolls?

A society of pious "apocalyptic" Jews, now generally identified with the Essenes.

What light do the scrolls throw on the subject of Christian origins?

That is largely a matter of interpretation, but by now scholars are generally agreed that the scrolls teach us for the first time: (1) the background of John the Baptist; (2) the exact date of Easter; (3) the nature and origin of the organization of the Primitive Church; (4) the significance of the strange language and teachings of John; (5) the origin of Gnosticism; (6) the nature of the Church as a continuation of an ancient apocalyptic and Messianic tradition ignored by Rabbinic Judaism; (7) the nature of the strange terminology of the New Testament as continuing an ancient tradition; (8) of the Christian community as following the pattern of earlier apocalyptic communities in the desert; and (9) the ancient Hebrew-apocalyptic background of the writings of Paul.

What light do the scrolls throw on the Book of Mormon?

This, too, is a matter of interpretation. But if there is any validity to the thousands of studies appearing on parallels between the scrolls and various biblical and historical writings, the perfectly staggering parallels between the Book of Mormon and the scrolls cannot be brushed aside nor explained away. Here are a few:

1. Many years ago this writer pointed out (*Improvement Era*, September 1954) that the peculiar manner of burying the scrolls indicated that they had been laid away for the purpose of coming forth in a future dispensation. Since then a number of scholars (such as Malik and Danielou) have confirmed this impression. The tradition of the sacred buried record meets us full-blown in the similar preservation of the scrolls and the Book of Mormon.

2. Lehi is clearly described as one of the prophets driven from Jerusalem because of his Messianic preaching, and seeking refuge in the desert, where he intended to found a

community. The community of Qumran was led into the desert by such a man centuries later, and there is considerable evidence that this was an established and traditional routine of great antiquity.

3. In a heretofore unparalleled situation we find the Qumran people offering animal sacrifice and observing the Law of Moses under the direction of legitimate priests and yet at the same time observing ordinances of a strangely Christian nature. It is a situation "difficult to visualize" (Cross), and yet its counterpart is found in the Book of Mormon.

4. The Qumran people denounce the Jews at Jerusalem for their corruption and laxity in observing the Law. They respect the temple and its traditions but despise the leaders of the Jews who have driven them from Jerusalem. This is exactly the attitude of Nephi.

5. They keep the Law of Moses but in everything *anticipate* the coming of the Messiah and the New Covenant. Their sacrament is "a liturgical anticipation of the Messianic banquet" (Cross), as are their baptisms and their white garments—all belong to "a church of anticipation." This parallels the Book of Mormon situation exactly.

6. They see a peculiar significance in going out into the wilderness and in choosing a site where they can establish a large and elaborate system of tanks and basins for washings and baptisms. One thinks immediately of Alma's community in the wilderness at the Waters of Mormon.

7. There they were organized into a general congregation with a council of twelve laymen headed by three priests. Scholars have agreed that we have here a definite tie-in with the organization of the Early Church. Its closest parallel is in Christ's organization of the Church in 3 Nephi.

8. Some scholars believe that the greatest single revelation of the scrolls is the existence of a great prophetic tradition that has been completely forgotten. Its greatest repre-

sentative is the mysterious "Teacher of Righteousness" or "Righteous Teacher," a major prophet whose very existence was unknown until 1950. How could a figure of such immense importance both to Christians and Jews have been completely forgotten? It was because his name was blotted out by Rabbinical or "official" Jews, who persecuted him severely and drove him into the desert because he preached the coming of the Messiah.

He was of priestly descent, being of the line of Zadok, another mysterious prophet, whom some believed lived at the time of Moses and who is the type of the true priest who looked forward to the Messiah. Allegro believes that the Teacher of Righteousness himself may have been called Zadok. The important thing is the discovery not of controversial individuals but of an undeniable tradition of a line of persecuted Messianic prophets. This is in perfect agreement with the Zenock and Zenos tradition in the Book of Mormon. Since one of the commonest phenomena in the apocryphal literature, including the scrolls, is the frequent duplication and corruption of proper names, it might not be too much to suggest that Zadok might even be a corruption of Zenock, since of course in Hebrew the vowels are not written, and the Hebrew "d" resembles the "n" closely enough (in the archaic script) to have been confused by an early copyist—a very common type of mistake. Be that as it may, the peculiar *type* of prophet represented by Zenock and Zenos is now fully established by the scrolls.

10. For the first time we now learn of the ancient Jewish background of (1) the theological language of the New Testament and Christian apocrypha, (2) their eschatological doctrines, and (3) their organizational and liturgical institutions. (Cross.) All three receive their fullest exposition in 3 Nephi, where the Messiah himself comes and organizes his church on the foundations already laid for it.

The strongest accusation against the Book of Mormon in the past has always been the presence in it of New Testament language, doctrines, and ordinances among people living in pre-Christian times. Today this objection not only vanishes but now furnishes powerful evidence supporting the Book of Mormon. The scrolls show a highly developed Messianism, very close to that of the New Testament. For example, it is now seen that Paul writes in the authentic Qumran pre-Christian style.

The most read, most available current books on the Dead Sea Scrolls are the following paperbacks, from which the above information was gleaned.

Allegro, John Marco, *The Dead Sea Scrolls* (Pelican, 1956).

Cross, Frank M., *The Ancient Library of Qumran* (Anchor Books, 1961).

Danielou, Jean, *The Dead Sea Scrolls and Primitive Christianity* (Mentor, 1958).

Davies, A. P., *The Meaning of the Dead Sea Scrolls* (Signet, 1956).

Gaster, Theodor H., *The Dead Sea Scriptures in English* (Doubleday Anchor, 1957).

Schonfield, Hugh J., *Secrets of the Dead Sea Scrolls* (A. S. Barnes, 1957).

11

Qumran and the Companions of the Cave: The Haunted Wilderness

Exactly at noon on the winter solstice of 1964, the writer stood at the entrance of an artificially extended cave at the place then called Raqim (now Sahab), a few miles south of Amman, with Rafiq Dajani, brother of the Minister of Antiquity for Jordan, who had just begun important excavations on the spot and duly noted that the sun at that moment shone directly on the back wall of the cave, a feat impossible at any other time of the year. The ancient picture of a dog painted on the cave wall had dimly suggested to the local inhabitants and a few scholars in an earlier generation the story of the dog who guarded the cave of the Seven Sleepers—hundreds of caves claiming that title—but nobody took it very seriously. Beneath Byzantine stones, older ruins were coming to light, suggesting that the place may have been another Qumran, the settlement of early Christian or even Jewish sectaries of the desert; the region around was still all open country, mostly bare rocky ground. There it was, the beginning of an excavation that might turn up something exciting. Professor Dajani had read the article below in manuscript form and obligingly taken me for a visit to the place, where I took some pictures which were published in the *Improvement Era.*

Compare those pictures with what you find there today! Twelve years later I returned to the spot with a tour group in excited anticipation of the wonders I would now see laid bare. What we found was that the excavations, far

"Qumran and The Companions of the Cave" first appeared in *Revue de Qumran* 5 (April 1965): 177-98.

from being completed, had actually been covered up, all but the cave; on the spot was rising the concrete shell of a huge new mosque, and a large marble slab, before the cave, proclaimed in Arabic and English that this was the Cave of the Seven Sleepers. The spot was being converted into a major Moslem shrine; our Christian Armenian guide was worried sick that there would be an incident, and at first hotly refused to stop the bus anywhere near the place. Naturally, I went straight for the cave and was met at the entrance by a venerable Mollah and his assistant, who were selling candles; I said I wanted to see the holy dog and they led me to the back of the cave where the wall was completely covered by a large old commode, through whose dirty glass windows they pointed out some ancient brown bones and their prize—the actual jawbone of the holy dog; a relic had usurped the place of the picture. So there it was: what had been a few scattered ruins, lying deserted and completely ignored on the heath, was now being promoted as a booming cult-center, rapidly foundering in the encroaching clutter of suburban real estate enterprises. To a student of John Chrysostom nothing could be more instructive; it had taken just twelve years to set up an ancient and hopefully profitable center of pilgrimage. So you see, all sorts of things go on in the haunted desert, as the following article will show.

While Jewish and Christian writings have been diligently searched for possible references, direct or indirect, to the Qumran tradition, the Moslem commentators on the Koran have been neglected as a source of information, and that for the very quality that renders their work most valuable, namely their "uncritical" reluctance to omit from their profuse and repetitive notes any tradition, anecdote, or rumor that might conceivably cast light on a subject. Packed in among their jumbled baggage are many items that bring Qumran to mind. Whether these are significant or not remains to be decided after some of them have been examined.

The most promising place to begin a search for possible

glimpses of Qumran is among the commentaries on the "Sura of the Cave" (*Sura* XVIII) and the most promising guidebook is that inexhaustible storehouse of oddities and surprises, Ahmad ath-Tha'labi's *Accounts of the Prophets.*[1] Following Tha'labi's lead, and eking out his reports with those of other commentators, we shall attempt to show that Moslem scholars were convinced that there had once been a singular community of saints living in caves in the Judaean desert, particularly in the region of Jericho, and that those cave people had a portentous message for the human race.

As the most fitting commentary to the thesis that all things of this earth are but "dust and dry dirt," the Prophet refers us to the *Ashab al-Kahf wa-l 'Raqim*, "The Companions (often rendered simply 'People' or 'Inhabitants') of the Cave and the Inscription." (*Sura* XVIII, 9-10.) This was a group of holy men who had sought retreat in the wilderness in flight from a wicked and godless community and in the expectation that God would guide them in a proper way of life, fill them with grace, and provide for their wants; in due time they were hidden from the knowledge of men, and their bodies were miraculously preserved in a cave, where they were at length discovered when a youth, by the providence of God, circulated old coins in a nearby town and thereby brought a rush of treasure-seekers to the scene. (*Sura* XVIII, 10-22.) Such a tradition might well look back to the sectaries of the desert—but there is a catch, for most commentators are agreed that the People of the Cave were the Seven Sleepers of Ephesus. That would settle the matter were it not that the Ephesus tradition itself rests on the flimsiest of foundations, archaeologically and philologically.[2] It is "une de ces légendes vagabondes qui n'ont pas d'attache fixé et prennent pied sur les terrains les plus divers, sans qu'aucun fait connu semble justifier le choix."[3] Scholars ancient and modern who have tried to get to the historical kernel of the story have found themselves confronted by countless conflicting traditions, and the Koran and its commentators note that every essential element of

the history of the Companions is a subject of hopeless controversy among the People of the Book, who cannot agree
as to where the cave was, how many people were in it,[4]
what their religion was,[5] how long they stayed there, or
in what condition.[6] In short, nobody really knows their
history.

The main source of the confusion is not far to seek:
there was more than one cave story because there was
more than one cave—as the extremely popular legend
spread abroad in the world, the tale had to be adjusted to
the interest of local patriotism, which from Andalusia to
Persia enthusiastically and profitably exploited local grottoes as the authentic and original sites of the Seven Sleepers or the Companions of the Cave.[7] But amid a welter of
conflicting legends and claims, two main traditions have
always been recognized—an Occidental, containing clearly
marked pre-Christian Classical elements as its distinctive
ingredient, and an Eastern or Arabic tradition, based prin-
cipally on Jewish apocryphal lore.[8] The clearest distinction
between the two versions is preserved by Tha'labi. He
knows the Ephesus tradition as well as anybody: the pre-
Christian legends of youthful sleeping heroes are well represented in his pages;[9] he knows the resurrection miracle-
stories of the early Christian apocrypha;[10] he and the other
Arabs give an accurate description of the state of the Church
both when the Sleepers fell asleep and when they awoke;[11]
and they know the name of the mountain near Ephesus
where they slept—a name that Christian scholars apparently
do not know.[12]

But knowing the Ephesus version as he does, Tha'labi
still gives priority to an entirely different story about a party
of three refugees who were looking for a place for their
families to settle when "the sky smote them"; they took refuge in a cave, only to be trapped by a rock-slide that sealed
the entrance. Being thus caught, each one of them re-
counted some pious deed he had done in this lifetime, and

with each successive story a fissure in the wall opened wider until they could all escape.[13] This tale has nothing to do with Ephesus—the men in the cave tell Jewish stories and do not even fall asleep.[14] The violence of the elements, the sliding down of the mountain, and the opening of fissures in the earth suggest an earthquake, and the sequel is that the people settled on the spot, since they left their records there.

The story of the Three is an Arabic contribution, designated by Huber as the "Raqim" version, that being the uniquely Arabic name for the locale of the Cave.[15] Since it is a perfectly plausible tale, one wonders why the Arabs, who insist on placing al-Raqim in Syria or Palestine, bother with Ephesus at all. It is because Ephesus had loudly advertised its claim to the Seven Sleepers ever since the middle of the Fifth Century, and our commentators are not the men to leave anything out.[16] Ephesus, however, gets into the picture only by usurping the much older credentials of Antioch—a circumstance that has been overlooked by researchers. The hero of the Arabic accounts of the Sleepers is one Tamlikh, whose name does not appear in the standard Western lists of the Seven: When he turns up in the Syriac versions his name makes an eighth in the established list, so that the older Syriac and Arabic accounts uniformly insist that there were really eight Sleepers.[17] The origin of the intruder is indicated by the epithet that Tha'labi gives him of *Ibn Falastin*—the Palestinian.[18] His Greek name of Iamblichus usually appears in Latin sources as Malchus, while the Arabic writers point it variously as Tamlikh, Yamlikh, and Namlikh: all that remains is Bamlikh to remind us that, as Huber long ago suggested, the name Iamblichus-Malchus is simply Abimelech.[19] What brought Huber to that observation was the long-established identity, or at least very close parallel, between the Seven Sleepers and Abimelech, the friend of Jeremiah who slept for seventy or one hundred years.[20] Abimelech in turn has long been identified with Onias-Honi the Circle-drawer.[21] Onias, Abimelech, and Jeremiah all fell into century-long slumbers as they sat in the shade of a tree, and the tree is a peculiar detail that the Arabic writers introduce into their version of the Seven Sleepers,[22] and just as Onias was driven with his workmen to seek shelter from a storm in a cave, so the Arabs say the Cave of the Companions was discovered by a shepherd escaping from a storm, who ordered two laborers to open the mouth of the cave for him.[23] This Onias has in our day often been put forth as the leader of the Zadokite forerunners of the Qumran community in the days when they were being persecuted by Antiochus Epiphanes, and even as the founder of Qumran.[24] So we have Tamlikh, the leader of the Companions of the Cave, identified through Abimelech, with Onias, the leader of the Qumran society.

The earliest mention of the Seven Sleepers of Ephesus is in the *Itinera Theodosi*, 530 Anno Domini, which states that the Seven were brothers and that their mother was Felicitas.[25] When one recalls that one of the first female martyrs was St. Felicitas, who heroically endured the extinction of her seven sons, and that these seven have been identified in ancient and modern times with the seven young Jewish heroes of IV Maccabees, martyred at Antioch by the brother of Antiochus Epiphanes,[26] and that Byzantine Christians also identify the Seven Sleepers with the martyrs of Antioch,[27] and when one further considers that Decius, the villain of the Ephesus story, goes by the name of Antiochus in an eastern version of it,[28] one begins to wonder if the Fifth-Century Ephesus story might not reflect a much earlier Syrian version. The confusion of Antioch and Ephesus is apparent in the strange insistence of our Arabic informants that the city of Ephesus changed its name to Tarsus after its conversion from paganism. Scholars have found no explanation for this strange aberration, and indeed it is hard to see how well-traveled men could have confused two of the best-known cities in the world.[29]

But there is evidence that the name of Tarsus was indeed changed to Antiochia in 171 before Christ in honor of the pagan Antiochus Epiphanes, in which case it was back to Tarsus after his demise.[30] Zonaras, in a rhetorical play on words, calls the city Epiphanes,[31] and one wonders if the confusion of Tarsus-Epiphanes with Ephesus might not be a typical slip: the Arabs knew that the city had once had another name—and what could it have been but Ephesus, since they favored Tarsus as the site of the cave?[32] The year that the name was changed, 171 B.C., also saw a migration of Jews to Tarsus,[33] and one Arabic commentator suggests that Tarsus got its name at the time of the Cave People from a group of colonists from Tripolis in Syria.[34] At about the same time, it is surmised, the Bene Zadok were first being driven by Antiochus Epiphanes under their leader Onias III.[35] Thus there is some evidence to associate the founding of the Cave community with persons, times, places, and circumstances that have become familiar in the discussions of the founding of the Qumran community.

While quite aware that the Seven Sleepers story is Christian property, our Arabic informants are inclined to favor a *pre*-Christian date for the Companions of the Cave, explaining that they later become disciples of Jesus and flourished "in the days of the kings of Tawaif, between Jesus and Mohammed."[36] This implies that the society had a fairly long life, a thing entirely out of keeping with the brief and violent episode of the Ephesians. Another thing to note is the dependence of our Arabic informants, especially Tha'labi, on Jewish sources.[37] While it was Jacobite and Nestorian leaders arguing about the People of the Cave who first asked Mohammed's opinion on the matter,[38] those who really claimed a monopoly of knowledge on the subject were the Jews. According to one account, the Quraish sent a delegation to Medina to gather intellectual ammunition against the Prophet from the local Jews, who loudly insisted that they alone were qualified to speak on prophetic matters. They suggested some test questions to embarrass the new prophet, the prize one being about the People of the Cave.[39] In another version it is the skeptical Jews themselves who send the delegation to investigate Mohammed.[40] But the account favored by Tha'labi is that of a delegation of three holy men who came not to Mohammed but to Omar, looking for a true prophet. These were not the smart, proud, skeptical Jews of Medina but sincere and humble seekers, who gladly accepted the Prophet as soon as they were made sure of his calling.[41] The impression one gets is that of Hasidic Jews interviewing the sympathetic Omar during his campaign in Palestine—he calls them "brothers," and he must send back home for Ali in order to answer their questions.[42] The peculiar questions they put to him moreover bear the characteristic stamp of the nonconformist sectaries: they ask about the keys of heaven, the moving tomb of Jonah, the warning minister who is neither spirit nor man, the things that walk the earth but were not created in the womb, the speech of animals and its spiritual message, and above all "about the people of a former age who died 309 years, and then God revived them—what is their story?"[43]

That the story of the devout delegates goes back to the early sectaries is indicated in a report attributed to Ibn Abbas, the nephew of the Prophet and the star witness in all matters concerning the People of the Cave: "The followers of Jesus remained on the sacred path for 80 years after his ascension," and then "Yunus the Jew came among the Christians wearing a hermit's or monk's gown [this well before the days of Christian monasticism]. . . . His devout life produced great confidence among the Christians, and . . . he said, 'Send me three of your learned men . . . that I may divine a secret before each of them separately.'" As a result "the Christians were divided into three sects" forever after—the very sects that argued about the Cave People in the presence of Mohammed.[44] Here we have a counterpart both to the three malicious questions that the Jews put to Mohammed (in nearly all the commentators the questions are three) and the delegation of three pious Jews that came to him. The oldest Syrian version of the Seven Sleepers, which some hold to be the original, places their history around A.D. 60, thus taking it entirely out of the later Ephesian setting and putting it in the orbit of the early sectaries.[45]

Tha'labi is quite at home with certain pre-Christian communities in the desert. He tells us among other things how the infant Mary was taken to be reared by "the priests of the sons of Aaron," and how the priestly society cast lots for her, standing on the banks of the Jordan to see whose rod would sink and whose would float, they being "the reeds with which they used to write the Torah." Zacharias, the father of John the Baptist, and, according to Tha'labi, "the chief of the scholars and their prophet," won the lottery; but when a famine came he could no longer support the child, and it was necessary to have another casting of lots, won this time by Joseph the righteous carpenter.[46] Since "Brownlee argues that the mother of the Messiah is the 'Essene Community,'"[47] Mary's prominence in such a community as this may not be without significance. The story of Joseph's winning of Mary is told in the *Epistle of I Clement,* c. 43, and indeed Tha'labi's general familiarity with Clementine motifs should be studied in view of the importance of the latter in understanding the background of Qumran.[48] His tracing of Zacharias's genealogy through both a Saduq and a Sadiq indicates access to early source material[49] and is quite relevant to the Seven Sleeper investigation, since the oldest Western version, that of Gregory of Tours, reports, on the authority of "a certain Syrian" that the mission of the Seven Sleepers was to correct certain errors not of the Christians but of the Sadducees—a term often confused with Zadokite in the early Middle Ages in designating nonconformist sectarians among the Jews.[50]

Why should the Seven Sleepers of Ephesus be emissaries to the Sadducees, of all things? The Zadokite background of Qumran needs no demonstration.

A significant aspect of the Seven Sleepers' history as told by the Arabs is that nobody ever sees them alive.[51] Even in the Western legends the ruler merely embraces the youths as they sit on the ground, and after a short and formal benediction by one of them they promptly fall asleep again.[52] The miracle that proves the resurrection is never the animation of their bodies but only their preservation;[53] no capital is made of the rich store of Jewish and Christian apocryphal lore, the "testaments" of various prophets, patriarchs, and apostles who come to life to tell of wonderful things in the worlds beyond. This remarkable reserve suggests what many students have pointed out, that the Sleeper stories may well have originated with the actual discovery of human remains in caves. The Mediterranean world had never been without local hero-cults and their grottoes: Arabic writers report visits to a center in Andalusia that had all the fixtures and purported to be the original home of the Companions of the Cave,[54] and such a shrine and cult survived at Paphos on Cyprus down to modern times.[55] But the cave best known to the Arabs was one near Tarsus, where thirteen cadavers in a remarkable state of preservation were annually propped up and groomed—their clothes brushed, their nails manicured, their hair dressed—and then laid down to sleep for another year before a devout host of Christian pilgrims who believed they were in the presence of the Seven Sleepers.[56] This reproduces exactly the drama of the original Sleepers in the presence of Theodosius and his people, and strongly suggests a cult of the dead. In the "Hunting" version of the Sleepers story, which has all the marks of the Classical Endymion cycle, our Arabic informants comment on how the spring dried up and the trees all withered while the youths slept, only to be miraculously revived at their awakening.[57]

Such obvious cult-motifs serve to set the Ephesian tradition apart from the more down-to-earth "Raqim" accounts of the Arabs, which indeed contain rather surprisingly nothing of a miraculous nature.

In a much-cited passage, Ibn Abbas tells how on a campaign with Mu'awiyah or Habib ibn Maslamah he passed by a cave containing bones that were said to be those of the Companions. His friend wanted to take a look, but Ibn Abbas protested that that would be sacrilege; some men who were sent to the cave to investigate were driven away in terror by a fierce wind.[58] Ibn Abbas is quoted as saying that the cave was "near Aelia," and al-Qurtubi explains that they passed by it on the way to Rum.[59] The latter authority also reports that when Ibn Abbas made a few fitting remarks at the cave site, a Syrian monk who was standing by observed with surprise, "I didn't think that an Arab would know anything about that!" to which the company proudly replied by introducing Ibn Abbas as their Prophet's nephew.[60]

The key to the location of the Eastern Cave is the mysterious name of *al-Raqim*. The great Ibn Abbas confesses that the word is one of the four things in the Koran that he cannot understand, but is quoted by Tabari as saying that Raqim is "a wadi between 'Asfan and Aelia beyond Palestine; and it is near Aelia";[61] while Damiri has him say: "it is a wadi between Amman and Aelia, beyond Palestine between the Ghatfan (tribe) and the country beyond Palestine; and this is the wadi in which the People of the Cave live, but Ka'ab says it is their village."[62] Most Arabic authorities locate al-Raqim in the plain of Balq in southeastern Palestine, and the geographer Istakhri mentions a small town by that name in the area, apparently near the Dead Sea.[63] Some writers, however, favor the region of Damascus and others that of Amman.[64] Clermont-Ganneau noted that the village of al-Raqim seven kilometers south of Amman is identified by Usama with a place called el-Kahf, where there are some remarkable tombs cut into the living rock—hence *Ashab al-Kahf wa l'Raqim*. In December of 1964 the writer visited this site with Mr. Rafiq Dajani of the Jordan Department of Antiquities, whose forthcoming book on the subject treats at length the features of the newly excavated site which render it in our opinion by far the most likely candidate for the original Raqim. Even Huber concedes that this was probably the al-Raqim of the Arabic commentators but hastens to point out that it cannot possibly have been the cave of the Seven Sleepers of Ephesus.[65] But then no one says it was—our Arabic authors readily admit that they are dealing with other caves, and what interests us here is not the mythical cavern of Ephesus but real caves in the Judaean desert.

Distant candidates in Nineveh and Yemen need not detain us, though we should not overlook the suggestion that the Companions were originally wandering artisans *(sayāqala)*.[66] Tha'labi reports that when writings inscribed on metal plates (and we shall presently see that the "inscriptions" of the Cave were such documents) were found in a cave in Yemen no one could decipher them until one of these traveling smiths or artisans was consulted.[67] This is noteworthy because some scholars have seen in these nomadic craftsmen the descendants of the Rekhabites and hence the possible ancestors of the Qumran community.[68] The earliest Oriental versions of the Seven Sleepers stories actually do come from Nejran, the borders of Yemen. Massignon explains this by showing that the feast of the Martyrs of Nejran falls on the same day as that of the Seven Sleepers of Ephesus, making it easy if not inevitable for Jacob of Sarug to confuse the two; and since Ephesus was inconveniently far away, Massignon reasons, Eastern Christians simply moved the shrine to Nejran, whence it was transplanted to "military garrisons and the hermitages of anchorites on the fringes of the deserts."[69] The objection to this theory is that the men of Nejran will have nothing whatever to do with *Seven* Sleepers, but only three or five, which is strange indeed if they imported the magic Seven directly from Ephesus.[70] Plainly the Nejran version rests on another tradition.

Al-Raqim, so Lane informs us, means writings engraved or scratched on something, "a brass plate, or stone tablet, placed at the mouth of the cave," Sale suggests, though he is not sure,[71] or else it is two lead tablets in a sealed copper box—with silver seals,[72] or it is simply a book, or even a golden tablet,[73] or perhaps it is an inscription over the cave door,[74] or else the name of the cave itself, or of the wadi where it is,[75] or possibly the mountain,[76] or it may have been the stone that blocked the entrance,[77] or else it is the ruins near the cave or even the village where the Cave People lived;[78] or it may refer to water holes or running water in the wadi.[79] On the other hand, it may refer to coins, or to an inkstand or writing desk found on the spot;[80] or it may be the dog that guarded the cave,[81] or any number of regions claiming to possess the Cave.[82] Strangely enough, no one seeking to locate the cave ever mentions the church or mosque that is supposed to have marked the spot with perpetual ritual observances—this most obvious clue of all has no place in the Raqim tradition. Instead we are confronted with a combination of caves, writings, bones, ruins, coins, inkstands, wadis (there is no mention of a valley in any of the orthodox Ephesus stories), and so on, suggesting that the would-be interpreters of al-Raqim all have in mind a type of archaeological site that the modern reader most readily associates with Qumran.

The general consensus is that al-Raqim refers to secret buried writings containing the history and even the teachings of the Companions but "whose meaning God has kept from us, and whose history we do not know."[83] These were deliberately hidden away to come forth in a later age when "perhaps God will raise up a believing people."[84] There was a tradition that Jeremiah with the same purpose had hidden such treasures in a cave near Jericho,[85] as Peter had done near Jerusalem (according to Baidawi it was Peter who discovered the documents of al-Raqim),[86] and the theme of buried holy books has a special appeal to Tha'labi, who carries the custom back to the remotest times.[87] The recently recognized possibility that the library of Qumran was deliberately buried in "a solemn communal interment" to come forth in a more righteous age thus supplies another link between Qumran and the Companions of the Cave and the Raqim, while putting a new stamp of authenticity on their existence.[88]

Let us recall how the question was put to Omar: "Tell me about the people of old who died 309 years and then God revived them—what is their story?" One wonders in passing why Jews should be so interested in a purely Christian story, and why they alone should claim to know its details, which according to Tha'labi were all to be found in Jewish books: plainly they were not asking about Ephesus at all.[89] The length of the famous sleep is reported at anything from 70 to 900 years. The Christians favor 372, while the Moslems accept the 309 years of the Koran.[90] The true meaning of the 309 is a great mystery, which only a true prophet can explain;[91] it comes from the beni Israel, and "the Christians of Nejran say, 'As for the 300 years we already knew about that, but as for the 9 years we know nothing about it.'"[92] But all are agreed that it represents the period of darkness during which the blessed Companions slept, like Onias, to awaken only at the dawn of a new age of faith.[93] Such was also, whatever the actual years may have been, the significance of the 390 years of the *Damascus Document* I, 5-6, "the Era of Anger" and darkness. Massignon shows the lengths to which Christians and Moslems will go to see significance in 309; it is the "anagram of the total of the 14 isolated initial letters of the Koran," namely 903, as also, of the name of Jesus: *'Isa* = 390.[94] The free juggling of figures does not draw the line at arranging them in any order, just as modern scholars are not embarrassed by the difference between 390 and 393 years or the necessity of adding or subtracting 20 or 40 to suit one's calculations. It has been recognized that the 390 of the *Damascus Document* is a symbolic number having "no more than a schematic value," and the same is held for the Koranic 309.[95] Since both have the same significance and are equally vague, distant, and mysterious, a possible confusion of the two may furnish yet another link between the two societies.

The consensus of opinion that al-Raqim were *metal* plates containing the writings of the Companions, as well as Tha'labi's preoccupation with metal documents in general, is moved from the realm of pure fantasy by the recent discovery of a number of metal documents in Palestine and Syria, the most notable being the Copper Scrolls from Qumran Cave IV. Tabari tells of a shepherd who discovered inscribed tablets that no one could read but an old holy man of the desert—like the Copper Scrolls, these tablets contained lists of buried treasure.[96] Another peculiarity of the Companions that does not fit with the Ephesus scene is the emphasis put on the formal organization of the society. After individually receiving enlightenment in the shade of a tree—like Onias, Abimelech, and the Buddha—the Seven reveal to each other their likemindedness and resolve to form a community with a nearby cave as their headquarters. They have a president and spokesman, Maximilianus, and a secretary and a treasurer, Tamlikh, the star of the play.[97] Each member fetches his property from his father's house and, after giving lavishly to the poor, turns the rest over to a common fund, to be shrewdly administered.[98] Such a community of property is one of the best-known features of the Qumran society.

In taking to the wilderness, the Brethren set up (according to the Arabs, but not to the Greeks) at a place where there were a good spring and some fruit trees, subsisting as did many a pious anchorite in years to come on the water and dates of an oasis.[99] "They left their homes and lands, families and children . . . and entered the caves [plural] in the year of the prophets."[100] Here we have a definitive religious movement, as against the adolescent escapade of Ephesus: in the latter case the youths (who are very young) flee to the wilderness expressly to escape the emperor, while in the former their society flourishes before the emperor ever hears of it.[101] Part of the heroic allure of the Companions is that they are high-ranking officers in the imperial army, which seeming inconsistency suits well with the image of the men of Qumran as "dedicated holy warriors."[102]

Considerable emphasis is placed by our Arabic authors on the north-south orientation of the Sleepers, who must face the north to preserve their bodies against the day of their arising. Here is a reminder of the north-south orientation of the burials at Qumran, whatever may be its significance.[103] The bodies of the Sleepers were turned from side to side by angelic ministers (to avoid corruption) every seven days, or seven years, or twice a year, or (in most writers) every year on New Year's Day.[104] Also, the sun shines into the cavern on just two days of the year—suggesting the equinoxes—and it is the sun that finally awakens them.[105] The emphasis here on a solar (resurrection) cult and calendar is a reminder that the Qumran people were peculiar for their zealous adherence to an archaic solar calendar.[106]

It was in the ancient practice of incubation at healing shrines that E. Rohde sought the origin of the Seven Sleepers tradition, and indeed our Arabic and Syriac sources tell how God speaks to the Companions as they sleep, and how one calls upon their names for healing dreams.[107] It is just possible that Qumran itself may have been such a healing shrine:" The idea of a place of healing by the Dead Sea was well established in Jewish tradition and gives added reason for the Essenes' ('Physicians') choice of Qumran (Mesillah) for their desert home."[108] In this connection, Allegro dwells on the ancient designations of Qumran as meaning "shady," "sheltered"—which puts one in mind of the elaborate arrangements described by the Arab scholars for keeping the sleeping Companions in the shade,[109] though admittedly far-fetched.

The one truly moving episode in the history of the Seven Sleepers as the Arabic commentators tell it is the manner of their falling asleep. The indefatigable Tamlikh returns from the town in tears of anxiety to report to his friends that the monster (*jabbar*, a Jewish word) has returned to Ephesus and is coming out against them. This calls for a general lamentation until Tamlikh tells the brethren to dry their eyes, lift up their heads, and "eat what God has given," an expression suggestive of an exhortation to martyrdom. Accordingly, we behold the Brethren of the Cave partaking of their last sorrowful supper as the sun sets (the setting of the sun receives special emphasis), and then, as they sit upon the ground, preparing and exhorting one another in holy conversation, quietly yielding up their souls to God.[110]

The celebration of a last supper and love-feast as the sun sets brings to mind Philo's account of an Egyptian branch of the Essenes holding their solemn feast at sundown,[111] as well as al-Biruni's report that the Jewish sect of the Magharia celebrated their rites at sunset—a circumstance that could easily lead him to omit the single *nuqfah* that makes the difference between Maghariba ("Sundown-people") and the familiar Maghariyah or "People of the Caves."[112]

The reference in *Sura* LXXXV, 4 to "the people of the pit" *(ashabu 'l-ukhdud)* deserves mention because in the past it has commonly been interpreted as referring to the persecutors of the Christians of Nejran. This explanation was seriously questioned, and the now familiar designation of the "people of the pit" in the Dead Sea Scrolls indicates an earlier origin of the concept.[113] At the same time it vindicates the Christian Nejran tradition as an authentic echo of the old desert sectaries: it was the Christians of Nejran, it will be recalled, who first mentioned the Companions of the Cave to Mohammed.

The name given by the Companions to their settlement, according to the Arabic sources, was Hiram or Khiram, meaning "sectarians" or "separation," but also an appropriate designation for forbidden ground.[114] The wonderful dog that spoke with a human voice and faithfully guarded the threshold of the Cave usually goes by the name of Qatmir, though we also find him sharing the well-nigh universal name of Raqim, explained by Damiri's note that the Arabs often called a dog Raqmah, meaning a wadi with water in it, which he believes to be the source of the name Raqim.[115] Since the name of the dog is thus confused with that of the society, the cave, the valley and what-not, one wonders if the second commonest name of the dog might not represent a like confusion—for the name is Khumran, the closest parallel yet to "the meaningless Arabic name Qumran."[116]

Let us now briefly summarize some of the main points of resemblance between Qumran and the Companions of the Cave. First of all, the experts favor a pre-Christian origin for both; each begins its history with a persecution and migration under (possibly) Antiochus Epiphanes, at a time when both societies seem to have the same leader; both have ties with wandering artisans—the ancestors and/or descendants of desert sectarian groups; they have the same apocalyptic-mystic teachings, familiar alike from the early Jewish and the early Christian apocryphal writings; both have connections with a priestly society on the Jordan before the birth of Christ; the activities of both are reflected in the Clementine writings; both are identified with the Zadokites by name; both are near Aelia and even nearer to Jericho; both leave behind the same peculiar combination of archaeological litter; both engage in the odd practice of burying sacred records to come forth at a later time as a witness; both make use of metal plates for such records; each thinks of itself as the righteous remnant; the numbers 309 and 390 have for the Companions and Qumran respectively the same significance; both societies are well organized and practice a community of property; each community has its buildings, spring, and fruit trees as well as its caves; both are ritually oriented, dedicated to good works and religious exercises, controlled by a special solar calendar; in both the dead are laid away facing the north; both practice healing and incubation and seem to have had a solemn ritual feast at sundown; the members of both are dramatized in a military capacity; both sites are linked in later times with the mysterious word *Khumran-Qumran*. In both cases everything is very vague, far away, and strangely portentous.

The great mystic and symbolic appeal of the Sura of the Cave, which is recited every Friday in every mosque, rests on the concept of the Seven as intercessors for man in a wicked and dangerous world.[117] But there may be more than abstract symbolism or allegory involved here. Scattered references in Jewish and Christian writings, such as the Karaite texts and the letter of Bishop Timotheus, indicate at least a dim awareness down through the centuries of the existence and the peculiar significance of writings found in caves near Jericho. When the red herring of Ephesus is removed we are faced with the very real likelihood that the people who left those records were those very "Companions of the Cave and the Writing" who made such an indelible imprint on the Islam.

The purpose of this brief exploratory study has been to raise rather than settle issues. The Arabic commentators cited are, of course, only a sampling, since the Arabic sources available at present in the Far West are limited, though increasing very rapidly, thanks to the titanic efforts of Professor Aziz S. Atiya. But they have given us enough to indicate that many questions still await and deserve investigation. We have not even touched upon the knotty and intriguing question of the identification and status of the all-knowing Tha'labi, nor have we examined the possible paths by which the Qumran tradition reached him and other Arabic writers; nor have we considered the wealth of literary tradition and folklore that surrounds the wonderful dog Qatmir, nor sought to trace the mysterious and significant line of Zadok in the Arabic sources; nay, we have not even mentioned the many other possible references to the Qumran tradition in the Koran itself. What we have done is simply to indicate the possibility that echoes of Qumran still reverberate in the pages of many Moslem writers, who may yet prove valuable informants to students of the Dead Sea Scrolls.

NOTES

1. "Abu Ishaq Ibn Mohammed Ibn Ibrahim ath-Tha'labi of Nishapur, the celebrated commentator, was the outstanding [Koran] interpreter of his time; he composed a great commentary which was without equal for fullness." (Ibn Khallikan, *Kitab wafayat al-aiyan* [Paris: 1842], I, p. 30. "Ein besonders heiss umstrittenes Feld waren altarabischen, jüdischen und christlichen Legenden des Korans und der Tradition. . . . So kommt es, dass der bedeutendste Korangelehrte deiner Zeit, der im Jahre 427/1036 gestorbene Ahmed eth-Tha'labi, als bedeutendstes Werk seine 'Prophetengeschichten' erfasst hat." (A. Mez., *Die Renaissance des Islams* [Heidelberg: 1922], p. 190.) His "History of the Prophets" gives all the stories in very great detail. (*Encyclopedia of Islam* [1934], IV, p. 736. Cf. C. Brockelmann, *Geschichte der Arabischen Literatur* [Weimar: 1898], I, pp. 350-51.)

2. Baronius and Tillemont both declared it spurious. The Austrian archaeologists working at the supposed site discovered "pas un nom ni un symbole, indice d'une tombe vénérée." (*Analecta Bollandiana* 55 [1937]:351.) Philology is no less nonplussed: "Il ne faut pas oublier que les noms de la grotte et de la montagne de la légende ne se retrouvent pas aux environs d'Ephèse." (Ibid., 24 [1905]:503.)

3. *Analecta Bollandiana* 55 (1937):351. Cf. ibid., 39 (1921):176, commenting on the "systèmes déjà échafaudés autour de cette littérature foisonnante." There is no apparent reason why the legend should have become the special property of Ephesus, according to Bern Heller ("La Légende des Sept Dormants," *Revue des Etudes Juives* 49

[1904]: 216, n. 6), though it is understandable that the city once in possession should exploit the legend to the fullest.

4. For location, see below, notes 61-65. The number of sleepers is a subject of endless debate. (*Sura* XVIII, 22; al-Nasafi, *Tafsir al-Qur'an al-jalil* [Cairo: 1936-1942], II, p. 286; al-Hijazi, *al-Tafsir al-wadih* [Cairo: 1952], XV, pp. 53-54.) It is one of the great mysteries, known to but a few. (Al-Tabari, *Kitab jami' al-bayan fi tafsir al-Qur'an* [Cairo: 1910], XV, p. 150; al-Nasafi.) The Jacobites said there were three sleepers, the Nestorians five, the Moslems seven. (Al-Qurtubi, *al-Jami' li-ahkam al-Qur'ran* [Cairo: 1935?-1950], X, p. 382; al-Damiri, *Hayat al-hayawan* [Cairo: 1867], II, pp. 353-54 [pages are incorrectly numbered, but we follow the numbers given]; al-Nasafi, II, p. 285; al-Baydawi, *Anwar al-tanzil* [Cairo: 1899-1902], IV, pp. 98-99.) Yusuf Ali, a modern authority, says that Mohammed "*suggested* that the youths were seven in number." (*The Holy Qur'an* [New York: Hafner, 1946], II, p. 730, note 2337.)

5. Some say they lived before Christ and were idolaters, others that they were Christians, others that they were Moslems (Tabari, *Tarikh al-Tabari* [Cairo: 1961], II, pp. 6-7; *Jami' al-bayan*, XV, p. 137); some even that their people were *majus* (Damiri, II, p. 353). Yet the Jews have a special claim on them. (Ibn Kathir, *Tafsir al-Qur'an al-asim* [Cairo: 1954], III, p. 74.) See below, note 37.

6. See below, note 90, for the length of the stay. As to their condition, the main discussion is whether they were sleeping or dead. (Baydawi, IV, pp. 97-98; Qurtubi, X, p. 388; Damiri, II, p. 358, etc.) See Michel Huber, *Die Wanderlegende von den Siebenschläfern* [Leipzig: 1910], pp. 79-99.)

7. Huber pp. 17, 122. Thus after favoring Ephesus (though Ephesus is not mentioned in the Koran), Ibn Kathir, III, p. 75, concludes: "We are not told what land the cave was in. . . . But Ibn Abbas says it was near Aelia, and Ibn Ishaq says it was near Nineveh, while others say it was in the land of Rum and others that it was in the plain of Balqā [southeastern Palestine], but God knows." See below, note 59.

8. Discussed by Huber, pp. 552-56. The distinction is clear in Huber's classification of sources into the Classical Endymion and Epimenides legends (pp. 378-90), as against the Onias-Abimelech-Ezra tradition (pp. 403-47) of the Orient. The Arabic commentators themselves admonish against confusing the two traditions. Thus Al-Shirbini, *al-siraj al-munir* (Cairo: 1868), II, p. 350, assures us that the three pious refugees (below, note 13) are "another group entirely from the [traditional] People of the Cave." (Cf. al-Qurtubi, X, p. 357, and Ibn Kathir, III, p. 75.)

9. The Endymion motif, in which E. Rohde, *Die sardinische Sage von den Neunschläfern*, in *Rheinisches Museum für Philologie*, Neue Folge, 35 (1880): 158-59, 162-63, sees the origin of the Seven Sleepers of Ephesus, is one of the four distinct versions of the Sleepers reported by Tha'labi and others. It is the "Hunting" story in which youthful nobles go forth to hunt and celebrate a great pagan festival only to end up falling asleep in a cave, guarded by their faithful dog. The fullest account of this is in Tha'labi, *Qisas al-anbiyah* (Cairo: 1921), pp. 289-90, 292-93. (Cf. Ibn Kathir, III, pp. 74-75; al-Qasimi, *Tafsir al-qasimi* [Cairo: 1957-60], X, p. 4032.) Typical of the cycle is Tha'labi's account of Saint George, pp. 299-300.

10. One of the four versions (see preceding note) is the tale of the Bath Attendant (Tha'labi, p. 293; Tabari, *Tarikh*, II, p. 8; *Jami' al-bayan*, XV, p. 136; Damiri, II, pp. 344-45; Qurtubi, X, pp. 359-60), which consists of familiar motifs from the early apocryphal *Acts of John, Thomas, Andrew, Peter*, etc. (See Huber, pp. 306-10.) Also the well-known talking-dog motif, found in all the above-named Arabic sources, is familiar from the pseudo-*Acts of Andrew, Thomas*, etc. Damiri, II, p. 344, says that the official story of the People of the Cave was written down by Andrew (Mandrūs) and Thomas (Dūmās), and others say that it was "a righteous ruler of the people called Peter (Bīdrūs)" who ruled for sixty-eight years who discovered the document. (Baydawi, IV, pp. 87, 90.)

11. The moral decline of the Christians just before the Decian persecution, to which Eusebius and Cyprian attribute that persecution, is passed over in silence by Christian commentators on the Ephesus story but is very well described by the Arabs: Tha'labi, p. 293; Tabari, *Jami' al-bayan*, XV, p. 133; Nasafi, II, p. 284; Shirbini, II, p. 351; Damiri, II, pp. 339-40. The state of things under Theodosius is equally well described. (Huber, p. 567; *Analecta Bollandiana* 72 [1954]: 265.) The risen youths seem to the emperor like the ancient disciples come to life, and he rejoices in the restoration of the old religion. (Tabari, *Jami'al-bayan*, XV, p. 147; Shirbini, II, p. 362; Damiri, II, p. 349.) The righteous leader who greets the Saints on their awakening sometimes bears the name of Arius. (Tabari, XV, pp. 145-47; Shirbini, II, p. 361.) Tha'labi, pp. 297-98, reads it *Armús*.

12. In Greek sources it is Chaos, Chileton, Chileon; in the Latin, Chilleus, Celius, Mons Celeus. (*Analecta Bollandiana* 41 [1923]:374; 55 [1937]:350.) In the Syrian tradition it is always Mount Anchilos, of which Huber, pp. 222-23, notes that "um Ephesus herum kein einziger Berg einen auch nur halbwegs ähnlichen Namen trägt," surmising that the Christians could readily borrow the name of Mons

Caelius near Rome for their Sleepers, "da der Berg selber nicht existierte," p. 58. The Arabs ring the changes on Anchilos with *Yanjilūs* (Baydawi, IV, pp. 85-86, 89), mispointed to read *Banāhīyūs* and even Manhilūs (Damiri, II, pp. 343, 350), but most commonly written as *Banjilūs* (Tabari, XV, p. 135; Shirbini, II, p. 353; Ibn Kathir, III, p. 73), this being nearest to the modern Turkish name for the real mountain east of Ephesus, Panajir-Dagh. (*Analecta Bollandiana* 55 [1937]:350.)

13. Tha'labi, p. 287, attributing the story to Mohammed. It was *thalātha nafrin*, which can mean either a party of refugees or a military detail. That it was the former may be inferred from the nature of their mission: *yarla-dūna li-ahlihim*, "looking about for some place for their families"—seeking asylum. (See Damiri, II, p. 341.)

14. The stories have been analyzed by B. Heller, pp. 199-202, and classified as Haggidic.

15. "So ist eine genaue *Scheidung* zwischen den Höhlenleuten [of Ephesus] und den Genossen des Er-Raqim festzuhalten. . . ." (Huber, p. 239.) See below, notes 61 and 62.

16. It is now definitely established that the story was first fastened on Ephesus by a *"pia fraus"* of Bishop Stephanus of that city in the year 449 or 450, according to *Analecta Bollandiana* 72 (1954):265, citing E. Honigmann, *Patristic Studies* (Rome: Vatican, 1954).

17. M. Huber, pp. 593, 503; *Analecta Bollandiana* 39 (1921):177; 66 (1948):195. The Arabs explain the discrepancy by having the Seven joined by a shepherd on their way to the Cave. (Tha'labi, p. 293.) Tabari, *Tarikh*, II, p. 6; Baydawi, IV, p. 48; and Damiri, II, p. 339, all tell straightforward stories of eight Sleepers, in spite of *Sura* XVIII, 22.

18. Tha'labi, p. 292.

19. "Schon der Name Abimelech weist auf den Jamlich-und-Malchus hin." (Huber, p. 22.)

20. Heller, pp. 207, 214.

21. Huber, pp. 418-26. (See the article *Onias [Honi]* in *Jewish Encyclopedia* [1901], IX, pp. 401-5.)

22. For the three Hebrews, see B. Heller, pp. 202-6. For the tree episode, see Tha'labi, p. 292; Tabari, XV, p. 136; Baydawi, IV, p. 86; Ibn Kathir, III, p. 74; Qurtubi, X, p. 359; Shirbini, II, p. 355.

23. Heller, p. 206; Cf. Tha'labi, p. 295; Tabari, *Tarikh*, II, p. 8; Baydawi, IV, p. 87; Damiri, II, 357. Down to modern times, the Seven Sleepers have been protectors against storms. (*Analecta Bollandiana* 68 [1950]:248.)

24. Whether a later Onias is preferred (R. Goossens, "Onias le juste . . . lapidé en 65 avant J.-C.," *La Nouvelle Clio.* 1-2 [1949f], pp.

336-53), or the earlier Onias III, *circa* 170 B.C.(M. Black, *The Scrolls and Christian Origins* [New York: Scribner's, 1961], p. 20), there is general agreement on a connection between Onias and Qumran. (See H. H. Rowley, "The Zadokite Fragments, and the Dead Sea Scrolls," *Expository Times* 63 [1951/2]:382; M. H. Segal, "The Habakkuk Commentary and the Damascus Fragments," *Journal of Biblical Literature,* 70 [1951]:145.)

25. " . . . civitas Epheso ubi sunt septem fratres dormientes . . . quorum mater Caritina dicitur graece, latine Felicitas," text in *Analecta Bollandiana* 41 (1923):372. Cf. Gregory of Tours, in Migne *Patrologiae Latinae* 71, col. 787: "Septem vero germanorum. . . . "

26. The identification is recognized in *Analecta Bollandiana* 57 (1939):3. Heller, p. 217, believes that the Seven heroes of Antioch are the most instructive of all parallels to the Seven of Ephesus.

27. Namely at Paphos on Cyprus. (*Analecta Bollandiana* 26 [1907]: 272.) The Christians of Antioch built a basilica over the tomb of the Seven Jewish brothers, just as those of Ephesus did at the shrine of the Seven Sleepers. (Heller, p. 217.)

28. In an "Antiochus-Gedicht" of 1527, that ruler is designated throughout as Decius. (W. Bacher, *Jewish Quarterly Review* 16 [1904]: 529.) "Voilà la fusion des deux légendes," cries Heller, p. 218, commenting on this.

29. Tha'labi, p. 287. Some writers simply speak of Tarsus without even mentioning Ephesus. (Nasafi, II, p. 282; Shribini, II, p. 358; al-Zamakhshari, *al-Kashshaf* [Cairo: 1890], I, p. 469.) Heller, p. 200, note 5, can make no sense of this.

30. Böhlig and Steinmann, in Pauly-Wissowa, *Realencyklopädie,* IV A, col. 2419.

31. Ibid., col. 2431.

32. Below, note 56.

33. *Realencyklopädie,* IV A, col. 2420-421.

34. Al-Qasimi, X, p. 4028.

35. H. H. Rowley, "The Covenanters of Damascus and the Dead Sea Scrolls," *Bulletin of the John Rylands Library,* 35 (September 1952): 137-45; P. Kahle, *The Cairo Geniza* (London: 1947), p. 19.

36. See Tha'labi, p. 288; Damiri, II, p. 349; Tabari, *Tarikh,* II, pp. 6-7: "Some say they worshipped Jesus . . . and some say their history . . . was before Christ, and that the Messiah taught his people about them, and that God woke them from sleep after he had raised up Jesus, in the time between him and Mohammed, but God knows." (Cf. Qurtubi, X, pp. 359, 388, and Huber, p. 21, citing Ibn Qutaiba.) Damiri, II, p. 357, says they fell asleep, following one tra-

dition, until the land became Moslem; and Ibn Kathir, III, p. 74, notes that if they had been Christians, the Jews, who do not mention such a thing, would certainly have reported it.

37. See B. Heller, "La légende biblique dans l'Islam," *Revue des Études Juives* 98 (1934):7, and ibid. 49 (1904):202-12. Tha'labi knows of specific Jewish informants of Mohammed (pp. 77, 137), and refers to his own Jewish teachers (pp. 137, 152, 241, 254, 257, etc.). He often betrays a distinctly pro-Jewish and anti-Christian prejudice, as in the long story of Jesus' vain attempt to convert a Jew, pp. 276-79. He even knows the Pumbeditha scandal-story that Mary was once a ladies' hair-dresser. (P. 131.)

38. "The seyyid and the Jacobite and their Christian companions from Nejran were visiting *(kānū 'inda)* Mohammed" when the matter came up. (Baydawi, IV, p. 98; Cf. Nasafi, II, p. 285; Damiri, II, p. 354.)

39. Shirbini, II, p. 351; al-Hijazi, XV, p. 54; as-Suyuti, *Lubab al-nugul* (Cairo: 1935), p. 144, emphasizes the boastfulness of the Jews.

40. Ibn Kathir, III, p. 74; as-Suyuti (in note 39); Sayyid Qutb, *Fi zilal al-Qur'an* (Cairo: 1953?), XV, p. 81.

41. Tha'labi, pp. 288-89. Heller, "Légende des Septs Dormants," p. 200, believes this story to be a unique contribution of Tha'labi.

42. Ali and Omar in the story both address the delegates as "brothers of the Arabs," who in turn are "the brothers of the Jews." (Tha'labi, p. 289.) The way in which Ali is greeted by Omar as he arrives wearing the robe of the Prophet suggests that he has been summoned from a distance. (P. 288.) As both the conqueror of Palestine and the would-be rebuilder of the temple (H. Nibley, in *Jewish Quarterly Review* 50 [1959]:118-120), Omar would be sympathetically received by the "Hasidic" sectaries of the desert.

43. The questions are given in full in Tha'labi, pp. 288-89. Most Arab writers mention only three questions: "about the Spirit, the Companions of the Cave, and Dhu 'l-Qarnain." (Hijazi, XV, p. 54.) On the apocryphal-sectarian nature of the questions, see M. Huber, pp. 454-56; K. Ahrens, "Christliches im Qoran," *Zeitschrift der Deutschen Morgenländischen Gesellschaft* 84 (1930):163.

44. H. Wernecke, *The Monist* 15 (1905):467-68. They became "the three chief sects of Syria." (Pp. 466-67.)

45. This is Jacob of Sarug, discussed by Heller, "Légende des Septs Dormants," pp. 260-61, who is at a loss to explain the surprisingly early date.

46. Tha'labi, pp. 260-61.

47. M. Black (note 24), p. 149.

48. Tha'labi, pp. 122-23, also tells the Clementine story of the

blossoming staff. On the influence of the Clementine writing on the Koran, see K. Ahrens (in note 43), pp. 56-60, 64, 174; on their importance for Qumran, see H. J. Schoeps, in *Zeitschrift für Religions- und Geistesgeschichte* 3 (1951):333-34; 6 (1954):277-78; 10 (1958):15; and especially "Das Judenchristentum in den Pseudo-klementinen," 11 (1959):72-77.

49. Tha'labi, p. 259. Onias, as the grandfather of John the Baptist, belongs to the same line, that of the Sadiqqim. (R. Eisler, *Iesous Basileus* [Heidelberg: 1930], II, p. 49.)

50. Gregorius Turonensis, in *Patrologiae Latinae*, 71, col. 788. On the confusion of Sadduccees and Zadokites, see H. H. Rowley (in note 35) pp. 129-32. The Moslems designated nonconformist sectarians as *Zandakiyah*, and though the origin of the word is obscure, a *zindiq* is, according to Lane's *Arabic-English Lexicon*, I, p. 1258, "one of the thanawiyah [or asserters of the doctrine of Dualism]: or one who asserts his belief in [the two principles of] Light and Darkness: or one who . . . conceals unbelief and makes an outward show of belief." How well this applies to the dualistic theology and secretive policies of Qumran needs no illustration. Our Arabic commentators often refer to the Companions of the Cave as *thanawiyah*. When a Moslem victor asked some sectarians, "Who are you?" they replied, "Harranites." "Christians or Jews?" Neither, was the reply. "Have you holy books or a prophet?" To this they gave a guarded and confusing answer *(jamjamū)*, whereupon the official observed, "You must be Zandokiyah." So in order to survive they changed their name to Ssabians. (D. Chwolson, *Die Ssabier und der Ssabaismus* [St. Petersburg: 1865], II, p. 15.) Sabaean denotes "irgend eine täuferische Sekte," according to K. Ahrens (in note 43), p. 154. Could Zandokite and Zadokite not have been as easily confused as Zadokite and Sadducee?

51. The entire company falls asleep as soon as Tamlikh announces the approach of visitors; the entrance of the cave then becomes invisible, or else all who attempt entry are driven out in terror. (Thal'labi, p. 292; Tabari, *Jami'al-bayan*, XV, p. 143.) Some say the purpose of the shrine is to keep anyone from entering the cave (Nasafi, II, p. 284; Zamakhshari, I, p. 724); others that the youths walled themselves in, or were killed in the city and taken to the cave for burial (Qasimi, X, p. 4051). Only one informant reports that they "arose and went out to the king and exchanged greetings," and then returned to the cave and promptly expired; but even he adds that "most of the scholars say" they died as soon as Tamlikh gave them his message. (Qurtubi, X, p. 379.)

52. So in the Syrian and Western texts supplied by Huber, pp.

118-27, 155-56. The same in Tha'labi, p. 298; Ibn Kathir, III, p. 77; Baydawi, IV, p. 90; Nasafi, II, p. 284. Tha'labi also tells this story, but quickly qualifies it by adding that "no man could enter into them," explaining, on the authority of Ali, that as soon as Tamlikh went in to his friends, God took their spirits and concealed their hiding place. (P. 298.) The most convincing of all Tha'labi's accounts is his vivid description of the greedy citizens and the wild-eyed and be-draggled youth who told them the fantastic story of his grisly companions in a nearby cave—companions that nobody ever saw alive. (Pp. 296-97.) Here we have a story that bears the marks of plausibility.

53. "And behold their bodies were completely unchanged, except that there was not breath (arwah) in them." So the king said, "This is the sign which God has sent you." (Tabari, Tarikh, II, pp. 9-10, and Jami'al-bayan, XV, p. 147; Damiri, II, pp. 349, 357.) Much is made of their eyes being open, giving them a frighteningly lifelike appearance. (Shirbini, II, p. 356; Baydawi, IV, p. 95; Nasafi, II, pp. 280-81; as-Sa'di, Taysir al-karim al-rahman fi tafsir kalam al-mannan [Cairo: 1954-1957], V, p. 10.)

54. Qurtubi, X, p. 358. Huber, pp. 231-33, supplies translations of descriptions of this shrine by Idrisi, Qurtubi, and Yaqut.

55. Analecta Bollandiana 26 (1907):272.

56. Al-Biruni, Kitab al-athar al-baqiya 'an al-qurun il-khaliya (Leipzig: 1923), p. 290. Many other sources are cited by Huber, pp. 225-26, 228-31. The extra cadavers were readily accounted for as those of devout monks who had chosen to live and die in the presence of the Seven (ibid., p. 231). M. J. DeGoeje maintained that the story of the Seven Sleepers originated with the finding of human remains in a cave near Arabissas in southeastern Asia Minor, the place being known to the Arabs as Afsus—hence Ephesus. (See "De Legende der Zevenslapers van Efeze," Verslagen en Mededeelingen der Koninklijke Akademie van Wetenschappen, III (1909), pp. 9-33, of which there is a lengthy summary in Huber, pp. 233-38.)

57. Tha'labi, pp. 291, 293; Huber, pp. 276-77.

58. Tabari, Jami'al-bayan, XV, p. 143; Damiri, II, pp. 338, 353; Shirbini, II, p. 365; Ibn Kathir, III, p. 77.

59. Qurtubi, X, p. 388; Damiri, II, p. 352. Though Ibn Kathir, III, p. 77, says the cave was in the bilad of Rum, he explains, "We are not told in what land the cave was. . . . But Ibn Abbas says it was near Aelia, and Ibn Isaac says it was near Nineveh." (Ibid., p. 75.) Ibn Isaac is a notoriously imaginative informant.

60. Qurtubi, X, p. 388. This may be an embellishment of an older version in which Ibn Abbas expresses some skepticism as to the pos-

sibility of recognizing bones three hundred years old. (Ibn Kathir, III, p. 77; Huber, p. 233, citing Tabari and Tha'labi.)

61. Qurtubi, X, p. 356; Tabari, *Jami'al-bayan*, XV, p. 131.

62. Damiri, II, p. 342.

63. Al-Qazwini, *Al-atharwa 'l-bilad* (Göttingen: 1848), I, p. 161: other sources in Huber, pp. 235-38, Al-Istakhri, Al-masalik wa 'l-mamalik (Cairo: 1961), p. 47.

64. Huber, p. 224, citing Yaqut and Qazwini. About the year 751 there was great excitement throughout the East in anticipation of an immediate appearance of the Seven Sleepers in a cemetery of Damascus, according to Al-Biruni (in note 56), p. 285. (Cf. *Analecta Bollandiana* 68 [1950]:253. On Amman, see Huber, p. 237.)

65. Clermont-Ganneau, *El-Kahf et la Caverne des sept Dormants*, in *Comptes Rendus de l'Académie des Inscriptions et Belles-Lettres, 4e série*, XXVII (Paris: 1899), pp. 564-74. Huber, pp. 238-39, accuses Clermont-Ganneau of following a false scent, yet the latter specifies that he is *not* seeking the original cave of the Seven Sleepers but only the favorite Moslem site of it. (*Analecta Bollandiana* 19 [1900]:356-57.) L. Massignon accepts his location of al Raqim. (*Analecta Bollandiana* 68 [1950]:254.)

66. Damiri, II, p. 340; Qurtubi, X, p. 367.

67. Tha'labi, pp. 102-3. Tabari (cited by Huber, pp. 254-55) tells of a shepherd who found an inscribed tablet in a cave, which no one could read but an old holy man of the desert.

68. R. Eisler (in note 49) II, pp. 35, 182-84, 190-93, 197-99. On a possible Rekhabite background for Qumran, see H. J. Schoeps, *Theologie und Geschichte des Judentums* (Tübingen: 1949), pp. 247-55.

69. *Analecta Bollandiana* 68 (1950):254. It was the leaders of the Nejran Christians who first questioned Mohammed about the Cave. (Nasafi, II, p. 285, etc.)

70. Above, note 4.

71. The quotation is from Sale's note to *Sura* XVIII, 8, though Sale is not sure of the explanation and leaves the word *raqim* untranslated. Tabari, *Jami'al-bayan*, XV, p. 131, says it was stone tablet.

72. Tha'labi, p. 298; Baydawi, IV, p. 83 (lead or stone). The box was sealed with a silver seal. Al-Bokhari, *Jami'al-Sahih* (Leyden: 1868), III, p. 276, says there was just one lead plate.

73. Tabari, suggests a book; Qurtubi, X, p. 357, a golden tablet.

74. L. Massignon, in *Analecta Bollandiana* 68 (1950):252, discusses the significance of this.

75. Hijazi, XV, p. 50; Qurtubi, X, p. 357; Ibn Kathir, III, p. 73 (it is the wadi); Tabari, *Jami'al-bayan*, XV, p. 131; Baydawi, IV, p. 83. Al-Raqim designates "the people of the Cave who were confined [or

trapped] in it" *(ashāp al-ghāri alladhi intabaqa 'alayhim).* (Qurtubi.)

76. Ibn Kathir, Tabari, Baydawi.

77. Qurtubi, IV, p. 357, citing al-Saddi.

78. Baydawi, IV, p. 83, and Qurtubi, X, pp. 356-58, suggest both.

79. "It is said that al-Raqim is a wadi beyond Palestine in which is the Cave; [the name] is taken from Raqmah, a wadi with water-holes in it." And Ibn Atiya says, "It is in Syria, according to what I heard from many people; it is a cave with dead people in it." (Qurtubi, X, p. 357.) It means running water in a wadi. (Damiri, II, p. 341.)

80. Qurtubi, suggests both.

81. Qurtubi; Hijazi, XV, p. 50; Nasafi, II, p. 277.

82. It was the name given to the Andalusian site (above note 54), and to "a region of Rum" where there was a cave containing "twenty-one souls as if they were sleeping." (See Qurtubi, who does not believe that this is *the* Cave.)

83. Qurtubi. Most commentators (including those mentioned in note 84) note that the tablets contained the names and history of the Sleepers, and Qurtubi would even include in the writings "the rule which they embraced from the religion of Jesus" *(al-shar'tamassakūhu bi-hi min dini 'Isa).*

84. Tha'labi, p. 295; Tabari, *Jami'al-bayan,* XV, p. 135; Baydawi, IV, pp. 86-87; Damiri, II, p. 344, according to whom the book itself is to come forth as a new revelation.

85. *2 Maccabees* 2: 4-8. At the time of the First Crusade, local reports located this cave near Jericho. (Fulcher, *Historia Hierosolymitana,* edited by H. Hagenmeyer [Heidelberg: 1913], p. 289.) When the Patriarch Timotheus was informed, about the year 800, of the discoveries of documents in caves near Jericho, he assumed that it was those buried by Jeremiah. (J. Hering, in *Revue d'Histoire et de Philosophie Religieuse* 41 [1961]:160.)

86. E. A. W. Budge, *The Contendings of the Apostles* (Oxford: 1935), pp. 394-96; Baydawi, IV, pp. 87, 90. See above, note 10.

87. He takes the custom back to the burial of Aaron, p. 171. He tells of a book sent to David from heaven sealed with gold and containing thirteen questions to be put to Solomon (p. 202); of an apocalyptic writing sealed in an iron box (p. 246); of another buried in a mountain (p. 242); of gold tablets containing the history of a vanished empire found in a cave in Yemen (p. 102); of magic books dug up from beneath Solomon's throne (p. 35).

88. M. Black (in note 24), p. 12.

89. Tha'labi, p. 288. When Ali finishes his story, the most skeptical Jew confesses that he has not added nor removed a single letter from the account in the Torah. (P. 292.)

90. Various estimates are given by Huber, p. 102. (Cf. *Analecta Bollandiana* 72 [1954]:266; B. Heller (note 3), pp. 205, 211.)

91. It "belongs to the secrets of heaven and earth." (Tabari, *Jami'al-bayan*, XV, p. 152; Shirbini, II, p. 366.) The Prophet spent forty nights trying to comprehend it. (As-Suyuti, *Lubab al-nuqul* . . . [1935], p. 145.)

92. Qurtubi, X, p. 386, who quotes Tabari as saying that the Jews also could not agree about it. It could hardly have been a Christian invention, since no amount of manipulating can fit the conventional three centuries of sleep into the century-and-a-half interval between Decius and either Theodosius. (Cf. *Analecta Bollandiana* 66 [1948]:195.)

93. Heller (note 3), pp. 206-7. Onias slept from the destruction of the First Temple to the completion of the Second:" The parallel with the Seven Sleepers . . . is of course obvious," comments the *Jewish Encyclopedia* (1902), IX, p. 405. Some say the Seven fell asleep until the land became Moslem. (Damiri, II, p. 351.)

94. *Analecta Bollandiana* 68 (1950):351.

95. H. H. Rowley, in *Expository Times* 63 (1951/2):381; M. H. Segal, in *Journal of Biblical Literature* 70 (1951):146, note 59, and p. 130; Ysuf Ali, *The Holy Qur'an*, II, p. 720, note 2337. The 390 and the 20 years "belong to the remote past. . . . Their writers lack any real knowledge of the origin and early history of the sect; hence the nebulous atmosphere pervading all the documents . . . the characters . . . appearing as types rather than individuals." (E. Wiesenberg, in *Vetus Testamentum* 5 [1955]:304-5.)

96. Above, note 87, Tabari's story is discussed by Huber, pp. 254-55.

97. Tha'labi, p. 292. They say *nakūnu 'alu amrin wahadin*, Tabari, *Jami'al-bayan*, XV, p. 132, where the last word suggests the much-discussed *"yahad"* of the Scrolls.

98. Nearly all Arabic sources mention this. Tha'labi, pp. 292-93, even notes that they gained the repute of being money-changers.

99. Tha'labi, p. 291. See above, note 79. Huber, p. 455, sees a Jewish tradition in the spring and the trees, and Heller, note 37, p. 201, notes that the society eschewed pork.

100. Qurtubi, X, p. 360; Nasafi, II, p. 278. Both mention caves in the plural. (Cf. Tabari, *Jami'al-bayan*, XV, p. 132, 151.)

101. On al-Raqim as a going concern, see Tabari, XV, p. 135: Ibn Kathir, III, pp. 74-75. In some Western versions Tamikh is only twelve or fifteen years old, and in all of them the youths must fetch all their food and drink from the city—they were *not* self-sustaining. There was a tradition that the activities of the Cave included even

dancing, according to Qurtubi, X, p. 466, who describes the pious exercises of the community.

102. Tha'labi, pp. 289, 294; Ibn Kathir, III, p. 74, who mention the dramatic episode of the stripping of their military insignia by the enraged emperor. This is a characteristic episode in the cycle of youthful military heroes who are martyred by the emperor but then come alive to prove the resurrection. Such were St. Mercurius, St. Victor, and St. Sebastian. Tha'labi's St. George, pp. 299-305, clearly belongs to the cycle.

103. Tha'labi, p. 291; Qurtubi, X, p. 369; Ibn Kathir, III, p. 75; as-Sa'adi, V, p. 10, etc. On Qumran, see M. Black, note 40, p. 141.

104. Once a week (Tabari, cited by Huber, p. 279); every seven years (Qurtubi, X, p. 370); twice a year (Baydawi, IV, p. 94); once a year at New Year's (Tha'labi, p. 291; Nasafi, II, p. 281; Qurtubi).

105. Tha'labi, p. 291; Nasafi, II, p. 281; Qurtubi, X, 369; Baydawi, IV, p. 93. Ibn Kathir, III, p. 75, see astronomical significance in these arrangements. Huber, p. 295, discusses the awakening by the sun.

106. S. Talmon, in *Revue de Qumran* 2 (1960): 475; E. Ettisch, in *Theologische Literaturzeitung* 88 (1963):186, 188, 191-92.

107. E. Rohde, in *Rheinisches Museum für Philologie*, Neue Folge 35 (1880):157-59, 162-63. Their names have great *"valeur prophylactique"* throughout the Moslem world. (Massignon, in *Anal. Boll.* 68 [1950]:249-50); for their healing offices, see ibid., pp. 247-48, and for dreams, see Huber, p. 135.

108. J. M. Allegro, *The Treasure of the Copper Scroll* (New York: Doubleday, 1960), p. 73. The Essenes specialized in "Traumdeute-und Weissagekunst"; R. Eisler, note 49, II, p. 17.

109. Allegro, pp. 70-71. (Cf. Tha'labi, p. 291; Nasafi, II, p. 280; Qurtubi, X, p. 369; as-Sa'adi, V, p. 10.)

110. Tha'labi, pp. 294-95; Tabari, *Jami'al-bayan*, XV, p. 131; Damiri, II, pp. 339-40; Shirbini, II, pp. 352-53; Baydawi, IV, pp. 85-86: ". . . lift up your heads, eat, and trust in God." On the Hebrew origin of *jabbar*, see K. Ahrens, note 43, p. 19.

111. Epiphanius, *Adv. haer.*, Haer. 29, no. 5, in *PG*, 41, col. 397.

112. Al-Biruni, note 56, p. 284. The added evidence of the Companions of the Cave tips the scales against the reading *maqariba*, favored by N. Golb, in *Journal of Religion* 41 (1961):42-44.

113. This expression puzzled Huber, p. 283, as the only purely Christian tradition in the Koran, where it is accordingly strangely out of place. But J. Horovitz, in *HUCA* 2 (1925):178, showed that "it is by no means assured that . . . Mohammed really meant the martyrs of Najran," and that the only reason for such an assumption

is lack of evidence as to what else the "People of the Pit" could refer to. The Dead Sea Scrolls now supply that evidence.

114. Baydawi, IV, p. 91 (Khiram); Damiri, II, p. 350 (Haram, Khadam); Qurtubi, X, p. 367 (Khiram). The usual difficulty with pointing is apparent.

115. Damiri, II, p. 341. Nasafi, II, p. 285, also says the dog was Raqim. Tha'labi, p. 290, gives a list of suggested names, not including this one.

116. Ibn Kathir, III, pp. 73, 78; Qurtubi, X, p. 360. The quotation is from Allegro, note 108, p. 70.

117. This has been discussed by Massignon, in *Anal. Boll.* 68, pp. 245-60.

Scripture References

Index

287